THE ASHBY GUIDEBOOK FOR STUDY OF THE PARANORMAL

THE ASHBY GUIDEBOOK FOR STUDY OF THE PARANORMAL

What to read, where to go,
names you should know
plus
exercises to improve your own
ESP and psychic abilities

Robert H. Ashby

Revised edition
edited by
Frank C. Tribbe

Published in collaboration with

Spiritual Frontiers Fellowship

Samuel Weiser, Inc.
York Beach, Maine

Originally published in 1972 as
The Guidebook for the Study of Psychical Research

This revised and enlarged edition
first published in 1987 by
Samuel Weiser, Inc.
Box 612
York Beach, Maine 03910

Library of Congress Cataloging in Publication Data:

Ashby, Robert H.
      The Ashby guidebook for study of the paranormal.

      Rev. ed. of: The guidebook for the study of psychical
research. 1972.
      "Published in collaboration with Spiritual Frontiers
Fellowship."
      Bibliography: p.
      1. Psychical research. 2. Psychical research—Bibliography.
I. Tribbe, Frank C. II. Ashby, Robert H. Guidebook for the study
of psychical research. III. Spiritual Frontiers Fellowship. IV. Title.
BF1031.A8 1987   016.1339'072   86–34033
ISBN 0–87728–660–4

Printed in the United States of America

CONTENTS

For Jenny and Mrs. P.
who made this book possible

Acknowledgments

Spiritual Frontiers Fellowship is grateful to all those who made this *Guidebook* revision possible.

Most especially, we are indebted to Jennifer Ashby, M.D., for giving the Fellowship permission to republish this seminal work in the field of psychical research.

We also deeply appreciate the special contributions of the following persons: Rhea A. White, for both her extensive knowledge and the data from her PSI Center which she graciously shared with us in updating several listings in this volume; Harold Sherman, for the use of his "Exercise In Relaxation and Visualization"; Gertrude R. Schmeidler, Ph.D., for her material on "How to Investigate a Haunted House"; Louis J. Matacia, for his material on "How to Dowse"; William G. Roll, for his material on "How to Investigate a Poltergeist"; and Frank C. Tribbe, for his material on "How to Do Token-Object Psychometry."

And, of course, our thanks go to Mr. Tribbe, for serving as General Editor for this revision.

Having known Bob Ashby for many years, I hope that this revision by Spiritual Frontiers Fellowship may help pay posthumous respects to Bob for his dedication, his loyalty and his service as SFF's director of Education and Research. His untimely death on August 22, 1975, left SFF with a great void in the direction of its educational and research program, for we all recognize the great contribution Bob could have made to the future of Psychical Research.

My personal hope and expectation is that this revision will not only pay tribute to Bob, but will also, by its potential for inspiration, secure in the minds and hearts of readers everywhere the significance of Robert H. Asbhy's work in the field.

Elizabeth W. Fenske, President
Spiritual Frontiers Fellowship

Spiritual Frontiers Fellowship

Spiritual Frontiers Fellowship was founded in 1956 as an inter-faith, non-profit fellowship by a group of religious leaders and writers who had a deep concern for the rising interest in mystical and paranormal experiences. Though SFF is Christian in its origin and orientation, it has always recognized that the "numinous" mysteriously moved within all religious traditions.

The goal of SFF "is the development of spiritual growth within the individual and the encouragement of new dimensions of spiritual experience . . . ." It is precisely this goal which gives SFF its uniqueness among other organizations and movements and its very reason for existence. Though the boundaries of the soul's consciousness within each individual transcend the limits of time and space, the heritage of SFF is rooted in, but not limited to, the Judaic and Christian traditions which are rich in mystical and paranormal experiences. To understand these experiences and to help interpret them to others, both within and outside organized religious structures, is to understand Jesus's sayings: "Ye shall know the truth, and the truth shall make you free," and, "Greater works than these shall ye do."

SFF has sought to express its goal through an emphasis and exploration of the three ares of mystical prayer and meditation, spiritual healing, and survival of consciousness. This means that SFF is dedicated to the expansion of consciousness which leads toward the realization of a person's intrinsic spiritual nature.

EWF

IN MEMORIAM—ASHBY REMEMBERED
by
*Martin Ebon**

My last discussion with Bob Ashby was concerning Sir Arthur Conan Doyle. It was the year of a charming bestseller, *The Seven Percent Solution,* which elaborated upon the historic fantasy that Sherlock Holmes went to Vienna for treatment by Sigmund Freud, and they joined hands in solving a mystery and preventing a criminal conspiracy. It was the sort of thing that Conan Doyle might have enjoyed, and it brought the personality of this grand author–physician–spiritualist into renewed prominence.

Robert Ashby was a Sherlock Holmes fan and something of a Conan Doyle scholar. In the spring of 1975, we discussed a projected collaboration on a book dealing with Sir Arthur's spiritualist involvements, his fighting spirit, his vigor, imagination, and limitations.

Ashby brought his own experiences in Scotland and England, his personal researches in Edinburgh and London, to this proposed project. Conan Doyle's skills, disciplines, and excesses clearly fascinated Bob. There is in all of us, and that includes Ashby and Conan Doyle, a struggle between caution and daring. And when it comes to the subject of life after death, this struggle often turns into a tug-of-war within our very souls. Where, we often wonder, do facts and wishful thinking create a more hopeless tangle? Conan Doyle's ulti-

*This eulogy appeared as the lead-article in the SFF journal, *Spiritual Frontiers,* Winter 1982 (XIV-1). The issue was dedicated to the memory of Robert Howe Ashby (July 5, 1930–August 22, 1975).

Mr. Ebon, former editor and frequent contributor to the journal, was the first executive secretary of the Parapsychology Foundation created by Eileen J. Garrett. Ebon is the author of more than sixty books, mostly in the psychic field, as well as a lecturer and raconteur par excellence. His recent anthologies, *The Signet Handbook of Parapsychology* and *Miracles*, were followed by *The Threat of Psychic Warfare.*

mate conversion to spiritualism took place during World War I, in the summer of 1916, when he received what he felt was a clear message from a medium, originating with the spirit of his wife's brother, Malcolm Leckie, who had died in battle in 1914.

What fascinated Bob was Conan Doyle's failure to publicize the—to Bob, convincing—details of this message. After all, he felt, much of what Sir Arthur had written in his books amounted to autobiographical confession. Why was he silent on this crucial point? He noted that John Dickson Carr had written in *The Life of Sir Arthur Conan Doyle* (1948): "It was reminiscence or reminder so intimately personal that it could have been known to no person in the world except to Malcolm Leckie and himself. In it he found the objective proof which he had been seeking for nearly thirty years."

In the midst of discussion of our Conan Doyle project, Ashby's symptoms were diagnosed as stemming from a terminal illness, and he became too weak to continue his researches. At the same time, I was sidetracked into a hospital for an operation, and when I returned to work, Bob had already left us.

But in the few years since his return from London in 1971, Robert H. Ashby had been a vibrant force in Spiritual Frontiers Fellowship. His impact was such that now, nearly seven years later, this tall and handsome figure is still vivid to many of us. Bob Ashby had dignity. Yet, he was boyish even at the age of forty-five; and, yes, he could be playful, crack a smile, tell a funny story.

But he was serious about psychic phenomena, their meaning to human development and existence and to the spiritual content of life. As SFF's Director of Research and Education, he supervised its Survival Research Project and stated his principles this way:

> The desire and determination to investigate the mystery of life, to bring order out of chaos and knowledge out of ignorance, are inherent in man. It is the person of bold probing and daring inference who trailblazes for mankind in the quest for meaning. And of all the enigmas we face, none is more baffling or overarching in its significance than that of death and its impact. How we view death determines in large measure how we view life, because our conviction about death is based upon our view of man, God, and the universe.

This was the theme of Bob Ashby's search and his life, which began in Springfield, Kentucky, on July 5, 1930, and ended in Shawnee,

Kansas, on August 22, 1975. The beginning and end of his life placed him firmly in Mid-America. His years in the British Isles provided that international touch, the grounding in the traditions of the Society for Psychical Research, London, which gave his work and quest additional dimensions.

Ashby's key work, *The Guidebook to the Study of Psychical Research* (1972) was in great part based on studies he had made in the archives of the London SPR. And, just as Bob Ashby influenced the lives of many of us, so was he indebted to the help of others. Among these was the resident Grande Dame of the London Society Rosalind Heywood. She took the young American visitor under her wing, served him tea, and made him the eager recipient of her intellectual generosity. (When I visited London in the summer of 1980 and hoped to make my own regular pilgrimage to the Heywood residence, Rosalind had just died.)

Mrs. Heywood provided Bob Ashby's personal linkage to the traditions of the SPR, to the beginnings of psychical research in the nineteenth century, its triumphs as well as its unavoidable quarrels and missteps. To the degree that we are all the sum total of the people we have admired, Rosalind Heywood's knowledge and experience became part of Bob's approach and attitude.

Ashby's style combined curiosity about people and things and ideas with an inborn gift to communicate, to teach and share knowledge. He did this in talks and writings, and by encouraging others to realize their own potential. As our search is unending, we ought not to look back in sadness (or even anger) that he died so early because he also knew that we won't find ultimate answers during our existence on this earth. And yet, it is clear by now that none of us has been able to replace Bob Ashby. Sure, we are all unique. But to paraphrase George Orwell, Bob was more unique than others. . . .

Just look at that man's credentials and potentials! He had taught history, French, speech, English, and Latin from 1955 to 1968. He was headmaster of the American School in Tangier, Morocco, from 1968 to 1969, and director of the high school of the American School in London from 1970 to 1971. After his return to the United States he became chairman of the SFF Research Committee and later the Fellowship's Director of Education and Research. In another civilization, he would be called a "guru"; to us, he was a teacher, as well as a fellow student.

What is too difficult to put into words is the manner in which Robert Ashby did his teaching, his talking, his arousing of enthusiasm and participation among audiences. His manner, in the innermost meaning of the word, was engaging; that means, he succeeded in capturing the individual listener, in "engaging" him or her in the subject he was talking about, in making each member of an audience a participant.

The key to all this, I think, was sincerity. Here was a man who meant what he said, who cared about the things that puzzled him and that he sought to explore. And he was sincere in wanting to share this quest with others, engaging them right along with himself in the search.

And, to be totally candid, I used to envy these gifts. I used to think to myself: "He's a better man than I am." I still think so. In our narcissistic age that is, I suppose, the ultimate praise. . . .

PREFACE TO THE FIRST EDITION

This book is intended for the person interested in Extrasensory Perception (ESP) and related topics who determines to investigate psychical research. I have written it because during the years of my involvement in the field, I have often been approached by people who are genuinely concerned about ESP and an invariable question is: "How do I find out about such matters?" They have wanted to know which books they should read; where there were libraries with substantial collections on the subject; which bookshops specialized in works dealing with the topics of psychical research; which organizations were devoted to psychical research or connected issues and how they could join such groups. There have often been queries regarding mediums: What exactly is a medium? How does one find a medium? How does one deal with a medium in a sitting? And how does one judge the quality of a medium and the significance of the mediumistic material from a sitting?

It is obvious that the beginning student of psychical research needs some guidance as to where and how to proceed with his studies, and those who already have some knowledge of the field need to decide at which point to undertake further study of a very puzzling mass of data, interpretations, theories, and disagreements. It is in the hope of helping to meet these needs that this volume has been prepared.

In response to the rapidly growing interest in ESP, there is a definite improvement in library holdings concerning psychical research. There has been a spate of volumes dealing with ESP during the last few years, and the serious student of the discipline may well be confused as to the relative merit, seriousness of purpose, and soundness of scholarship behind many of these popular treatments. Because of this difficulty, I have prepared in Chapters Three and Four two separate annotated bibliographies. The first is a list of approximately forty books which should prove useful for those without previous experience in studying psychical research. The second of approximately forty books is for the student who has learned the basic facts and procedures of the discipline and feels that he is ready to proceed into more complex issues and deeper, more subtle discussions. Works in both chapters have been grouped according to major topics and coverage. They are, of course, of varying difficulty and I have tried to indicate something about this in the annotations.

In addition to the annotated works, in both chapters I have listed a considerable number of other books which I feel are worth consulting. I did not wish to make the bibliographies either exhaustive or exhausting. They are merely possible and, I believe, sound starting points for the student. His own particular interests will then lead him on to further reading. The information in the bibliographies is as accurate as I could determine; however, readers may well find that some important books are no longer in print or that they are available only in a hardback or only in a paperback edition.

I am grateful to Dr. J. B. Rhine and the Editor of *The Journal of Parapsychology* for their kind permission to use some of the Glossary definitions from their publication. The two quotations from SCIENCE DIGEST are reprinted with the permission of SCIENCE DIGEST, © The Hearst Corporation. I have benefitted greatly from the sound criticism and constructive suggestions given by Miss Renée Haynes, Mrs. Rosalind Heywood, and Mrs. Ena Twigg. Mr. Leslie Price has been of enormous assistance in clarifying bibliographical points and in gaining information about library holdings. The staff of The College of Psychic Studies have been most cooperative and patient with my use of their fine library; my appreciation also goes to Mrs. Laura F. Knipe of The American Society for Psychical Research and to Mrs. G. Babusis of the Eileen J. Garrett Library at The Parapsychology Foundation for their assistance. Finally, in this undertaking, as in all, my wife's constant encouragement, understanding, and perceptive suggestions have been indispensable.

For the opinions expressed and any errors I am, of course, solely responsible.

Robert H. Ashby, 1972

CHAPTER ONE

THE NATURE OF PSYCHICAL RESEARCH

T HERE IS SURELY NO field of study in which the concepts, beliefs, and biases of our "common sense" world clash so violently with the data collected and analyzed by scholars as psychical research or, as it is frequently termed today, parapsychology. Nor is there any discipline which aims at following the scientific methods whose data and theories are so widely disclaimed by orthodox scientists. Indeed, a sizeable majority of scientists would doubtless contend that psychical researchers have not established that there is anything to investigate. In short, the scientific community at large still rejects the data that indicate that "paranormal phenomena"—earlier called "psychic phenomena"—i.e., occurrences which do not fit into currently known patterns, behavior, or theories, ever occur. Dr. George R. Price may be cited as typical of this school of thought. He is quoted in *Science Digest* for November, 1965, as saying:

> My opinion concerning parapsychologists is that many of them are dependent on clerical and statistical errors and unintentional use of sensory clues, and that all extra-chance results not so explicable are dependent on deliberate fraud or mildly abnormal mental conditions.[1]

Such a situation in scientific circles, following ninety years of careful research into psychic phenomena might be termed a paranormal phenomenon itself. It is, however, true that this attitude has gradually changed during the last twenty-five years and that an increasing number of younger scientists in many fields are open-

---

[1]"See, however, his letter to the editor of *Science*, January 28, 1972, retracting his charge of 1955 that Rhine and Soal were guilty of fraud."

minded about Extrasensory Perception (ESP) and feel that psychical research is an important area of study. The changing climate of opinion was indicated in a most encouraging manner in December of 1969 when the American Association for the Advancement of Science accepted the Parapsychological Association as an affiliate member.

Why has this fledgling science aroused such scientific hostility and skepticism? The scientific method utilized in scientific disciplines can be summarized as one in which the phenomenon under study must meet the following criteria:

1) Isolation from other phenomena in nature

2) Observation under conditions controlled by the scientist

3) Repeated experimentation

4) Results both statistically assessable and obtainable by any other scientist replicating the experiment and its conditions precisely.

Thus, one must have isolation, observation, control, experimentation, measureable data, and repeatability both of experimentation and of results in order to establish the reality of the phenomenon. It is true, of course, that this method is more readily applied with some types of phenomena than others. Chemistry and astronomy cannot be approached in exactly the same manner; and behavioral sciences like psychology have had to modify the methodology somewhat. Nevertheless, these canons of evidentiality and predictability undergird the acceptance of phenomena by the scientific community.

The central problem is that paranormal phenomena have very rarely conformed to this pattern. They have most often been "spontaneous," occurring without prior planning or preparation for observation, control, or experimentation. In such instances, researchers have had to depend upon witnesses to the phenomena to describe what they believe occurred as carefully as possible, and as soon as possible after the "ostensibly paranormal" phenomenon occurred. The phrase "ostensibly paranormal" is used to show that whether the experience was, in fact, paranormal is a judgement to be made *only* after all of the evidence has been analyzed and all "normal" explanations have had to be rejected. Many critics of psychical research may not fully realize how many reports of strange happenings have been proven by parapsychologists to be explicable by perfectly normal means, or have been rejected as inadequately supported by convincing evidence. Probably few more than one out of a hundred reports received have ever been found worthy of publication.

Such witnessed accounts of phenomena possibly paranormal in nature do not satisfy the scientist as meeting either his usual methods or his standards of evidence. Hence, parapsychologists set out to devise experiments which would conform to the scientific method. While there were numerous earlier attempts, it is during the last forty years, beginning in the United States with Dr. J. B. Rhine at Duke University, that researchers in many countries have conducted such controlled laboratory experiments and have garnered impressive evidence that ESP does occur under controlled conditions, that these experiments can be repeated by other researchers, and can sometimes yield similar extra-chance results.

These experiments have centered upon using a pack of test cards consisting of twenty-five cards with five different designs. The person trying to demonstrate ESP, the "subject," would try to guess which card was being held by the experimenter in another part of the room, another room, or another building. Since there are five cards of each of the five designs in the pack, the chance result would be one out of five, or five right in the pack of twenty-five. If a subject could obtain appreciably more than five right in each test over a considerable number of tests, this showed that something other than chance was operating; and since there was no opportunity for the subject to use his five senses to ascertain the correct card, there was sound statistical evidence to indicate that "something" other than chance and other than the five senses were responsible for the accurate "guessing." That "something" has been termed Extrasensory Perception.

Dr. Helmut Schmidt, formerly a physicist with the Boeing Scientific Research Laboratories and successor to Dr. J. B. Rhine as Director of The Foundation for Research into the Nature of Man, caused a sensation by publishing in 1969 and subsequently precognitive and PK results of experiments conducted with randomness assured by using "single quantum processes." Subjects tried to guess which of four bulbs would next light and indicated their choice by pressing the appropriate button. Three subjects performed a total of over 63,000 trials with precognitive success at odds of two billion to one against chance. In a second test of 20,000 trials, subjects could choose either to press the button of a lamp that would light or one that would not, and the results were equally impressive. The scientific community seems to have been more impressed by Dr. Schmidt's work than that of any other parapsychologist of recent years; and his sophisticated use of highly complex technology to guarantee both randomness and accuracy of recording results is an important development.

Yet, despite this statistical evidence, many scientists still reject the reality of ESP. Why? First, because, as Dr. Price said, there *could* be errors made by the researchers in recording the results of the tests, and because of the researcher's bias in favor of ESP, such errors would tend to support rather than to deny it. Second, where the researcher and the subject were close, it *might* be possible that the subject had "sensory clues," i.e., heard the researcher inadvertently mumble the name of the design on the card, or saw through a badly printed card and so learned which design was being held, or noticed that the researcher tended to act in a particular way when a certain design came up in the pack. Third, since we do not know a great deal about how we learn, there *may* be a perfectly physical explanation which is possibly "mildly abnormal" or unusual, but still within the sensory system. Last, there *might* be "deliberate fraud" either by the subject or the researcher or both. Obviously, one cannot absolutely refute such an allegation unless one were present during all the experiments and observed both parties involved very carefully; even then, of course, by another scientist, one could be suspected of fraudulent conspiracy with the original two, and so on *ad infinitum*. In short, the accusation of fraud is impossible to disprove completely, however honest and meticulous a researcher has been. But one may fairly ask, what would either the researcher or the subject gain by such fraud? Certainly not financial rewards: there is very little money available for research, and most subjects have been volunteers; possibly fame either as a scholar or as a gifted psychic, but such reputations have more generally been viewed as notoriety than renown in the scientific community; possibly self-esteem, but this would be absurd since the fraudulent person would know better than anyone that he was a fraud. It is most difficult to see what end would be served by such alleged collusion. It assumes either dishonesty or *naïveté* to an extraordinary degree over decades by hundreds of intelligent and responsible people who had no reason to cheat; but it remains the final, unanswerable criticism which has been faced by psychical researchers for ninety years.

The scientists have issued those criticisms partly because they found that the experiments described above did not prove so repeatable or so conclusive in terms of results as Dr. Rhine and his associates claimed. Why? The enormous amount of research during the last twenty-five years into the psychological states conducive to the operation of ESP has established firmly that this faculty (generally termed "*psi*" and covering all aspects of the paranormal ability) is elusive, unpredictable, emotionally triggered and repressed, sensitive to surroundings, conditions, and especially, to attitudes towards psi itself. Psi is much more likely to operate if the subject and the researcher are predisposed to believe that psi does or may exist, and if both the conditions and the experimenters are relaxed, comfortable, and cheerful. Parapsychologists have found that some subjects perform better with certain researchers than with others; that results depend upon the subject's health and mental state; that subjects tend to lose interest in the numerous repeats of the test and boredom suppresses psi; and that many other generally uncontrollable variables can affect the performance of psi.

Now for a scientist to achieve the kinds of results which seem to demonstrate statistically that psi does exist, it is clear that he would need something other than the detached, skeptical frame of mind with which he prides himself he approaches his experiments. He might need different surroundings from the sterile, utilitarian, stark laboratory; he must hope that he could establish a warm rapport with the subject; he must realize that if the subject was distraught in some way, psi might well not evidence itself; and he must recognize that most of these variables he could not control. In short, it appears that to establish for himself psi as a reality, the scientist must already believe, partially at least, that it *could* exist. This has proven too much of a departure for most scientists, and it is not surprising that their attempts to repeat Rhine's experiments have not been generally successful. And so they have gathered far less evidence of psi than psychical researchers when, for conviction, they have needed far more. Psychologist Ernest R. Hilgard explains why in *Science Digest*, November 1965:

> To demonstrate something highly implausible requires better evidence than to demonstrate something plausible. The reason is that supporting evidence for the plausible finding comes from many directions, while the implausible one must hang from the slender

thread of nonrandomness until certain systematic relationships are found that tie it firmly to what is known.

Despite the widespread denial of the reality of psi by the scientific community, psychical research continues amidst rapidly growing interest in its findings and its significance among the general public. This is because *if* psi and its manifestations do exist a revolution in general scientific and "common sense" thinking will be necessary. Psychical researchers ask whether some people can:

1) Exchange ideas via some extrasensory means termed "telepathy"? If so, does this indicate anything about the extent of the mind's powers and range?

2) Perceive objects, persons, or happenings without the use of the five senses, sometimes at great distances? If so, does "clairvoyance" demonstrate anything about the nature of man's perceptions?

3) Foresee events in detail without any inferential or logical reasons? If so, does this "precognition" signify anything about man's free will?

4) Apparently "step back in time"? If so, does this "retrocognition" indicate anything about the quality, or even the existence, of time itself?

5) Perceive accurate visions of persons known and unknown, alive or dead? If so, do these veridical "apparitions" mean anything in terms of man's dramatic faculties, or possibly of his basic essence, the so-called "soul"?

6) Cause objects to move without touching, pushing, or throwing them in any normal manner which science considers necessary by the laws of motion? If so, does this "telekinesis," "psychokinesis," or "PK" demonstrate anything about the power of thought or human will?

7) Perceive detailed data about an unknown person by touching objects once in that person's possession? If so, does this "psychometry" show anything about the tactile faculty and about any normally imperceptible residue of an intimate and unique character upon an object which the sensitive's fingers seem to detect?

8) Communicate with "personalities" which claim to be, and sometimes seem to be, the spirits of deceased persons? If so, does this,

"discarnate communication" indicate anything about death and the possible survival of human personality?

Do a whole range of other ostensibly paranormal phenomena occur—including "poltergeists," dream phenomena, animal phenomena, "apports," "materializations" (by means of a strange substance termed "ectoplasm"), "table tipping" (wherein the table seems to move of itself and to tap out meaningful messages), "levitation" (wherein an object or a person seems to rise without any known means of doing so), "astral projection" or "out-of-the-body experiences" (wherein the percipient claims to have left his physical body and while in his "astral body" to have perceived persons, places, and events which he could not have perceived normally from the location of his physical body) and "spiritual healing"? If so, do such phenomena shed any light upon the scientific framework within which we usually move and think?

In view of such questions and the documentation gathered since the close of the last century which suggests that some of these things do happen on occasion, it is hardly surprising that the scientific establishment has not reacted kindly to psychical research. Yet, as Dr. Rhine has pointed out, it is surely unscientific to term something "impossible," especially in the face of the extant evidence available for careful and critical scrutiny. Unfortunately, far too few scientists have examined the evidence in such a manner. The prevalent attitude has very often been that of the Cambridge don of chemistry who, in debating the reality of psychic phenomena with Sir Arthur Conan Doyle, based his rejection of their actuality upon the fact that "I once attended a séance." Doyle retorted that were he to debate a topic in chemistry, how absurd his position would be were he to base his conclusions on the statement, "I once visited a chemistry laboratory."

It is apparent that the establishment of psi as a reality has posed very real problems during the ninety years of psychical research and that its occurrence remains a matter of considerable controversy. And within psychical research itself there is a disagreement as to the likelihood of different types of phenomena. Few parapsychologists today are convinced about most so-called "physical phenomena" which flourished in the last half of the nineteenth and the first quarter of the twentieth centuries. This category includes such things as materializations of "spirit forms" which were claimed to be composed of an unknown, semi-physical substance termed "ectoplasm" by the distinguished French phsyiologist Charles Richet; "apports," or small objects such as stones, flowers, or even small animals which seemed to appear at a séance without any normal means of doing so; "levitation" of objects and people, as quite a few researchers and laymen claimed to have witnessed, sometimes in good light, especially as performed by the most remarkable medium of all, Dunglas Home; "psychic" or "spirit" photography in which faces and forms of deceased persons would appear on the photograph, supposedly without any normal means of doing so; and a whole spectrum of strange happenings occurring in the dark or semi-dark, which the psychics—termed "physical mediums"—insisted was essential because "ectoplasm" was generally allergic both to light and to touch by any witness.

The principal reason for the widespread doubt as to the reality of such physical phenomena are first, that virtually every physical medium was disclosed at some point in his career to have produced fraudulent phenomena, and these disclosures naturally placed in doubt all the other phenomena produced: were they genuinely paranormal or also fraudulent? Second, very few physical mediums ever agreed to scientific examinations under conditions controlled by the researchers (although there have been some remarkable exceptions to this statement); and, third, such phenomena seem extremely rare today, when the techniques of investigating such claims are greatly advanced over those available when such phenomena flourished. Whether this present rarity of physical mediums is due to the greater risk of detection in fraud or to some other reason is not certain.

There is far better evidence that "poltergeists" (literally, German for "noisy spirits"), termed Recurrent Spontaneous Psychokinesis or RSPK by parapsychologists, do, in fact, occur. The large number of well-attested instances of strange movements of objects in full light, odd noises in houses, sudden feelings of a cold breeze, etc., precludes hoax or imagination as the only explanations. However, some parapsychologists feel that such phenomena can be explained in many, if not all, cases by such causes as underground water, rats, mice, youthful pranks, and overly active imagination. It is interesting that in such poltergeist manifestations, there is generally a child near the age of puberty present and that the phenomena seem to center around the adolescent. Whether, in a genuinely paranormal instance, there is intentional use by the adolescent of some psychokinetic faculty to make objects move, whether there is a completely unconscious use of such an ability remains a matter of doubt and controversy. Since poltergeists are location centered, the investigator can rarely observe the phenomena under laboratory conditions, but delicate recording devices, motion picture cameras, and other equipment enable the modern parapsychologist to investigate thoroughly such RSPK reports. And some of the adolescents who have been at the psychic vortex of such phenomena have been found in laboratory tests to be gifted with a strong psi faculty.

While poltergeist phenomena do not lend themselves to laboratory experimentation, PK has. Dr. Rhine and other researchers have conducted lengthy experiments over a considerable number of years to see whether subjects in the laboratory under controlled conditions could "will" dice to fall a certain way; and statistical evidence that PK has operated has been published. It is interesting to note that subjects attempting to demonstrate PK have been tested at various distances from the dice and, generally, the results have been in accordance with the individual subject's belief as to whether distance has any effect on PK: i.e., a subject who thought it did not matter would score just as well twenty feet from the dice as one foot away; one who believed the opposite declined in score as his distance increased. This shows again the bearing of belief upon the psi faculty. The acceptance of such evidence among parapsychologists has been mixed: replication of the results has not been easy or frequent, giving rise to doubt among some that the case for PK has been statistically proven.

The other large category of the paranormal, besides the physical, is termed "mental," and this has received by far the greatest attention during the last forty years of research. Under this heading would come telepathy, clairvoyance, precognition, retrocognition, and mediumistic communications. Psychometry and apparitions seem to span the two general categories of physical and mental: whether the object the psychometrist handles actually does contain a "psychic residue" from its possessor which the psychometrist perceives by handling it or whether the object acts merely as a catalyst or focal point for his own psi faculty is not yet clear. Thus psychometry may be entirely mental or partially mental and partially physical in nature. Similarly with apparitions: is the verifiable figure and/or scene which is perceived by the witness a spatial one, that is, is "something there" in an objective sense, as when one perceives a table in the middle of the room; or is the apparition a "veridical hallucination," that is, a mentally constructed and projected image really "seen within" but *seeming* to be "outside" one, hence not objective but subjective in nature? The theoretical difficulties inherent in apparitions pose one of the most fascinating and complex problems in psychical research.

Within mental phenomena there are divisions between spontaneous, experimental, and mediumistic data. The first yields documentary evidence which must be assessed in terms of the quality and quantity of the witnesses, the time lapse between the occurrence and the report, the possibility of normal explanations, such as subconscious memory, logical inference based upon known but consciously forgotten information, discrepancies between accounts, elaborations due to dramatic tendencies, faulty memory, poor light, or fraud. It can well be appreciated that a perfect case in which the evidence passes every such criterion with flying colors is so rare as to be virtually nonexistent: one can always find some flaw in human testimony. But if researchers can gather thousands of such accounts from a wide variety of countries and cultures, covering the entire spectrum of ages, social, economic, religious, and political types and predilections over a period of almost a century; and if these accounts when closely analyzed disclose striking similarities in characteristics—both in terms of what they include and what they exclude—then, even if individually there are flaws in each, the cumulative effect of such a collection can be most impressive, and to many convincing.

As we have seen, however, spontaneous phenomena are neither repeatable at will, statistically measurable, controllable, nor entirely free of human bias and error of observation. Also, such phenomena are difficult to categorize because each is unique in terms of its time, place, and conditions of occurrence. Consequently, a great many different interpretations of these accounts are possible. While these phenomena are very frequently of a lasting importance and conviction to those who participated in or witnessed them, for someone investigating or reading about them, such evidentiality is greatly diminished if not totally lost. Add to this the "implausibility" of such occurrences in terms of scientific and common sense experience, and the hope to convince either the scientific community or the general public of the reality of the paranormal through this type of evidence becomes remote.

Furthermore, if the psi faculty is as widespread as the various surveys taken at different times have suggested—approximately ten per cent of the representative groups polled said that they had had some ostensibly paranormal experience during their lifetime—one would suppose that in the United States alone hundreds of thousands of people each year should experience paranormal phenomena. If they do, why are not the psychical research organizations inundated with such reports which they could then publish in a steady steam to confound all their critics? Henry Sidgwick, the distinguished Cambridge philosopher, who was the principal leader of the Society for Psychical Research from its founding in 1882 for twenty years, pointed out almost ninety years ago that it was incumbent upon the new discipline to discover, investigate, verify, and publish accounts constantly. Why, then, are so few new cases published each year? Why are the same impressive cases cited in book after book as demonstrating some type of phenomenon, and why are these excellent cases mostly very old rather than contemporary? There are several reasons for this most unfortunate state of affairs. First, because, as we have seen, the general climate of opinion regarding the paranormal has remained hostile, people who do experience such phenomena are understandably most reluctant to come forward and report them; when they do, it is frequently many years after the occurrence, documentation is difficult, if not impossible, to obtain or to verify, and they often request anonymity to avoid annoyance and abuse. Second, before publishing any report, researchers must investigate it, gather all the evidence, analyze and weigh it, and prepare a careful, scholarly report. All this takes a great deal of time and would necessitate an enormous staff of trained parapsychologists. Yet, there are very few funds to support such an enterprise. Nevertheless, within the last twenty-five years there have been some collections of such spontaneous cases published in English; for example, both the Society for Psychical Research in Great Britain and the American Society for Psychical Research undertook such surveys, while in recent years Dr. Louisa E. Rhine in the United States and Mr. Andrew Mackenzie in Great Britain have prepared several books reporting such cases. Anyone reading these carefully compiled works will realize that such occurrences do still happen, and that thousands of people have taken the time and trouble to report them and to answer detailed questionnaires and follow-up correspondence. Still, such collections probably represent but a tiny portion of those manifestations of psi that happen daily, become nothing more than a vivid memory and, eventually, an elaborated ancedote as part of a family's lore.

It is because of the inherent difficulties of the spontaneous phenomena carrying conviction to the scientific community that the laboratory approach was initiated and has dominated parapsychology in recent years. Even the experimental data, as already indicated, have produced their own full crop of problems. Assuming that the psi faculty does exist and, under certain conditions, can and will operate, how does one set about determining which facet of the faculty—telepathy, clairvoyance, precognition, or retrocognition—is being used? The answer is very complex and only a brief outline can be given here. In testing for telepathy, the experimenter will lift one card at a time from the pack of twenty-five and look at it while the subject notes his guess as to which of the five designs is printed upon that card. Since the experimenter knows which design is on the card, the subject may obtain the correct design through telepathic reaction with the experimenter. In testing for clairvoyance, the experimenter lifts one card at a time, but does *not* look at it; hence, as he does not know which design is on that card, if the subject guesses correctly, the correct information cannot have come by telepathy, but by the subject's extrasensory perception of the card itself, hence clairvoyantly perceiving the design. Precognition can be tested by asking the subject to guess not the card the experimenter is holding, but the next one; or to ask the subject to guess "down through" the entire deck of twenty-five cards, or guessing the order of the designs before they are checked, or guessing the order even before they are shuffled by the experimenter or by a machine.

In fact, however, the process cannot be this simple. Suppose, for example, that the experimenter himself unconsciously and unintentionally perceives the cards in the deck clairvoyantly or precognitively; then, even though he may not look at them, in a test for clairvoyance on the part of the subject, the experimenter unconsciously knows them and the subject may be in telepathic rapport with the experimenter rather than perceiving the cards himself by clairvoyance. Because of this difficulty of separating telepathy, clairvoyance, and precognition, the term "General Extrasensory Perception" or "GESP" was coined to denote a situation wherein there is good evidence for ESP, but one cannot definitely decide which facet of the psi faculty was used.

Eventually, very complicated and circumventing experiments were devised to demonstrate only one of these three facets; randomizing machines and procedures were used to avoid hand shuffling and to minimize the possibility that, by means of PK, the subject was influencing the fall, and hence the order, of the cards. Thus, the techinques of the parapsychological laboratory have become very refined and precise to deal with this most elusive psi; and, as is to be expected in any discipline, there is not complete agreement among researchers as to the facets of psi and their characteristics. One school of thought tends to the view that what has passed for clairvoyances can be adequately explained by telepathy and recognition; another that clairvoyance is the underlying faculty and can account for what has passed as telepathy.

The final large category of mental phenomena consists of the records of mediumistic data. The term "medium" has been used by the spiritualists—a religious group who believe in frequent, if not constant, ability to communicate with the "discarnate" surviving spirits of those who have died—to denote a person who has a highly developed psychic ability. By far the majority of mediums have been women, although some of the very finest have been men. The medium believes that she can, either in a self-induced state of trance, through clairvoyance while awake, or through "automatic writing"— an involuntary writing generally done while in a slightly dissociated state—obtain messages of a "veridical," i.e., verifiable, nature from the discarnate entities which will prove that they survive as self-conscious, remembering, distinctive personalities. In sum, the medium is a go-between, a means of communication between our world and theirs. Psychical researchers often prefer the term "sensitive" or "psychic" because neither of these words implies acceptance of the fact of survival, as "medium" does. In any case, the three terms denote the same type of person.

There are various kinds of sensitives. "Trance mediums" generally go into a self-induced hypnotic state, varying from a very light dissociation to a very deep one; and while in this state, another "personality," termed the medium's "Control," manifests, claiming to be a spirit who will control the medium's body and vocal cords while she is in trance and will "introduce" the spirits who wish to communicate with the "sitter," the person who has arranged the meeting with the medium. Many of these Controls claim to be American Indians, Orientals, and Blacks, maintaining that these peoples have more highly developed psychic abilities. Sometimes, while in trance, there are striking changes in the medium's voice, facial expressions, vocabulary, and gestures from those when awake. Whether the Control may be, in fact, what he claims, or is merely a secondary personality of the medium, is an issue that has been hotly debated for many years. Word Association Tests given some mediums while awake and their Controls while in trance which showed striking countersimilarities, the use of false names of supposedly deceased persons who were really alive and yet were accepted as spirits by the Controls and other "spirits" are among the items of evidence which point to the secondary personality theory. Yet, there have been some highly trained, experienced, and critical investigators who have maintained that while some Controls may fall into this category, others of truly outstanding mediums seem much more likely to be, in part at least, a discarnate entity. Authorities like Salter and Tyrrell have argued that we must, above all, avoid simplistic concepts of personality construction based upon daily experiences and possibly misleading experimentation in dealing with the complexities of mediumship. Whichever may be the case, that which the sitter seeks and must ultimately judge the medium by is whether he obtains from her veridical information which she could not have obtained normally.

A special category of the trance medium is the "direct voice" medium. This rare type is one who, while in trance, seems to be "taken over" directly by the ostensible communicating spirit, rather than working only through the Control. Some of the most dramatic instances of highly veridical information have occurred with direct voice mediums; and some investigators who have been fortunate enough to sit with a good medium of this nature have written how extraordinarily the voice changed; the idiosyncrasies of the purportedly discarnate entity have sometimes been reproduced with uncanny accuracy, and those present have testified that they felt that another personality, entirely distinct from that of the medium or the Control, was present and had often succeeded in convincing the sitter who should know best that he or she was in fact, and not in pious or desperate hope, the surviving spirit of a loved one. One can well imagine how impressive and moving such an experience would be; yet, as with other spontaneous phenomena, the vicarious impact of the incident upon those who merely read about it is seriously lessened. One's critical faculty rejects such an occurrence as implausible at best, impossible at worst, and says, "I'd have to see it for myself."

And this may well be out of the question. Very few have ever had this kind of evidential sitting, although they may have visited many mediums. If such ever did really happen, why cannot it occur regularly? We do not know.

Much more common than the two preceding types is the "clairvoyant" medium, who besides claiming to "see" spirits psychically, often claims "clairaudience" (psychic "hearing" of spirit voices), and/ or "clairsentience" (the "sensing" of unseen presences). It should be noted that trance mediums are generally clairvoyant when awake. The clairvoyant demonstrates her ability while awake; sometimes she may want to hold an object belonging either to the sitter or to the deceased person the sitter hopes to communicate with: we see again the close connection between clairvoyance and psychometry. Clairvoyants vary enormously in quality. Many give only the vaguest kind of generalities with a string of common first names, frequent illnesses and problems, generalized descriptions of the supposed spirits, etc. Some of these items are bound to apply to almost anyone. Such is hardly convincing evidence of survival. However, there have been, and are today, some clairvoyants who have demonstrated a remarkable ability to furnish very specific and unusual veridical information about the sitter, his family, and some of the deceased relatives or friends he wished to learn about.

Among the most convincing evidence for survival from mediumistic data has been that of a few really fine "automatic writing" mediums. One of these, Mrs. Piper, was possibly investigated more thoroughly over a great many years by trained investigators than any other medium. Often, the trance handwriting has varied sharply from the medium's normal script; it has changed sometimes to approximately that of the purported spirit communicating; the vocabulary, foreign phrases, and eccentricities of expression of the supposed discarnate have, on occasion, been reproduced quite accurately; and highly veridical information has been provided.

The principal question with reference to mediumistic material is: what is the source of any veridical data? Could the medium have obtained the information in some normal way, e.g., through the newspapers, obituaries, subtle enquiries about the sitter's family; through the use of leading questions which cause the sitter to give more information than he realizes about the deceased with whom he wishes to communicate; through shrewd observation of the sitter himself—his clothing, use of language, accent, etc.; through the sitter's unintentionally offering information from which the medium can make logical inferences? Assuming that fraud, inference, and observation can be ruled out for a given item, what could be the source? The most straightforward answer, that of the spiritualists, is that obviously the information comes from the one who claims to furnish it, the surviving spirit of a supposedly dead person, thereby establishing the fact of survival. And this answer has been accepted as valid in some instances by some very distinguished psychical researchers after many years of investigating mediums of all varieties and qualities. But as knowledge about psi has grown, including evidence of its power ranging over human experience with, seemingly, no restraint from either time or space, this simplistic view has been increasingly attacked as inadequately eliminating all possibilities.

Veridical data means data which can be verified. How does one set about verifying an item given by a medium? One can refer to one's own memory, or to the memory of someone else who should know the facts; one can examine books, other publications, objects, or documents. Therefore, *if* an item is verifiable, some person must be able to prove its accuracy by human knowledge, by some object, or by some document. But if psi is not limited by time or space, if telepathy, clairvoyance, precognition, and retrocognition are at the medium's command unconsciously, it is *possible* theoretically that the medium could telepathically tap the memory of *any* extant document or object, or precognize *any* future event, and then present this true information to the sitter as coming from a discarnate the convincing personality of which she subconsciously constructs through the use of her intricate dramatic and imaginative mechanism. Such a theory has been termed the "Omnibus," "Extended Telepathy," or "Super ESP" hypothesis. While there seems little, if any, laboratory data to support the willed use of psi in such a complex manner, this hypothesis does mean that there is a theoretically viable alternative to the surviving spirit as the source of any veridical information. Consequently, it is an ironic twist that as the evidence for the reality of psi has increased, so too have the difficulties of proving conclusively that such a faculty demonstrates a non-physical facet of human personality which could survive physical death.

Suppose that such odd phenomena as we have briefly described, as well as others possbily even stranger, do sometimes happen? Of what possible importance are they, other than to demonstrate that the world gets "curiouser and curiouser"? Besides being vaguely intriguing and faintly amusing anecdotes of absurdly unlikely events, why should anyone take the time to study them seriously? Why have some of the world's greatest scientists, mathematicians, philosophers, and scholars of many diverse disciplines devoted years to their investigations? Because these occurrences and the little-known faculties which underlie them may throw some light upon the most basic queries which every thinking individual must sooner or later pose for himself. Who am I? What does it mean to be a human being? Is man some sort of cosmic jest, chance occurrence, or a carefully wrought creature as part of a larger universe plan? Are time, space, cause, effect, and physicality really the basic characteristics of life and any others wishful imagination? Is the "I-ness" of each person merely a psychological awareness entirely dependent upon the brain, or is it a non-physical faculty which utilizes the brain but which, as the essence of a person, could possibly survive the dissolution of the body and brain at death? Is there any fundamental meaning to human life or is it merely "sound and fury, signifying nothing?"

Psychical research as such does not aim or pretend to answer such questions; its *raison d'être* is the scholarly establishment and analysis of paranormal phenomena which, at the moment at least, do not fit within the known patterns of physical "normality" or scientific explanations currently available. However, insofar as psychical research does demonstrate the existence of such occurrences, and gives evidence that the psi faculty seems independent of known physical, spatial, and temporal limitations, it provides data that bear significantly upon the above questions and any tentative answers one postulates. So it is that those who have studied psychical research thoroughly inevitably turn their attention to the theoretical, philosophical, and possibly religious issues raised by its documented findings.

Surely any field of investigation which can shed light upon the most basic questions a human being can ask must be important, indeed essential, to a thinking person's deliberations; and it is this that has attracted so many of distinguished intellectual gifts and attainments to psychical research. This does not mean, however, that psychical research is an esoteric or elitist field; rather, it is one open to anyone who will take the time to study the findings—spontaneous, experimental, and mediumistic—with an open, critical mind, and decide for himself its significance to him.

The entire purpose of this volume is to assist people to begin and to continue such a study. There is no area which holds such fascinating instances of human testimony, sound and faulty, such an admixture of paranormal and fraudulent phenomena, such possibilities for developing one's critical faculties and broadening one's frame of reference. If, as many of us believe, psychical research is one of the most important disciplines in the world, and if, as is the case, among its students one finds distinguished and sensitive people from around the world, it clearly behooves the thoughtful man to give attention to its records.

No task is more difficult or more worthwhile than the considered attempt to determine the meaning of human existence. The challenge of psychical research is not to be content with the obvious, the commonplace, not to equate physical actuality with ultimate reality, but to delve into all possibilities, however curious they may appear, however disparate from the accepted norm, however obliquely or subtly they may bear upon the search, and to synthesize for oneself a world-view and a philosophy which bring fulfillment. Such a quest may well require of us all that we have and all that we are. No one can expect any more; no one, least of all ourselves, should give any less.

CHAPTER TWO

GUIDANCE FOR INDIVIDUALS AND GROUPS

S OME TWO TO THREE HUNDRED persons in the world consider themselves professional parapsychologists and psychical researchers, so the data in this book is already available to them. This volume, however, has been written for those many thousands who are "interested" in psi research, who wish to understand it better, or who would like to read more deeply in order to do some research on their own—informally or formally. This book will guide them in such pursuits. And accordingly, in this revision of the *Guidebook*, eight new sections of the bibliography, titled "Self-Help and Development" and "Textbooks," were added.

Additionally, the following material in this chapter, which is all new, was written especially for this revision of the book as a "how-to" chapter. The sections were written by specialists, so that, with this professional guidance, readers can learn to visualize with confidence, investigate a haunted house, dowse, investigate a poltergeist, do token-object psychometry, conduct target-picture tests, and intelligently sit with a medium.

THE ROLE OF PERSONAL RESEARCH
IN THE SPIRITUAL QUEST
Robert H. Ashby

Any conviction we may develop regarding paranormal abilities and occurrences as they relate to spiritual growth can only be attained by a combination of study, meditation, and personal experience. Otherwise, some major part of the spiritual quest has been bypassed. Study is essential to form a background and framework within which we can experience and learn both safe and unwise avenues of exploration based upon others' experiments and experiences.

Meditation is basic to the unfolding of our psychic potential, for it leads to a vital subjective awareness without which we can hardly judge the validity of the accounts others give. Personal experience adds depth to study and meditation—it develops critical standards, and individual goals in the spiritual quest.

Research is all too often thought of as a dry, dull, ho-hum sort of process carried out by slightly odd persons who have nothing better to do. In fact, however, it can (and should) be exciting since it is an endeavor thoughtful individuals are engaged in regularly, for all that research actually entails is *repeated searching* for information. The more precise the information, the more focused the effort, the more deeply we can probe. And, the deeper we study, the wider our curiosity grows, so that depth of knowledge and breadth of interests are not, as some suppose, mutually exclusive.

Why should questing individuals engage in personal research? First, because that is bound to be the undertaking as we become interested in the paranormal and how it bears on Christianity or other religious tradition. We must discover what ESP and related topics are really about, and that can only be done by research—by inquiry. Second, while the initial stage of research will probably be in the form of reading and discussing, we will inevitably wish, and need, to have first-hand experience with the occurrences we have read about. Third, as we commence this stage, we can make personal research more meaningful to ourselves and to others if we have guidelines as to what to expect, what to avoid, simple procedures, safeguards, controls, and evaluation standards. Without these, we may simply be confused, frightened, or bored, as so many have been as they plunge into a complex field without any prior training. The purpose of this discussion is to point to such tools.

DO YOU HAVE ESP?

The research in dozens of countries by hundreds of professional experiments, together with the thousands of world–wide reports of paranormal experiences give sound reasons to believe that ESP (or, psi, the broader term used today, which expands extrasensory perception to include psychokinesis, which is the movement of objects by will-power alone) is probably a universal faculty, innate, but usually latent, in each individual.

This does *not* mean, necessarily, that everyone is a potential medium or sensitive, as has sometimes been claimed by persons who promise to train anyone to that end for a goodly sum. It *does* mean that you can discover your psi potential, find which facet of it seems strongest or easiest, the conditions under which your psi works best, and increase thereby your sensitivity toward others, not only in the psychic sense of obtaining information paranormally, but in the even more important sense of awareness of others' needs.

How do you set about determining whether you have ESP and to what degree? Do you think you have never had a psychic experience—have never ever known anyone who has had such an experience? You may be quite wrong! Just try the ESP questionnaire that follows and think back carefully over your life's experiences:

1) Have you or a member of your immediate family ever had a "prophetic dream" that seemingly "came true?" Was the dream discussed before the event occurred?

2) Have you or a member of your immediate family ever had a "premonition" or inexplicable flash of knowledge about a then-happening distant event, usually a tragedy such as a death or bad accident? Was the premonition discussed before verification of the event?

3) Have you ever had the certain feeling, "I've seen this person before," when inquiry indicates you probably had not?

4) Have you ever visited a place for the first time, but felt, "I've been here before?" Did that seeming "pre-knowledge" accurately "show" you additional scenes a few minutes or more before you actually saw them? Did you tell anyone of this before the confirmation?

5) Do you *frequently* say or start to say the same thought—even the precise words—that another person speaks? Is this usually with reference to a member of your immediate family or close friend?

6) Do you know that all denominations of Christianity and many other religions throughout history have taught that we have "souls" which survive bodily death? Is this your personal belief?

7) Do you know that the Bible reports the experiences of dozens of persons, from kings to beggars, who were able to receive definite and useful messages from "departed souls" or "higher entities," either by their own abilities or through a "medium"? Have you or a member of your immediate family had such an experience?

8) Have you ever known of a case where recovery from a sickness seemed to be *only* explainable as an answer to prayer? Have you heard ministers or physicians recount such stories?

9) Have you ever observed a "gifted" or "lucky" person throwing dice, who seemed to "command" the appearance of specific scores—beyond all reasonable expectations?

10) Have you ever read newspaper accounts of poltergeists or hauntings in an ordinary home, where for days or weeks there were cups and vases, etc., flying around corners, and heavy furniture was moving without physical explanation (sometimes with police authentication of specific events)?

11) Have you personally known of instances when a dog or cat "followed" their owners to a new home many miles away, where the animal had never been?

12) Have you ever known a person who could remove another's headache in two or three minutes by holding or stroking the throbbing head—and who was usually successful in doing so, time after time?

13) Have you ever briefly held another person's hat, ring, comb, or the like, and suddenly felt a strong emotion about that person, or felt a sure knowledge of some specific fact about the person?

14) Have you ever awakened from a nap or during a night's sleep and found (or imagined) yourself floating near the ceiling looking down on your body (regardless of whether you later decided that you had been dreaming)?

All of the above are known as "psychic phenomena." If you answered "yes" to as many as six questions, then you have had some knowledge of such matters, although you may never have consciously totalled or evaluated your knowledge. *Knowing* that such things *do* happen, as well as having a rationalized *belief* in this phenomena, can favorably affect your own ability to score well in a psychic exercise or test.

There are simple tests that will determine your ESP and enable you to determine the odds against chance of your test results. These tests are easily taken, easily scored, and can be used to test your telepathy, clairvoyance, precognition, or psychometric talents. An excellent, clear and simple description of and instructions for various such tests are contained in Martin Ebon's *Test Your ESP* (New American Library, 1970). Other references regarding quantitative testing will be found in the Bibliographies.

QUALITATIVE TESTING

In experiments of controlled quantitative card-testing, researchers have noted that it is impossible in most experiments to determine exactly whether telepathy, clairvoyance or precognition is being exercised in making a correct "guess"; hence, the term "General Extrasensory Perception" (GESP) was coined for tests that do not attempt to specify the type of psi that is operating. Testing of the qualitative type does not lend itself so readily to statistical analysis and evaluation, but there are methods which can be used for this purpose. The reader is referred in this connection to writings by Pratt, Roll and Owen, cited in the Bibliographies.

Qualitative testing is highly useful for several reasons. 1) It may reveal unsuspected psi abilities among members of a group. 2) It will demonstrate how careful such tests must be to eliminate the alternative explanations of unsuspected sensory cues (unconscious gestures, murmurings, etc.) or chance. 3) It will show how tedious, time-consuming, and even boring such tests can be, thereby illustrating some of the reasons for the "decline effect," i.e., the tendency for ESP abilities to diminish with use, rather than to increase as is the pattern with other aptitudes. 4) It can, however, be designed to be far more interesting than quantitative tests, through the use of targets with higher emotional content, thereby increasing the subject's motivation to achieve. There are various qualitative experiments which groups or individuals can undertake, as are described in various books such as that of Ebon.

Exercise in Relaxation and Visualization
Harold Sherman

Mr. Sherman describes the following exercise as "how to image your future." He says that its use enables us to attract the sort of future we want. It is a meditative exercise that involves the holding of a mental picture, or series of pictures, which clearly show the desired result; it should be repeatedly practiced, and he explains that we must feelingly apply each thought in our consciousness. The exercise can be used with a large audience, repeating the statements aloud, or with a small group, or by an individual in private. It is designed to place us in touch with the creative power of our subconscious:

I now relax my body. . .

I make my feet and legs comfortable. . .

I rest my hands and arms in my lap. . .

I let the seat hold my entire weight. . .

I let go of my body, with my mind. . .

I leave all fears and worries behind. . .

I feel lighter—all physical tenseness is gone. . .

I close my eyes and shut out the world around me. . .

I turn the attention of my thoughts inward and become unselfconscious of my body. . .

I now feel that I am existing only in consciousness. . .

A feeling of great inner peace and quiet begins to come over me. . .

In this moment of quiet—this inner stillness—I describe in words, and also present in mental picture form, what I feelingly desire. . .

If it is better health—I picture healing energy permeating every cell and organ of my body—renewing and revitalizing it. . .

If I seek new opportunities and achievements—whatever they may be—I picture myself already having received them. . .

Then, through an exercise of faith, I set up in myself a confident expectation that what I have visualized will come to pass in my outer life. . .

That all the resources and developments I need are on their way to me, in time. . .

That I will be led by my creative power and my intuition to be at the right place at the right time. . .

And that I will be protected and guided every day thoughout my life.

How to Investigate a "Haunted House"
Gertrude R. Schmeidler

Dr. Schmeidler is professor emeritus of psychology at City College of City University of New York, where she conducted credit classes in parapsychological subjects and parapsychology experiments for more than twenty-five years. She is currently president of the American Society for Psychical Research and has twice been president of the Parapsychological Association. The following material is adapted, with permission, from articles by Dr. Schmeidler in the Journal, ASPR (Apr. 1966, 60/2, pp. 137-149; Oct. 1968, 62/4, pp. 399-410, with Dr. Thelma Moss).

If a friend ever says, "I think my house is haunted; are you interested?"—what would you say? With the guidance given below, you might find such a project of investigation, conducted on a scientific basis, to be easier to perform, and producing more impressive results, than you might expect.

Your preparation need only include: 1) arranging for the permission and cooperation of the occupants; 2) the making of a simple floor-plan (approximately to scale) of each floor, adjacent buildings and area frequented by the ghost; and 3) arranging for an on-site "psychic tour" by three or more psychic-sensitives who agree to participate in accordance with your procedure. These psychic-sensitives should not know the persons or house involved nor anything about what was reported. A larger number of sensitives (up to ten or twelve) probably would ensure that coincidence does not explain any correspondences in the scoring.

You may wish to balance the efforts of the sensitives with a group of non-sensitive controls, who go through the same procedure. However, I find no need for such, and my reasons are given at p. 140 of my first JASPR report. Another way to effect a control-type of evaluation would be to use the same sensitives to tour a different house—preferably a fairly new one where the occupants feel sure there is no haunting. Whether the sensitives strongly sense a ghost's presence in the "new" house, or not, the variations and groupings of scorings among the sensitives can be compared with their previous scorings and comments—comparing scorings and comments for House A with those for House B. Neither the sensitives nor your associates should know whether both houses are supposed to be haunted.

Enough copies of the floor-plan sheets should be reproduced to provide one set to each occupant and visitor who has sensed the haunting effect, as well as one set each for the sensitives. Also, instructions should be drafted, followed by an Adjective Checklist to describe the personality of the ghost, and a Physical Appearance Checklist and multiple copies of these lists should be reproduced. Samples of all three forms of checklist follow this article. If preliminary discussion with the occupants indicates that this was a fairly active ghost, it may be desirable also to provide an Activity Checklist. Floor-plans and checklists should be scored by the occupants and visitors, together with any amplifying comments they can make, and should be collected before the visit of the sensitives. Occupants should mark the floor-plan with a red X where they sensed the frequent presence of the ghost, and with a blue X at the places where the ghost was sensed more rarely.

If preliminary interviews with the occupants indicate that visitors to the premises have had significant sensing of possible paranormal visitations there, such visitors should be requested (as just referenced above) to score the checklists and provide any amplifying statements they wish to add, since the observations of non-residents may be especially useful upon subsequent evaluation of results. The occupants should also be asked whether there are particular hours of the day or night, weather conditions, or any other factors which seem to be favored by the "ghost" or haunting effects. Specific "activity" that seems customary for the ghost should also be elicited. Any strong indication in these respects can be given consideration in scheduling the walk-through by participating sensitives.

When the on-site participation of the sensitives is scheduled, the principal investigator should be assisted by two or three associates who do not know what the occupants or visitors reported. Arrangements must be made for the occupants to be away from the premises at the time of the sensitives' visit to obviate contamination of the results by the way the occupants behave. An investigator should walk through the premises before the sensitives do, to ensure that necessary lights are on, etc., and that no sensory cues as to the haunting are left around. If statistical evaluation, formal reporting, and a scientific presentation of results is planned, the principal investigator should also absent himself from the premises for the same reason, and leave the on-site handling of the sensitives to his associates.

The sensitives should be kept at one point by an associate investigator (who has not seen the scoring data of the occupants), who will furnish a set of floor-plans to each of the sensitives *as they start* to tour the premises, *one at a time*. Each sensitive will be instructed to put his/her name on each sheet and to mark the floor-plan (while on the tour) as the places which feel as if they have been visited by a ghostly presence. Upon completing the tour, each sensitive will be taken by another associate investigator to an out of the way place— perhaps the backyard, if it's summer. It's important that each sensitive goes through the house alone. These precautions should preclude any conversation between sensitives who have completed the tour with those not yet finished.

As each sensitive completes the tour, the associate investigator will take the marked floor-plans, and give the sensitive the checklists for immediate scoring; the checklists should be promptly collected also. Sensitives should be encouraged to add any comments they wish to the checklists, for data not specifically requested might be meaningful.

The floor-plans and checklists are so simple that it will be very easy to look for correspondences. First, look for correspondences between the statements (scorings) of the occupants; then, between the statements of the visitors; then, between the occupants and the visitors. Commonalities within and between these two groups, and upon combining them, can readily be developed. Finally, one will look for commonality within the group of sensitives, and between them and the scorings of the occupants/visitors.

A statistician, especially one familiar with parapsychological experiment scoring, can provide chance-expectation and related statistics on the basis of the data developed by the above procedures. If very precise location statistics are desired, the floor-plan sheets can be lightly marked with a grid of squares, each relating to an approximate four by four foot area of each floor of the house, and these squares can be numbered on a master set of floor-plans, or can be identifiable by coordinates on the margins (e.g., numbers for the vertical columns and letters for the horizontal columns of squares).

Post-hoc investigations can sometimes provide interesting avenues for speculation or action, and possible conclusions. If any of the sensitives report a message, purpose, need, or identification from the ghostly presence, the investigator will wish to check the report data with the occupants to determine if there seems to be correlation with any present or past occupant of the premises. Since hauntings are usually place-oriented, the relationship may be with a prior occupant, which a special investigation might disclose. Not only identity, but also activities reported for the resident ghost may correlate with prior occupants.

But, as Mrs. Eileen Garrett once said in an alleged haunting case, since the lady of the house was "eminently psychic. . .she might be producing the shadows." This leads us to wonder whether a ghostly presence could be created unconsciously by a living person, perhaps by repressed needs, and whether this presence could be perceived by others. In this connection, one may consult *New Horizons* journal, 1974, 1, 6-13, for the discussion titled, "Generation of Paranormal Physical Phenomena in Connection with an Imaginary 'Communicator'," by I.M. Owen and M.H. Sparrow.

Checklist 1. Instructions to the Sensitive

In one way, this will be like any other investigation of a haunted house, where the sensitive tries to make contact with a spirit and records all impressions. But there is another way in which this particular investigation is different. The special thing about this one is that members of the family agree on two things: the *places* in the house where the ghost was, and the *kind* of a ghost that it was—its personality.

I'll therefore ask you to do two things, even before you write your own impressions. The first is to go all through the house (first floor, second floor, attic, cellar) and put an X on the floor plan for each place where you feel the ghost is or has been. There are separate floor plans for cellar, for first floor, etc.

Walk through the house, carrying the four floor plans. I recommend the following route, but of course the actual path you take will depend on the individual characteristics of each house.

1) Go in the front door and turn left to the study.

2) From the study, go to the living room, then the dining room, laundry, kitchen, dinette, and then go to the room, bath and closet at the rear.

3) Go up the front stairs to the second floor, and through the four bedrooms, baths, hall, etc. on the second floor.

4) Up the stairs to the attic, storeroom and unused room.

5) Then down the back stairs to the cellar, and all through the cellar.

6) Then out by the rear door, where the experimenter will meet you.

Mark each place where you feel the haunting. Make your marks very, *very* specific. If you want to mark an area just big enough for a person to stand on, make your X so that the lines cross at the place you mean. If you want to make a larger area, encircle the space with a thin line, so that your circle covers *only* the right area. Thus the center of the X or the space within your enclosing line will designate the places you note.

When you come out the back door with your marked floor plans, go to the garage. There you will be given the adjective checklist, and lots of blank paper for you to add whatever you choose.

And many, many thanks for coming to help!

Checklist 2. Adjectives to Describe Ghost

Respondent's name ———————————————————.

Before you write your own special impressions, would you check off the following list? Put a circle around every word that describes your impression of the ghost. Cross out (put a line through) every word that is definitely wrong, so wrong that it is the opposite of the impression you received.

active	dignified	leisurely
affectionate	distrustful	mature
aggressive	emotional	meek
alert	enterprising	mischievous
aloof	fearful	noisy
anxious	forceful	obliging
apathetic	forgiving	patient
arrogant	friendly	peaceable
bitter	gentle	quiet
calm	greedy	rigid
changeable	headstrong	shy
cold	helpful	stern
complaining	humorous	strong
confused	immature	submissive
contented	impatient	tolerant
cruel	impulsive	trusting
demanding	independent	vindictive
despondent	irritable	warm
determined	jolly	weak

Checklist 3. Ghost's Physical Appearance

Respondent's name _____.

Ghost's age _____ Sex _____ Height _____

Body build _____

_____

_____

Musculature _____

Hair color _____ Complexion _____

Teeth _____ Wears glasses _____

Hearing Aid _____ Face Hair _____

Obvious other physical characteristics _____

_____

_____

_____

Clothing, upper _____

_____

_____

_____

Clothing, lower (including shoes) _____

_____

_____

_____

Clothing, outer _____

_____

_____

_____

Checklist 4. Ghost's Activity

Respondent's name ⸺

Please put a circle around the activities which seem most like what the ghost appeared to be doing, and *cross out* (put a line through) those activities which seem most opposite (wrong) to what the ghost was doing.

Annoying someone	Playing a musical instruments
Attacking someone	Playing a game
Building something	Pursuing someone
Cooking something	Puttering around
Crying	Reading
Dancing	Repairing something
Eating	Resting
Floating about the ground	Revenging on someone
Flying in the air	Running
Gesturing	Searching for something
Getting rid of someone or something	Sewing
Helping someone	Singing
Hiding himself	Sitting
Insulting someone	Standing up
Laughing	Stealing something
Lying down	Talking
Mocking or imitating someone	Threatening someone
Musing	Walking in a definite direction
Pacing restlessly	Wandering aimlessly
Peering around	Writing

HOW TO DOWSE
Louis J. Matacia

Mr. Matacia is a certified land surveyor licensed in six east-central states who has spent more than twenty years as a professional dowser. During the Vietnam War he trained U.S. Marines to dowse for Viet-Cong munitions caches and tunnels, land mines, booby-traps and other military structures. He taught them to dowse with L-shaped, modified, wire coat-hangers; the Marines dubbed this instrument "Matacia's Wire Rudder."

Water dowsing is ages-old. Perhaps Moses was a dowser. Now we know that dowsing is not limited to finding underground water— we can find any structure made by nature or man. Attempts have been made to explain dowsing on conventional scientific bases, but sophisticated dowsing, even for water, is beyond physical explanation. Some have suggested that telepathy is part of the explanation, but map-dowsing with a pendulum for geological data (ores, oil, etc.), or for a sunken submarine, precludes mental or physical explanations. Dowsing involves some physical force because it is impossible to keep a nylon Y-rod or a forked-stick from pointing down when it is over the objective; dowsing also involves intelligence, for the rod or pendulum will accurately answer questions asked silently by the dowser when correct information is not known to any living person, but dowsing is more than either of these. Dowsing will locate unknown or lost objects and structures (either where one stands or at a distance), and will then provide detailed information about the object. Dowsing is limited only by the imagination and belief of the dowser—some people cannot dowse, though most can.

My wire rudder dowsing rods are easy to make and to use. Take two heavy wire coat-hangers and clip off the hook sections; straighten both rods. Measure 34 inches, clip both rods at this point, and throw away the short pieces. Now, measure 26 inches, and bend both rods there, making a right angle at this point; the result will be two L-shaped rods (one for each hand), with an 8-inch handle and a 26-inch pointer. Hold them loosely in your fists at chest-level with elbows comfortably bent, and with the parallel pointers aimed straight ahead, about four to six inches apart (fists touching). You are now ready to dowse. In your kitchen, tell yourself that you want to locate water-pipes, and walk slowly from the east wall to the west wall; if nothing happens, walk from the north wall to the south wall. There is a high likelihood that water-pipes are under the kitchen floor, and when your fists are exactly over one, the pointers will have swung right and left (respectively, in your right and left fists), forming together a straight line parallel and above the water-pipe. If your basement is unsealed, you can look up between the joints of the kitchen floor and see that the dowsing pointers located a water-line exactly.

Nylon Y-rods are a very effective modern substitute for the old-fashioned forked-stick, which was usually hickory or willow wood. The nylon dowsing rods are available from many specialty shops and are advertised in New Age periodicals. They can also be made quite readily from the small ends of two nylon fishing rods. Using two 18-inch lengths, placed side by side, bind the small ends tightly together for a distance of four or five inches by wrapping with nylon fishing line. The wrapped end will be the pointer. Then, spread the two butts apart, with them lying in your upturned palms at belt level; grip the butts firmly, moving your wrists slightly until the pointer is aimed horizontally and straight ahead of you. You are now ready to dowse. The nylon Y-rod is usually favored for field dowsing, and one talks silently "to the rod" as he walks steadily across the field. Water, sewer, electrical, and gas lines are usually convenient structures to search for while developing your skill. The rod is held under "balanced tension" in the horizontal position, and when the dowser reaches a point over the desired structure, the pointer will *forcefully* point downward.

If the Y-rod is to provide detailed information as well as to locate concealed structures, the dowser must learn extreme care in posing his questions correctly so that there can be no doubt as to the meaning of the answer. Usually, it is desirable for the novice to "program" his Y-rod so that both rod and dowser understand the meaning of its movements. Questions to which responses are *Yes* and *No* should be used as long as possible. At some point a more sophisticated technique of communication may be needed. Conventionally, a pointer turned down is *Yes* to the dowser's question, and a pointer turned up is *No*. If a direction is desired, the rod should be held in the neutral (straight ahead) position, while the dowser turns his body slowly in an arc or full circle asking the question: "Which direction?" This is often done to find the most favorable location of a structure or substance being sought. When the answer is "that way," the pointer will dip toward the ground. While standing still, the dowser can then silently "call off" distances (10 feet, 20 feet, 30 feet, etc.) and the pointer will dip at the approximately correct number, which the dowser can then step off.

In recent years dowsers have learned to save much time and effort and to expand the variety of problems they can solve by using the pendulum to supplement their dowsing rod. The pendulum consists of a small weight at the end of a short cord or chain. The weight can be literally anything — a coin, a lump of glass, ore, semi-precious stone, a ring. Many feel that crystal has special psychic properties and makes a good pendulum weight; some feel that the shape of the pendulum is important and opt for a sphere (like a marble) or a tear-drop shape. The cord or chain need be only six to eight inches in length. The dowser may wish to program his pendulum to suit his personal needs. There are common or conventional rules usually agreed-to between the dowser and the intelligence of his pendulum:

1) Hold the pendulum about breast-high and some ten inches from the body, perfectly still.

2) A "Yes" answer will be a fairly strong swing straight toward and away from the dowser's body.

3) "No" will be a straight side-to-side swing.

4) A diagonal swing (out to the right diagonal and back to the left diagonal) may mean yes *and* no, or "re-phrase the question."

5) The opposite diagonal (out to the left and back to the right) can be agreed as danger, or difficulty.

6) A clockwise rotation in a wide circle usually is a strong "Yes."

7) A counter-clockwise rotation usually will be a *definite* No, or "rephrase the question."

Odd-looking oscillating swings (figure-eights) sometimes appear when using the pendulum; if these are tight oscillations near the "No" meridian but swinging from one diagonal gradually to another, it is usually signalling, "the time is not right." Occasionally, the pendulum will respond to a question with wide, sweeping oscillations moving all around the circle. This frequently means that the basic information given the dowser is false, or the question posed will bring a misleading, undesirable, or unuseable answer.

The pendulum, like the dowsing rod, is a very personal tool and the dowser will need much practice and close observation to learn how the pendulum may be programming him (as well as the converse), so that he and the pendulum intelligence can become a smooth-working team. Obviously, the pendulum can be used in the search for all sorts of information and lost objects, etc. (Some people even use it to determine the better items on a restaurant menu!) For straight dowsing, however, its use is most helpful at the beginning and end of a standard dowsing search.

Typical in such regard is use of the pendulum for map-dowsing, which can reduce a search over thousands of miles to a very precise area in just a few minutes. With a basic map spread out before the dowser, his questions can quickly bring him to a larger-scale map so he can pin-point the desired location. Similarly, once at the precise location in the field, the dowser may take the pendulum in preference to the rod in working out some of the detailed information.

Water dowsing alone involves many tricky and difficult problems that the dowser learns only through study, work under a professional dowser, trial and error, many mistakes, and innumerable hours of practice. Some people quickly learn that they have a natural aptitude for dowsing, but there are no short-cuts to fully reliable work. For instance, in water dowsing it is very tempting to stake-out a drill site at the very center of the water perimeter found; however, very little subterranean water is found in pools (which is more typical of oil)— water is usually flowing, and is often meandering; actually the safe procedure is to *ask* the dowsing-rod intelligence for the best site on the *lower side* of the flow, because when the water flow diminishes in volume your well will be unaffected.

In water dowsing, there are many vital bits of information needed beyond the initial question of where to drill. One of the most obvious is the depth at which a reliable water source will be found, and the type of material that must be penetrated to reach it. The direction of flow of the underground stream can be important, and very especially it will be necessary to know the volume of water per minute that will be available. Sometimes it may be necessary to recommend two wells at a given site in order to produce the desired quantity. Will the water be clear, potable etc.? Will the well be safe from earthquake, from contamination? The problems are endless and, largely, can be anticipated and resolved only on the basis of the dowser's experience, study, and ingenuity.

How to Investigate a Poltergeist
William G. Roll

Mr. Roll is Director of the Psychical Research Foundation in Carrollton, Georgia, and editor of Theta. *The primary activity of the PRF is in the area of human survival of bodily death. Roll is a past–president of the Parapsychological Association. The following material is adapted with permission from the appendix of his book,* The Poltergeist *(Doubleday, 1972).*

To carry out a serious study of a suspected poltergeist, familiarity with the scientific literature is a requirement. It would also help the student or would-be investigator to contact professional parapsychologists, preferably before his investigation. People interested in such studies may become voluntary field reporters for the Psychical Research Foundation (write to Psychology Dept., West Georgia College, Carrollton, GA 30118).

It is not yet known whether the differences between hauntings and poltergeist phenomena are only superficial or whether they result from different psychical processes. In general, poltergeist incidents are connected with an individual, while hauntings seem to be connected with an area, usually a house. Physical disturbances predominate in poltergeist incidents, hallucinatory experiences in hauntings. However, hauntings tend to stretch over longer periods of time while poltergeist disturbances are usually of fairly short duration, rarely lasting more than a couple of months. A haunting may go on for years.

The investigator should try to prevent publicity, at least until a study has been made. If intensive research is to be undertaken, the investigator must arrive at the scene as soon as possible. He should try to get a good appraisal of the case before he arrives by talking to the family and others who have been present during the events. Dr. Pratt and I have developed a questionnaire for this purpose; it will be found at the end of this article. Its main purpose is to determine whether or not a case seems to be genuine and deserves serious investigation, and if so, what form this should take. In my opinion, it is best to begin a personal investigation in a low–keyed fashion. This means the investigator should try to blend in with the psychological and social situation in the home or area where the disturbances take place. Controls, tests, and instruments should be introduced gradually and inconspicuously. There is a need for physical instrumentation, such as the closed-circuit television monitoring of the active areas, particularly if this can be introduced without disturbing the psychological situation.

Poltergeist occurrences are "people happenings." However strange the events are, first and foremost they involve the people in whose homes or businesses they erupt. The poltergeist student soon finds himself intimately associated with several classes of people. The primary group, the people in whose territory the phenomena occur, usually wish them to end as quickly and painlessly as possible. It is therefore likely that they have asked the help of a second group, namely people whose professions or skills seem appropriate. Depending upon the educational and social background of the family, they may seek help from members of the building profession, from police officers, the clergy, and so on. The members of this second group have their own attitudes. If a police officer, or clergyman, or another individual has consented to enter the case, it is probably because he believes that his skills may help the family, and he will proceed on this basis. If his approach is balanced by common sense, his contribution may be useful, whether or not he finds an explanation for the phenomena.

If the occurrences have become generally known, a third group, consisting of representatives of the news media, such as press, radio, and television reporters, is likely to enter the picture. Their main responsibility is to their media and they are often expected to provide dramatic and entertaining stories. These, in turn, are likely to draw in a fourth group, namely curiosity-seekers whose presence and behavior is usually extremely disruptive both for the life of the family concerned and for the conduct of a serious investigation. A serious investigator usually must first resolve the social problems presented by these four groups of people and by their different needs and activities.

Usually the investigator/parapsychologist is the last to appear on the scene. His concern is basically to explain the phenomena. However, an investigation can best be carried out by examining the phenomena while they are occurring. If the family recognizes this need, they may be willing to follow his suggestions, even if these are not designed to put an immediate stop to the incidents.

To obtain a record of earlier occurrences in the case, which should be as complete and as accurate as possible, the parapsychologist or student investigator also needs the cooperation of the second group, the investigators and observers who have probably been involved from a practical rather than from a scientific point of view. Their collaboration may also be useful in gathering information about disturbances which take place while the investigator is on the scene.

When representatives of the news media have been alerted, the investigator must attempt an agreement with them, so that there will be as little publicity as possible during the investigation period. This is particularly important since the fact that the parapsychological investigation is being made is itself newsworthy, and likely to draw in additional reporters and curiosity-seekers, if it becomes generally known. If the investigator can deal satisfactorily with the representatives of the news media, then the fourth group, the curiosity-seekers, are not likely to present a serious disruption.

Poltergeist and haunting cases show different characteristics and have to be studied in different ways. The questionnaire at the end of this section will bring these out. The questionnaire should be answered by the people primarily involved. When there have been outside witnesses, they, too, should be interviewed. Especially in poltergeist cases, which are likely to be short-lived, the questionnaire should be given as soon as possible, either face-to-face or by telephone.

Sometimes the onset of the events coincides with a birthday or other significant date. If this date is particularly important to some person in the house, this may indicate that he is psychically involved in the events. If there are children at the age of puberty or adolescence, this may indicate that the events concern a poltergeist. If the people involved have had psychic experiences in the past, particularly if the experiences are similar to the present occurrences, this may indicate that the people are important for the phenomena.

A case is particularly promising if visitors to the house have been present during the incidents and are willing to describe their experiences. This is especially helpful if the visitors have some training or qualifications as investigators (such as police officers or reporters).

In my experience, these people are often much more cautious and objective than public reports sometimes suggest.

Usually people who have witnessed poltergeist incidents have a theory about them. It may be important to know what this is, and whether the theory has any basis in fact. The family's beliefs may also affect the investigation.

It is not always easy to determine whether sound and light effects are physical unless tape recorders, film, and other means of instrumental registration are used. The rule of thumb is to classify knocks, lights, etc., as physical if everybody who is in a position to see or hear them actually does so. If the event is noticed only by some of those present, it is not physical in the ordinary sense of the word, and should be classified under "nonphysical phenomena."

In poltergeist incidents, the objects in motion often seem to behave in strange ways, sometimes moving around corners, sometimes accelerating or slowing down. Such features, particularly if unexpected by the observers, make it more likely that genuine incidents are taking place. On the other hand, an object falling directly to the floor from its shelf may more easily be explained by tremors caused by traffic, settling of the house, and the like. Also, objects that move in poltergeist homes sometimes produce unusually loud noises when they hit. There may be thumps and bangs without visible physical causes. If objects move while somebody is watching, this is particularly significant. The watchwords of the investigator are: inquire, observe, record.

POLTERGEIST QUESTIONNAIRE

General Background

1) Where have the disturbances taken place?

2) When did the disturbances begin?

3) How recently has anything happened?

4) How does the frequency and severity at this time compare with earlier periods?

5) Who are the members of the household or group involved? What are their ages?

6) Have any of the persons who witnessed the phenomena had telepathic dreams or other psychic experiences in the past? If so, state who they are and describe the experiences.

7) Were any of the persons who witnessed the phenomena interested in psychic matters before the present disturbances began? If so, indicate their areas of interest.

8) Have attempts been made to find an ordinary explanation of the events? For example, is there reason to think that someone is doing these things as a prank or that they could be due to settling of the house, rodents, or similar causes?

9) Are there pets or farm animals in the area? If so, how do they react to the disturbances?

10) Have any visitors to the house or area witnessed the disturbances? If so, are they willing to testify? (Ask for names and addresses of such persons.)

11) Do you or others who witnessed the phenomena have any idea or theory about their cause?

Localization of Phenomena

12) Are events more frequent at certain times during the 24 hours of the day than at others? If so, state which periods.

13) Are they more frequent in certain places (for example, in certain rooms of the house) than in others? If so, state where.

14) Do the occurrences happen more frequently in the presence or vicinity of certain persons than others? If so, state which people. Do events take place when they are not in the area?.

15) Has anything been known to happen when no one was in the area?

Physical Disturbances

Answer Questions 16-23 only if there are physical disturbances, such as unexplained movements of objects.

16) Describe these disturbances.

17) How frequent are the disturbances?

18) If there have been unexplained movements of objects, was there anything strange about the manner in which the objects moved or stopped (for example, objects that moved around corners, hit with unusually great force, and so forth)?

19) Are unusually loud noises caused by the moving of objects? If so, describe these noises.

20) Are there noises not connected with the disturbances of objects? If so, describe these noises.

21) Has anyone ever seen an object *start* to move when no one was near it? If so, describe these occurrences.

22) Have things happened when no one was in the area or room in which the disturbances took place? If so, describe the occurrences.

23) Are special objects or kinds of objects disturbed more often than others? If so, which?

Non-physical Phenomena

Answer Questions 24-31 only if there are unusual phenomena not caused by the movements of objects or by other physical disturbances. (For instance, if there are "ghost," "footsteps," sensations of heat and cold, unexplained sounds, sights, smells, and touches.)

24) Describe these experiences.

25) How frequent are these experiences?

26) Who first noticed them and when?

27) What other persons, if any, have had these experiences and when did they have them?

28) Were the people who had these experiences aware that others had had such experiences in the area before they did?

29) Have there been instances where the ghost, footsteps, and so on were experienced by some persons in the room or area but not by others? If so, describe these cases.

30) Do the ghosts or images resemble actual persons and events from the past? If so, describe the evidence for this. Were these persons or events connected with the house?

31) Did the people who experienced the ghost or image know about the person whose ghost they saw *before* they saw it?

Future Investigation

32) Would the family or group welcome a serious investigation of the disturbances by someone who could make firsthand observations?

33) Has there been any publicity about the events? If not, can you be reasonably sure of not letting any get started?

34) If things are relatively inactive at this time and the prospects for a visit uncertain, will you telephone us collect at once if the events become more active?

How to Do Token-Object Psychometry
Frank C. Tribbe

Mr. Tribbe is editor of SFF's journal, Spiritual Frontiers, *and is Publications Chairman for the Academy of Religion and Psychical Research. In addition to dozens of articles, papers presented at scientific meetings, and book reviews published in journals and other periodicals, he is author of* Creative Mediation: A Leader's Manual with Guided Meditations *(S.F.F., 1975), and* Portrait of Jesus?—The Illustrated Story of the Shroud of Turin *(Stein & Day, 1983).*

Psychic sensing from a "token object" is called "psychometry." The "object" must be *intimate and uncontaminated*. To be intimate, it is usually necessary that the item has been regularly, if not constantly, in the possession of the subject for a considerable length of time—months, if not years. Preferably, the item should have been in actual contact with the subject's skin much of the time. To be uncontaminated, the item should be one that is almost never touched by others—especially for long periods, or recently.

Token objects should never be passed from hand to hand, on the way to the psychometrist who is reading for a group. These items should be passed in an envelope, or items from everyone in the group may be dropped into a receptacle so that no one but the psychometrist touches them.

"Good" objects for psychometry might be rings (never worn by anyone else), eye-glasses, watches, ear-bobs, necklaces, pendants, neck-chains, and wrist-bands. "Poor" objects would be pens (because they are frequently used by others), jewelry that is shared in the family, billfolds (because money and cards are touched by others), items from a woman's purse (both because they are touched only a small percentage of the time, and because they are often in contact with objects that are touched by others). Scientific experiments and inquiries frequently make use of locks of hair (in an envelope) or a drop of blood (on a piece of new, white blotter).

In group readings, it is always best to read an object "blind" which means that the psychometrist does not know the identity of the owner of the object. An additional reading (after identification of the person) will then more likely flow from the initial blind reading instead of from the sensory cues emanating from the person.

In group readings, psychometrists usually avoid contaminating one object by another by wiping their hands with a damp cloth between each object. Some cleanse themselves after reading one object by vigorously rubbing and shaking their hands.

A psychometric reading may consist of two parts: information about the object itself, how and where it was made and used; and information about the person who presently possesses it. If the object presented was that of a person now deceased, it is important that the object has not been used, worn or handled very much or very recently by survivors of the deceased. One of the most important rules of psychometry is for the reader never to hold back on ideas that come—they *must* be spoken regardless of how ridiculous they may seem to the psychometrist, else all additional thoughts will be stifled. He usually tries to improve his "sensing" by turning the object over and over, rubbing it between both hands, or by holding it to the forehead.

Psychometrists have sometimes given startlingly accurate readings for archaeological artifacts, even though unaware of where the item was found, or even that it was of ancient origin.

An interesting token-object to be given for a reading is a small photograph of the kind usually carried in a card-case. In spite of "contamination" by the owner and by the handlers of the cards kept in the case, it is frequently possible to get a surprisingly good reading for the person whose picture is on the photo. Photographs should be read face-down to preclude sensory cues misleading (or leading) the psychometrist.

How to Conduct Target Picture Tests
Robert H. Ashby

These simple and interesting tests can be easily conducted by anyone to test for ESP ability using pictures as targets; your "subjects" will guess the hidden targets. Follow these steps:

1) The Experimenter either draws or cuts out pictures for the targets. The pictures should be dramatic and colorful, with as much emotional content in terms of subject and treatment as possible. If pictures from magazines or newspapers are used, be sure there are no pictures on the reverse side of the paper for they may confuse the subject during the test and make judging the "hits" more difficult.

2) The Experimenter places a number on each picture. He then places each target picture in a thick, flat envelope with cardboard or other light-blocking material on each side of the target picture (inside the envelope). He then seals the envelope. Usually, ten pictures are used for an experiment of this sort.

3) The Experimenter has the envelopes containing the pictures randomized (shuffled) by someone unconnected with the experiment. After randomization, the Experimenter marks a letter in each envelope (in sequence, beginning with A, then B, etc.). Each subject

should be furnished a score-sheet on which is written his or her name, and a "guess" record sheet bearing only an assigned number.

4) The tests can be run to emphasize telepathy, clairvoyance, or precognition; it must be recognized that those three cannot be absolutely separated or identified under test conditions—we merely suggest one will be the likely faculty in a given instance.

To Emphasize Telepathy: All subjects write "Run #1" on their sheets. The Experimenter opens Envelope A in a manner so that the subjects cannot see its contents. He looks fixedly at picture A, and invites the subject to telepathize with him to obtain the picture. They are to either draw or describe the picture (or both), on their "guess" record sheets.

To Emphasize Clairvoyance: All subjects write "Run #2" on their sheets. The Experimenter lifts Envelope B from the pack and holds it, still sealed, in view of the subjects. The subjects are asked to see through the envelope and cardboard, and to perceive the target picture clairvoyantly. They are to either draw or describe the picture (or both), on their "guess" record sheets.

To Emphasize Precognition: The Experimentor re-seals Envelope A, replacing the envelopes in A, B, C, order. He tells the subjects that in a few moments he will again randomize (shuffle) the envelopes; before he does so, however, they are to "guess" the new order of the envelopes by letter (make a list of numbers 1 through 10, and note the envelope letters in new order). Then, he tells the subjects to clairvoyantly "see" the pictures inside the envelopes, and to draw and/or describe them next to the envelope letters on their "guess" record sheets. When this has all been done, the Experimenter will *now* randomize (shuffle) the envelopes to complete the test.

5) All phases of the above tests should be graded at once, with scoring on a separate page (on the score-sheet, not the "guess" record). The Experimenter will first write the numbers (in sequence) on the envelopes to establish their final order, and will be careful to keep the pictures with the proper envelopes. He will first lift out envelope A, open it, and show the subjects the picture so that they can score their telepathy "guess" as a hit, a near-hit, or a miss. He will then put envelope A back in the final order in the pack, and lift out envelope B. Opening the envelope, he will then hold up the picture to

show the target for the clairvoyance test, and give the subjects time to score their "guesses." Putting envelope B back in the final order in the pack, he will then go slowly through the pack, of envelopes 1 through 10 in the final order, reading off the matching envelope letters, and displaying the picture that goes with each. The subjects score both parts of the precognition test.

6) A second evaluation can now made by having the subjects exchange their "guess" record and score-sheets, and note a supplemental scoring where they disagree with their fellow's self-scoring. Often, the fellow-subject will find correspondences not noticed by the subject himself. At both times, during self-scoring and during fellow-subject scoring, ample opportunity for full discussion should be allowed.

7) During the discussion periods, two anomalies should be kept in mind, and all should watch for them: A) Cross-telepathy may occur where two subjects clearly miss the target picture, but record approximately the same wrong picture. B) A displacement-effect may be occurring—which means the subject clearly "hits" the picture ahead or the picture behind.

8) Keeping the envelopes in final order and all pictures in the proper envelopes, the Experimenter then collects all the "guess" records and score-sheets, for objective judging (optional). This will be performed by one or three persons who have had no connection with the tests. For the record, the letter and the number from the envelope (as evidence of the first order and the final order sequence of the envelopes) will be transposed, along with the picture-number, to a master list which the Experimenter will keep (example: 1-G-6). The Experimenter can then give the judge all the pictures (bearing only the picture-number), along with the "guess" record sheets. The judge will be "blind" as to the scores, the sequences, and other terms and conditions; he will score only on correspondence between drawings and descriptions noted by the subjects and the pictures themselves, being unaware of which were the targets on various tests.

When the judge's decisions are returned to the Experimenter, he should share this additional information with the subjects. The total data in the Experimenter's hands will provide the basis for quite a bit of statistical evaluation.

Sitting with a Medium
Robert H. Ashby

By and large, the most promising aspect of survival research for the layman is mediumistic data. Through the use of careful, time-tested techniques, controls, precautions, and report forms, it is possible that the student may garner significant evidence that will stand severe scholarly inspection and analysis. Principal attitudes and major precautions for sittings are given below:

1) When making an appointment with a medium, it is preferable to use a pseudonym to maintain anonymity. Explain to the medium that you are doing this to strengthen the evidentiary of the material received, *not* because of distrust of the medium. It is by far better to have a sitting alone, unless someone else is needed to take notes.

2) Realize that this research requires great perseverance and patience. Mediumistic material, from even the most gifted mediums, will contain a very large percentage of vague generalities, platitudes, common names, etc., while truly evidential, precise, verifiable data are rare. Have realistic expectations and know that more chaff than wheat will not dishearten, but spur you on to further research.

3) Whether the medium is clairvoyant, clairaudient, clairsentient (see, hear, or feel paranormally), trance (light to deep dissociative state), or direct voice (ostensibly discarnate voices sounding as if apart from the medium's mouth), be sure to follow the medium's instructions as to your actions during the sitting. If those directions are such as to weaken the evidential value of the material, this must be taken into account in judging the data.

4) If one is fortunate enough to locate a medium of quality who will cooperate fully in research, as your rapport and familiarity increase, you can suggest tighter controls or direct your questions to specific research targets or topics. This should not be attempted, however, until such support and mutual confidence are firm. Do *not* rush such a development; let it emerge gradually, with encouragement and patience.

5) If at all possible, obtain permission (before the sitting) to tape the entire session. A full, verbatim record of the material is essential for

accurate judgment of evidence. Many mediums are amenable to this so long as the the sitter does not annoy or distract by the manipulation of the recorder during the sitting. Be sure the recorder is operating properly before the sitting; use as large a tape as possible to preclude changing tapes during the sitting; check that the machine is quiet; be as unobtrusive as possible in operating it. In the absence of a recorder, take as full set of notes as possible. Note the medium's gestures, facial expression, and any peculiarities which seem significant or evidential. Even with a recorder, notes of the latter type should be made, since they will not appear on the tape.

6) Do not divulge any more information to the medium before, during, or after the sitting than is absolutely necessary to assist in a successful session. If the medium, for example, asks "Is your father in spirit?" (meaning, is he deceased?), answer, "yes" or "no." Do *not* reply, "Yes, he died in 1966 of cancer of the lungs, in St. John's Hospital, Detroit, on April 17, age 58." Such gratuitous information eliminates the possibility of the medium obtaining it paranormally; it may lead her astray in her subsequent impressions; and it may cause her to *infer* other facts which cannot then be admitted as evidence.

7) Corollary to the preceding (when asked by the medium), the sitter should clarify a point as briefly as possible; state frankly when a statement is wrong or confusing, but do so in an encouraging rather than a disparaging manner: "No, I'm sorry, that is not correct, so far as I can recall, but you have given some very interesting information. Please go on."

8) If the medium wishes to use a token object, ask beforehand which type of article she prefers: jewelry, leather, clothing, etc., and approximate that as closely as possible. It is preferable to use objects without initials, inscriptions, or dates upon them as these can give cues for inference by the medium, even subconsciously, which can invalidate data. The object should have strong emotional connotations for its owner. If it belongs to someone other than the sitter, handle it as little as possible. Preferably, wrap it and hand it to the medium to unwrap.

9) Since it may happen that the medium's attempts are abortive and nothing of consequence is given, the sitter should be understanding and sympathetic rather than critical; such attitudes are far more

likely to produce the rapport essential to eventual success. If, after several sittings, it seems clear that one cannot expect fruitful results with the medium, part amicably and seek another medium.

10) It is always wise *not* to tell the medium which, if any, of the informational bits are evidential, except when absolutely necesary to keep the sitting progressing, because if such items recur with another medium, it could be argued (and sometimes justifiably) that the first medium told the second which data would be personally evidential to the sitter.

Very early in the development of psychical research, it was found that mediums could and would report information as emanating from discarnates which was in fact obtained telepathically from the sitter. This "telepathic leakage" problem led to the development of the "proxy sitting." In such a sitting, someone acts as sitter on behalf of another, thereby removing, by one stage at least, the telepathic leakage. Since the proxy sitter should know nothing or very little of the discarnate with whom it is hoped to communicate, the medium cannot tap the proxy's memory or subconsciousness for information. It could be, and has been, argued that the medium could still have telepathic access to the memory of the persons for whom the sitting is held—either directly or with the proxy acting as a telepathic intermediary. While this theory cannot be obviated, the fact remains that evidential material from a proxy sitting is more impressive than that from the usual arrangement, because one must postulate a more precise and selective psi process on the medium's part to account for the veridical (i.e., "truth–telling") material. One should take the following steps in arranging a proxy sitting:

1) Obtain the medium's agreement beforehand. It should be explained as a research technique and *not* a slur upon the medium's integrity. If the medium does not wish to participate, that is her prerogative.

2) Choose as a proxy a sitter of considerable experience, but preferably one unknown to the medium. This is of less importance in cases where a medium is eager to cooperate in research and where there is an experienced researcher with excellent rapport gained through many sittings with the medium, like Sir Oliver Lodge or the Rev. C. Drayton Thomas. In such instances, it is unlikely that the medium

will be distracted by the proxy and inadvertently direct the reading to *him* rather than to the sitter *in absentia*. This error can occur, however, where such a long–standing relationship is not present.

3) The proxy should know as little as possible about the proposed discarnate communicator, or else the proxy's memory as a source is suspect.

4) If the medium uses a token object it should be of the type she prefers. It should have close association with the target communicator, and be wrapped in cloth or placed in a box. It should not be handled by the proxy any more than absolutely necessary. It is preferable to hand the target to the medium for unwrapping.

5) The proxy should take careful note of any gestures, facial expressions, or other peculiarities manifested by the medium but not showing on the tape recording. These should be presented to the sitter *in absentia* together with the tape.

6) The cross-matching technique described below can be used; it is interesting to have the proxy act as one of the judges to determine whether any of the medium's statements were particularly pertinent to *him* rather than to the sitter *in absentia*. If so, this may indicate inadvertent misdirection of information by the medium, which could mean that, if this proved a pattern, she is unsuitable for proxy sittings.

Many of the most evidential items from sittings are very personal, even intimate, in nature, and the impact of such information— often trivial, even banal, but most pertinent to the ostensible discarnate—is severely lessened when read by someone unfamiliar with the deceased. On the other hand, because of personal involvement, emotion, desire to believe in the survival of loved ones, far greater credence than may be warranted can be given such data by a sitter. Consequently, it is important to try to obtain some more objective judgment about its value.

There are various statistical methods for analyzing such "free verbal response" material. A widely used technique which does not require sophisticated statistical knowledge is cross-matching. The process is as follows:

Table 1. Medium Education Form

Medium (A pseudonym may be used, e.g. Mrs. X) Date of Sitting _____

Location: _____ Time of Sitting _____

Present: Name(s) of sitter(s)

STATEMENTS	True but too general	Too vague to judge	True in fact	True in character	Do not know	Wrong in fact	Wrong to character
1. A lady							
2. Mid-sixties							
3. Blue eyes							
4. Gray hair							
5. Hair blonde, almost white when young							
6. Thin face							
7. High cheekbones							
8. Medium height							
9. Strikingly pretty							
10. Dimple in middle of chin							
11. Very sensitive							
12. Took on others' troubles too much							
13. Name of Martha							
14. Aunt							
15. Died about three years ago							
16. Died of chest ailment							

1) Transcribe the tape recording verbatim. If you took notes at the sitting transcribe them as fully and as soon after the sitting as possible.

2) Break down the medium's remarks into single sentence statements. For example, suppose a section read as follows: "There is a lady here, mid-sixties, very fair, blue eyes, hair gray but was blonde, almost white when young, thin face, high cheekbones, medium height, strikingly pretty, dimple in the middle of the chin, very sensitive, took on the troubles of others too much, gives the name Martha, says she is your aunt, died about three years ago of something wrong in her chest." This would be broken down thus:

1. A lady
2. Mid-sixties

3. Blue eyes
4. Gray hair

5. Hair blonde, almost white when young
6. Thin face
7. High cheekbones

8. Medium height

9. Strikingly pretty
10. Dimple in middle of chin
11. Very sensitive
12. Took on others' troubles too much
13. Name of Martha

14. Aunt
15. Died about three years ago
16. Died of chest ailment

3) Opposite each statement draw columns labeled. "True but too general," "Too vague to judge," "True in fact," "True to character," "Do not know," "Wrong to character." The form is shown in Table 1.

4) Send these forms to as wide variety of persons as feasible but to at least four of different ages and backgrounds, with common qualities of thoroughness, critical acumen, thoughtfulness, and willingness to perform the task promptly. Ask each one to judge the accuracy of each statement *as it would pertain to him.* He is to imagine that *he* was the sitter and these statements were directed to *him* from an ostensible discarnate loved one, and check the appropriate column for each statement.

5) When the completed forms are returned, tabulate the replies to each statement in the various columns. If one finds that a statement

pertains to many for whom the sitting was *not* held, that statement's evidential value is very low or null; on the contrary, if the statement *does not* pertain widely, while it does to the sitter, its evidential value is much increased. The larger the number of judges and the larger the support or denial of specificity, the safer the extrapolation from the data.

6) It should be noted, however, with reference to this procedure—and, indeed, the statistical ones as well—that the process of separating the total mediumistic response into individual statements and judging them in isolation and out of context does reduce the overall evidentiality of a combination that seems to create a vivid *portrait of a personality*. In the case of such data, often the most impressive evidence is precisely such a portrait, a sense of *presence* which such a breakdown inevitably destroys. The student, therefore, must weigh the *objective* findings of such cross-matching with the more *subjective* experience of the sitting itself in framing his conclusions. Furthermore, given the same set of data, different students will probably come to different conclusions as to its evidentiality depending upon individual variables of personality, belief stance, etc. The best that one can do—and this he *must* do—is to view the material as critically and as sympathetically as possible. This paradoxical attitude—some might term it contradictory—is both essential and difficult, but it can be learned with experience.

Many mediums will give advice on personal, business, spiritual, or related issues and problems during the sitting. Should the sitter accept and follow their advice? This must, of course, be a personal decision; but there is no reason to suppose that a medium is, because of her psi gift, any more shrewd or wise than anyone else of like age, experience, training, etc. Psi alone does not impart either wisdom or omniscience, and the sitter must weigh the pros and cons of the sensitive's counsel, just as he would that of a minister, doctor, lawyer, or friend. Nor should he be unduly alarmed or excited if a medium predicts dire future events or astonishingly promising ones, for, while precognition does occur, it is relatively rare, and most predictions of this type are found to be baseless. Here again, the individual must keep his wits about him, use common sense and reason, and evaluate his personal situation before acting upon such purported glimpses of the future. Qualified and respected mediums may give general advice or may foresee some general pattern of developments for the sitter, but they will rarely be precise as to what the sitter should do; they realize that such decisions are not theirs to make.

Many able mediums will make distinctions between items they feel emanate from discarnates and those they obtain telepathically or clairvoyantly from the sitter or other living person. Because psi is not utterly controllable, a medium may, for reasons as unknown to her as to the sitter, be unable to obtain anything significant during a sitting. It is entirely unfair to judge any medium by one or two sittings, or indeed by her performance with a few sitters. Here as elsewhere, rapport is essential, and if the sitter and medium somehow clash in personalities, they may be unable to cooperate sufficiently for success, while with another person both sitter and medium may obtain exciting results. That is a reflection upon neither; it is merely the nature of the psi relationship.

Mediums, like everyone else, have their personal philosophies, religious viewpoints, opinions about the whole gamut of topics, including the nature of the afterlife, reincarnation, etc. These opinions will, of course, reflect their personal predilections, backgrounds, and psi experiences; and there will be considerable disagreement among mediums themselves over many topics. The sitter must reserve for himself the decision as to which and how many of those opinions he wishes to accept; but the sitting is no place for an argument over them.

It cannot be reiterated too often that success in mediumistic research will depend in large measure upon the material, trust, rapport, and the medium. While viewpoints as to the source and evidentiality of material may differ, the researcher must remember that a medium is sensitive (another term used for psychics), variable in mood, not in complete control of the psi gift, and generally *convinced of the discarnate source of much, if not all*, of her material. This latter conviction is for many mediums the very bedrock of their personal philosophy and religion; it must be treated with the respect due everyone's religious views, whether or not one agrees. The very difficulty of attaining such a stance makes mediumistic research so intriguing; and if one can, with the aid of the medium, shed further light in survival, the intense effort is manifestly worthwhile.

CHAPTER THREE

BIBLIOGRAPHY
FOR THE BEGINNING STUDENT

I N THIS CHAPTER AND the next, students will find listings of more than three hundred and eighty book titles, organized according to topic, which will be useful in the study of psychical research. For more than a hundred and twenty-five of these titles, descriptive summaries are provided to aid students in making their selections. The books have been carefully selected from a very large number of available volumes but, as with any such personal choice, omission does not, of course, mean that the omitted work is either unsound or worthless. From my experience with lecture and seminar groups, I have found that certain books seem clearer, more interesting, and more helpful than others, and I have based my selection upon those criteria.

The literature in psychical research is enormous, running into thousands of volumes and varying greatly in quality, approach, intent, readability, and importance. Also, many of the types of paranormal phenomena with which psychical research is concerned are integral parts of various esoteric and occult traditions and movements; and while these latter may have considerable value *per se*, their intentions and methodologies are quite distinct and markedly different from those of psychical research. I have not included any works occult in nature, but have limited myself to those which are within the recognized purview of psychical research. I have consulted many acknowledged sources, include bibliographies of research organizations and those in major introductory works, and the students will find, I believe, the most significant contributions to the field covered in either this chapter or the next. I have not, however, except in a few instances, listed any of the vast periodical literature from the *Journals* and *Proceedings* of the principal research bodies.

Because of the great interest in psi phenomena, there has been a constant torrent of popular books on the subject, especially in paperback, during the last several years. Some of these are very sound; many, however, are quite superficial, sensationalistic, overly anecdotal, and often factually wrong. Where I have been able to ascertain that there is a paperback edition of a recommended work, I have indicated this, but there may well be some books so noted that are no longer available in paperback, and, conversely, there may be other books now available in paperback but not so noted.

As with any discipline, the serious student must study the primary sources and assess them critically if he is to understand the material thoroughly. The chief sources in English for such material are the *Journals* and *Proceedings* of the Society for Psychical Research (SPR) and of the American Society for Psychical Research (ASPR), together with the *Journal* of *Parapsychology*. There are also now defunct publications such as the *International Journal of Parapsychology* which may be of interest to the advanced student. Libraries with sizeable holdings in parapsychological materials will have some, if not all, of these, and the student may learn about availability of both past and current issues of the SPR and the ASPR by writing those organizations, while information about the *Journal of Parapsychology* can be obtained from the Foundation for Research into the Nature of Man. Addresses of these organizations will be found in Chapter Five.

The pamphlet, *Psychical Research, A Selective Guide to Publications in English* (1959), available from the SPR, lists many sections of their *Journal and Proceedings* which pertain to specific topics and is a very useful guide to their use. The ASPR also has available a very recent bibliography, R.A. White and L.A. Dale, *Parapsychology in Print* (1971), and the Parapsychology Foundation published *A Bibliography of Parapsychology* by George Zorab in 1957 which is worth consulting. Probably the most thorough bibliography on experimental articles is found in Rao's *Experimental Parapsychology*, annotated in the next chapter.

The edition of the work cited either in the annotated section or in the Additional Reading may not be the latest or most easily available, and the student may find that the pagination will vary from edition to edition. Some of the recommended works are currently out of print, but many of the more important books are being reprinted to meet the increased demand, and accessibility of these major treatises is steadily improving.

GENERAL SURVEYS AND INTRODUCTIONS TO PSYCHICAL RESEARCH

Martin Ebon, *Psychic Warfare: Threat or Illusion:* McGraw-Hill, New York, 1983, 282 pages.

This volume is a combination of the Soviet beat, on which Ebon is an expert, and the psychic area on which he is a past master. One of the solid facts he is able to report is that both in the United States and in the Soviet Union high-government controversy actively exists over the issue of whether to be involved officially in psychical research, for warfare or otherwise.

No one familiar with psychical research can doubt the potential power and insidious advantage that would result if military uses could be perfected for reliable dispatch of messages by telepathy, for the reading of the secrets in another's mind, for the control of another's actions by mental manipulation, for distant spying by clairvoyance or "remote viewing," and for the activation of physical or electronic equipment by the psychokinetic power of the mind. Nor can one doubt that both American and Soviet military groups have made efforts in such directions—we need only remember the recent public uproar when the svengalian efforts of the CIA were disclosed respecting their attempts to make human robots by a mix of hypnotism and mind-altering drugs.

Ebon gives us many little-known facts and guidance for logical speculation in these areas (the weakness—not his fault—is the lack of official disclosures on the subject). We must hope that our governmental leaders are reading Ebon. At the same time he does not counsel that anyone push the panic button, and it is suggested that the reader keep four factors in mind: when high-scoring subjects are asked to perform for very long, the bore-quotient causes psi-hitting to drop drastically; psi performance most often is sporadic, not on–call; emotional and subliminal factors, as well as ego factors, often distort or wipe out psi effects; when a monetary, selfish, immoral, or criminal element is added, psi often disappears. This volume is important and is highly recommended.

Martin Ebon (Ed.), *Signet Handbook of Parapsychology*. New American Library, New York, 1978, 519 pages.

This author has written more than sixty books, most of them in the psychic field, and lectures extensively. His first years in this field were as Administrative Secretary for the Parapsychology Foundation at the time when Eileen Garret was its active head and the Foundation was one of the very few organizations in the world actively researching the psychic dimension. In this volume he has reprinted outstanding papers from thirty-four top authorities. The book's scope is far more than parapsychology, and in fact spans most of the paranormal, with sections devoted to the history of the psychic area and parapsychology's relationship to psychotherapy, religion, biology, survival of death, consciousness, dreams and other controversial sciences. For a reliable look at the entire area, the general reader cannot do better than this volume.

Alan Gauld, *The Founders of Psychical Research*. Routledge & Kegan Paul, London, 1968, 387 pages.

Dr. Gauld, a psychologist, was for some time Editor of the *SPR Journal*. This book recounts the conditions giving rise to the birth of psychical research, the founding of the SPR in 1882, its aim, standards, and problems. There are fascinating biographical portraits of key leaders of early psychical research like Meyers, Sidgwick, and Gurney, together with glimpses of other figures who loom large and honorable in the early days: Mrs. Sidgwick, Lodge, William James. The overall view which emerges is of a group of extraordinarily gifted people with a no less remarkable devotion to a search for the truth about contradictory, puzzling, and yet potentially vital phenomena. To understand the care with which psychical research has generally been carried on, one must learn of the tradition; and here Dr. Gauld has traced the genesis of that tradition. In doing so, he has implicitly undermined many of the less valid—and less humane—critics of the discipline. The book is splendidly written.

Rosalind Heywood, *The Sixth Sense*. Chatto and Windus, London, 1959, 224 pages, excellent index. Paperback, Pan Books, London,

1966. American edition, *Beyond the Reach of Sense.* E.P. Dutton, New York, 1961.

This is a first-rate introduction to psi phenomena and research by one of the leaders of the SPR. Written with a light, deft touch which is charming, there is equally apparent a rigorous balance and a care to assess the various possibilities inherent in any set of data. Mrs. Heywood has a delightful sense of humor, a wide background of general knowledge, and a thorough grasp of the field. The book is greatly enhanced by an appendix in which some of the major theories of psi in its many facets are summarized and analyzed clearly and cogently.

Raynor C. Johnson, *Psychical Research.* The English Universities Press, Ltd., London, 1955, 176 pages; Philosophical Library, New York, 1956; Funk & Wagnalls, New York, 1968

Dr. Johnson has produced a clear, readable, and thorough introduction to the field. The explanations are illustrated with some well-chosen examples from the annals of psychical research; the problems inherent in the discipline are discussed; and guidelines as to the evaluation of evidence are given. Johnson also offers some interesting personal theoretical hypotheses which may prick the reader's curiosity to probe deeper. Also, although the book is fifteen years old, there is a sound, if rather brief, bibliography following each chapter. A good index is highly useful.

Charles McCreery, *Science, Philosophy, and ESP.* Foreword by H. H. Price. Faber and Faber, London, 1967, 192 pages, index, glossary. Archon Books, Hamden CT, 1968, 199 pages.

This is an excellent book dealing with both physical and mental phenomena and offering some original hypotheses and definite suggestions for experimental designs to test them. McCreery, who is a Research Officer at the Institute of Psychophysical Research in Oxford, discusses, with long verbatim extracts, the impressive physical phenomena of Rudi Schneider and Eusapia Palladino, the famous Shackleton experiments of Dr. Soal, and the well-attested case of Larkin and McConnel's apparition. Following this, he adduces hypotheses regarding the characteristics of the state conducive to ESP, the role of EEG evidence regarding the correlation of the alpha rhythm and the ESP state, the influence of drugs, and other variables. His treatment of the knotty problem of repeatability and his suggestions as to its possible solution are important. He writes very clearly.

Thelma Moss, *The Probability of the Impossible: Scientific Discoveries and Explorations in the Psychic World*. J. P. Tarcher, Los Angeles, 1974, 410 pages.

This is clearly the best overview of the psychic field written for the general reader by a parapsychologist. Serious students of the field will also find this satisfying fare, spiced by three bonus sections at the back of the book: 235 references with full citations, a list of 48 items of "recommended reading," and an index.

Dr. Moss was a medical psychologist at UCLA's Neuropsychiatric Institute, where she also headed a parapsychological laboratory. Best known for her imaginative innovations in parapsychology, it comes as a pleasant surprise to see the breadth of her scholarship, with quotes from Jung/Freud and from Egyptian, Tibetan, Grecian, and East Indian literature, as well as SPR and ASPR beginnings. Her trips to East Europe (Moscow, Alma-Ata, Prague) have turned up more hard data there than quoted by any other Western parapsychologist. The scope of this book is quite broad, the subject matter embracing: dowsing, skin vision, acupuncture, energy fields, psychokinesis, Uri Geller, levitation, dreams, drugs, hypnosis, trance, prophecy, telepathy, clairvoyance, retrocognition, psychic photography, inspiration, automatic writings, prodigies, spiritualism, mediumship, multiple personality, possession, famous mediums, out-of-body projection, hallucinations, apparitions, ghosts, poltergeists, survival, reincarnation, age and life regression, meditation and biofeedback.

Gardner Murphy, *Challenge of Psychical Research: A Primer of Parapsychology*. Harper & Row, New York, 1961, 297 pages, index; paperback, Harper and Row (Colophon Books), 1970, 303 pages.

A general treatment by one of America's most distinguished psychologists and parapsychologists. Long in the forefront of psychical research, renowned as a scrupulously judicious scholar. Dr. Murphy is in an excellent position to present a balanced view of paranormal phenomena, their investigations and investigators. This volume is remarkable for the lengthy verbatim extracts of actual experimental and investigative articles. Especially noteworthy is the thorough section of key "cross–correspondence" materials. Murphy's careful and clear comments are thought-provoking and will encourage the reader to form his own views and to study further.

Gardner Murphy and Robert Ballou (Eds.), *William James on Psychical Research*. Viking Press, New York, 1960; Chatto and Windus, London, 1961, 339 pages, index.

This collection of the writings of Harvard's great pioneer in psychology and pragmatic philosophy is much enchanced by a very perceptive introduction and epilogue by Dr. Murphy who places James's work and influence within the context of his time. James's determined and courageous insistence that paranormal—or "supernormal" as he called them—phenomena did occur, and must be investigated with the same zeal, impartiality, and care as other ramifications of nature brought his immense prestige to the support of the struggling infant discipline of psychical research. The selections included range from James's important report of the Hodgson control sittings with Mrs. Piper, James's eloquent, yet critical, review of Frederick Myers's work, to his major essay in which he discusses the concept that the brain may be a transmitter rather than, or as well as, a source of consciousness, and his splendid *apologia*, "What Psychical Research Has Accomplished." James had a style that was most precise, yet never dry. This work is essential reading.

J. Gaither Pratt, *Parapsychology: An Insider's View of ESP.* E. P. Dutton, New York, 1966, 300 pages, brief index, brief bibliography.

Dr. Pratt, who has been very active in what he terms the "psi revolution" since 1936, is a highly trained, cautious, and critical parapsychologist who has played a vital role in the development of quantitative experiments and assessment techniques. This book recounts some of the central data for the reality of ESP and PK, discusses some of the principal difficulties in psi research, analyzes various theories, gives a detailed account of the famous Seaford poltergeist case in 1958 which he investigated, provides an especially good treatment of precognition, and includes some sage observations on the significance of the "psi revolution." Pratt writes simply and clearly.

Milan Ryzl, *Parapsychology—A Scientific Approach*. Hawthorn Books, New York, 1970, 216 pages.

This is a broadly popular account written by a Czech investigator who discovered the impressive subject Pavel Stepanek and who now lives in the United States. In this non-technical introductory work, Ryzl deals with both spontaneous and quantitative work and he gives rather more attention to European parapsychology than most surveys by non-Europeans, which is a welcome feature. There is also a sound summary of Russian research about which the author seems quite well informed. As with any treatment so brief that essays to be an overall view of so vast a field, there are flaws and questionable generalizations; but the book is particularly worthwhile as an easily accessible source of brief information about European work.

Susy Smith, *ESP*. Pyramid Books, New York, 1962, 189 pages.

Despite its rather exotic cover, this paperback provides a basically sound, if superficial, introduction to the discipline. It is neither so scholarly nor so thorough as Raynor Johnson's book, but it is very readable and, in America, probably more easily obtained. Unfortunately, there is neither an index nor bibliography. Miss Smith is a well–known free lance writer about psychical research.

G. N. M. Tyrrell, *The Personality of Man.* Penguin Books, London, 1947, 284 pages, index, bibliography.

One of the most complete and perceptive overall views of psychical research yet published is given by a leading student of the discipline. There are illuminating discussions of qualitative work, experimental efforts by Soal, Rhine, Hettinger, Carington, and others, automatic writing, cross correspondences, mediumship, psychometry, physical phenomena, and an interesting brief chapter on chance. While the treatment of each topic is of necessity rather general and brief, the illustrative instances are carefully selected and his observations are thought-provoking. Tyrrell wrote with great clarity.

Rhea A. White, *Surveys in Parapsychology: Reviews of the Literature, with Updated Bibliographies*. Scarecrow Press, Metuchen, NJ, 1976, 484 pages.

The nineteen articles of this collection have obviously been gathered with great care "to provide a sourcebook of parapsychological surveys." There are five categories, each with an original introduction that adds much to the book: basic areas of parapsychological study, special subject populations (animals, primitive groups, etc.), how psi operates, theories of psi, and criticisms of parapsychology. The articles are timely, meaty, excellent, and often exciting.

The lengthy bibliographies following each article have been extended and updated by Ms. White to provide the reader direction for further research. Generally speaking, journal articles in this field are not available to the nonprofessional, so that a special service is hereby done the general reader. This book does not offer sensational material, and while a few of the articles are highy technical in nature, most are very readable and provide interesting illustrations of the theories being discussed. Authors included are the usual familiar ones such as W. G. Roll, J. G. Pratt, Robert L. Morris, Robert L. Van de Castle, J. B. Rhine, Karlis Osis, Charles Honorton, and Stanley Krippner.

ADDITIONAL READING

Eric J. Dingwall and John Langdon-Davies, *The Unknown—Is It Nearer?* New American Library, New York, 1956.

Martin Ebon, *The Psychic Reader.* World Publishing Co., New York, 1969.

Simeon Edmunds, *Miracles of the Mind: An Introduction to Parapsychology.* Charles Thomas, Springfield, IL., 1965.

F. S. Edsall, *The Worlds of Psychic Phenomena.* David McKay Co., New York, 1958.

Fabian Gudas, *Extrasensory Perception.* Scribner's, New York, 1961.

Renée Haynes, *The Society for Psychical Research, 1882-1982: A History.* Macdonald, London, 1982.

Naomi Hintze and J. G. Pratt, *The Psychic Realm: What Can You Believe?* Random House, New York, 1975.

C. G. Jung, *Memories, Dreams, Reflections.* Pantheon, New York, 1963.

Edward F. Kelly and Ralph G. Locke, *Altered States of Consciousness and Psi: An Historical Survey and Research Prospectus.* Parapsychology Foundation, New York, 1981.

D. C. Knight (Eds.), *The ESP Reader.* Grosset & Dunlap, New York, 1969.

Thelma Moss, *The Body Electric: A Personal Journey into the Mysteries of Parapsychological Research, Bioenergy, and Kirlian Photography.* J. P. Tarcher, Los Angeles, 1980.

R. Omez, *Psychical Phenomena.* Burns & Oates, London, 1958; Hawthorn Books, New York, 1958.

H. W. Pierce, *Science Looks at ESP.* New American Library, New York, 1970.

Louisa E. Rhine, *Something Hidden.* McFarland, Jefferson, NC, 1983.

J. B. Rhine and J. G. Pratt, *Extrasensory Perception After Sixty Years.* Holt, Rinehart & Winston, New York, 1940.

W. H. Salter, *The Society for Psychical Research: An Outline of its History.* Revised by Renée Haynes, Society for Psychical Research, London, 1970.

Harold Sherman, *How to Make ESP Work for You.* Fawcett, Greenwich, 1964.

William O. Stevens, *Psychics and Common Sense.* E. P. Dutton, New York, 1953.

Spontaneous Phenomena

Christopher Bird, *The Divining Hand.* Dutton, New York, 1979, 340 pages.

This profusely illustrated, large format book is the last book you will need to buy on the subject of dowsing, because this is a most remarkable book and it should stand for many years as the definitive work on this subject. Unfortunately, it is rather overpriced for the average book buyer and thus may not enjoy the circulation it deserves. It is most impressively researched and very readable, tracing the 500-year history of dowsing from early times down to modern work in the United States, in Europe, and in the Soviet Union. Chris Bird is fluent in Russian and so has thoroughly investigated the work that has been done in dowsing behind the "iron curtain." This book contains some remarkable examples of the practical value of dowsing in the finding not only of water but also of oil, minerals, and in fact anything lost, buried, or missing as well as ailments of the human body. It is a most striking and valuable presentation of both the history of the art and of evidence respecting some of the little-known powers of the human mind and spirit. Among the book's valuable facets are its appendices that include Bibliography, Notes, and Index.

Bird's use of well-told anecdotes makes this a most readable book. These stories range from the work of Wayne Thompson, who has dowsed over 2,000 productive wells in the High Sierras with a record of 95 percent success and who saved a failing rice farm during the recent two-year drought in California, to a retired general who, with a second career in archaeology, dowses successfully all over Great Britain for buried cities.

Jule Eisenbud, *The World of Ted Serios*. William Morrow, New York, 1967, 357 pages, excellent index, extensive bibliography, 140 illustrations.

The "thoughtography" of Ted Serios has been hailed by some scholars in parapsychology as the most remarkable paranormal phenomena of our time. In this study of Serios, Dr. Eisenbud, a psychiatrist highly interested for many years in psychical research, explains the sessions in which Serios has produced his extraordinary photographs seemingly by "thinking the picture." In addition, Eisenbud discusses the reasons behind the scientific world's dismissal of paranormal phenomena from a psychiatric point of view which is enlightening. Dr. Eisenbud writes extremely well, with a delightful sense of humor and with an unusual ability to sketch clearly the personality of Ted Serios, his outlook, religious views, psychological make-up, and emotional problems. Altogether, this is a highly readable yet thorough treatment of a fascinating person and his production of remarkable phenomena. The student may wish to pursue his study of Serios's phenomena through the follow-up experiments by Pratt and Stevenson and by Eisenbud given in several issues of the *ASPR Journal* during the last two or three years.

Andrew Mackenzie, *The Unexplained*. Introduction by H. H. Price. Andrew Barker, London, 1966, 176 pages, index. *The Unexplained: Some Strange Cases in Psychical Research*. Abelard-Schuman, New York, 1970, 180 pages.

This collection of about fifteen cases is a very good instance of careful investigation, thorough scrutiny of evidence, and cautious conclusions. Mr. MacKenzie, a professional writer and journalist, is a member of the Council of the Society for Psychical Research and is a highly competent and respected researcher. Included in his selection is the Seaford poltergeist case, but all the others are British, among them the famous Versailles "adventure" with some new aspects presented, the very puzzling Vandy case, and the important cross-correspondence instance, the "Palm Sunday." This work is one of the few really carefully researched and cogently presented collections of cases in recent years. Mr. MacKenzie writes clearly and holds the reader's interest. There is an admirable brief sketch of the nature and aims of the Society for Psychical Research as an epilogue. This is a fine introduction to the study of spontaneous cases which are the largest and possibly the most interesting segment of the collected data of psychical research.

A. R. G. Owen, *Can We Explain the Poltergeist?* Garrett Publications, New York, 1964, 436 pages, extensive bibliographical notes.

Dr. Owen is a well-known British geneticist and mathematician, for many years a lecturer at Trinity College, Cambridge. Written with the encouragement and support of the Parapsychological Foundation, this is probably the most complete study of poltergeist phenomena in English. Dr. Owen has examined many cases covering virtually every phase of poltergeist activities, has discussed the alternative explanations upon spiritualistic, psychological, fraudulent, hallucinatory, illusory, and paranormal grounds and has presented his own considered—and tentative—opinions. The student will find this engrossing and essential reading, for Dr. Owen has an excellent literary gift and the reader is constantly aware of his erudition and of his judiciousness.

Walter Franklin Prince, *Noted Witnesses of Psychic Occurrences.* Introduction by Gardner Murphy. University Books, New Hyde Park, NY, 1963, 336 pages, index.

This compilation of approximately one hundred and seventy spontaneous cases is divided into categories of professions within which the prominent person who experienced a paranormal occurrence worked and gained his fame, e.g., "Men of Science," "Statesmen," "Theologians," etc. The accounts are generally short and in the original words of the percipient or experient. There is an excellent introduction and explanation by Dr. Prince of the criteria of his choice and of possible conclusions to be drawn. There are also exceedingly thorough indices by nature of phenomena (Apparitions, Premonitions, Raps, etc.) and by percipient. This is an intriguing collection, a good introduction to spontaneous phenomena and to Prince who was possibly America's shrewdest pioneer in psychical research.

Louisa E. Rhine, *ESP in Life and Lab: Tracing Hidden Channels* Macmillan, New York, 1967, 275 pages.

This is the second of Dr. L. E. Rhine's valuable collections of spontaneous cases taken from over 10,000 which she has gathered over the years. The author analyzes about eighty instances after categorizing them as dreams (realistic or unrealistic), hallucinations, intuitions, or PK cases. Dr. Rhine is known as a "common sense" authority who weighs cases objectively, analyzes them thoroughly, and places them within the context of their specific occurrence as well as within that of their bearing on major issues in psychical research. She also makes it abundantly clear why such anecdotal material often, if not always, unverifiable, is, nevertheless, important. Fascinating reading which raises significant questions about the place of psi within a world system.

Louisa E. Rhine, *Hidden Channels of the Mind*. William Sloane Associates, New York, 1961, 291 pages, brief bibliography.

This book represents the fruit of a ten-year study of Dr. Rhine's large collection of spontaneous cases sent to the Parapsychology Laboratory at Duke University. As her husband, J. B. Rhine, remarks in his Introduction, "The experiences in this book make the data from the laboratory more understandable by demonstrating them, as it were, in action and in life." They may also assist people who have had such experiences to understand what might have occurred. The organization is straightforward and clear. The individual cases are generally presented in the words of the percipients, giving them a lively flavor which exposition would lack. There are perceptive chapters regarding the role of "agent" and "percipient," the problems of time and space, and ostensible discarnate communications. A very fine collection of modern spontaneous phenomena for the student to explore and ponder.

Louisa E. Rhine, *The Invisible Picture: A Study of Psychic Experiences*. McFarland & Company, Jefferson, NC, 1981, 267 pages.

The late Dr. Louisa, and her husband Dr. J. B. Rhine, were responsible more than any others for creating the modern field of parapsychology in the decades following the nineteen thirties, and both lived to see the discipline validated by the A.A.A.S. and accepted by a majority of the general public, as well as by significant numbers in the conventional sciences. The Rhines also pioneered and developed experimental parapsychology, using strict scientific methods in the psi laboratory. However, much to her occasional chagrin, the author in more recent years found herself to be the darling of psychical researchers, phenomenologists and even occultists, because of her work since 1948 in collecting and analyzing spontaneous psi cases from ordinary life. That work has resulted in her writing twenty articles and four books on spontaneous psi, of which this volume is the best. In contradistinction to most books about experimental psi and laboratory scene, general readers will have no problem following the author's writing style in this book. One of the big pluses is the fact that the book is based on the world's largest collection of spontaneous cases.

W. H. Salter, *Ghosts and Apparitions*. G. Bell & Sons, London, 1938, 135 pages, glossary.

The author was a prominent figure in the Society for Psychical Research for half a century and knew all the key figures of several generations. A retired barrister, he combined a shrewd judgement of human testimony with great experience in all forms of paranormal phenomena and unusual clarity of expression. This book deals with hauntings, various types of apparitions, and poltergeists, illustrating the different categories of phenomena with about thirty-five instances from the *Journal and Proceedings* of the SPR. Salter examines group perception of apparitions together with the theories advanced to account for it, and in his chapter on poltergeists discusses the role of adolescents, trickery, and other factors, concluding that such phenomena seem rarely, if ever, paranormal. This is a good brief treatment of an important facet of psychical research; but as it was written before Tyrell's classic *Apparitions*, it can fruitfully be compared with that work and with Owens's *Can We Explain the Poltergeist?*

Diana Robinson, *To Stretch a Plank: A Survey of Psychokinesis*. Nelson-Hall, Chicago, 1981, 277 pages.

Psychokinesis (PK), of course, is the phenomena of mentally affecting the physical world, or mind-over-matter. The catchy title of this book comes from a Sufi legend about Jesus the carpenter in Joseph's Nazareth carpentry shop: a plank of wood was cut too short, so Jesus stretched it to fit the intended use. Public reaction was the same as would be expected today. Some said, "This is a miracle; he must be a saint." Others said, "We do not believe it—do it again in our presence," but saner heads opined, "It cannot be true, just exclude it from the record."

To insure a comprehensive scope, our author has included many areas beyond conventional psychokinesis, such as healing, physical mediumship, poltergeists, thoughtography, taped voices, "miracles," etc., for which this reviewer is thankful. Additionally, she has endeavored to show the possible interrelatedness of physical psi phenomena and mental phenomena (ESP), and to put in perspective that old bugaboo, the "experimenter effect." In discussing theoretical aspects of the phenomena, Mrs. Robinson carefully considers the possible unintentional effect of our thoughts on our environment, whether they be positive or negative thoughts—and whether fear of results can impede intentional or "natural" PK.

H. F. Saltmarsh, *Foreknowledge*. G. Bell & Sons, London, 1938, 120 pages, glossary.

The author discusses the evidence for precognition, the theories of Dunne, Price, Broad, Du Prel, and his own "specious present" concept as attempts to account for precognitive occurrences, and the philosophical implications such as free will and determinism. Like Saltmarsh's *Evidence of Personal Survival*, this is clearly written, cogently argued, balanced, and careful. No aspect of psychical research has caused more difficulty in terms of logic than precognition; yet, as Saltmarsh says, it occurs and must be faced. This volume is the best brief introduction to the issue we have, even though it is over thirty years old. Students will find the classification of cases and the criteria used by Saltmarsh illuminating. Comparison with Pratt's discussion of precognition in his *ESP: An Insider's View* would be useful.

Stephen A. Schwartz, *The Secret Vaults of Time: Psychic Archaeology and the Quest for Man's Beginnings*. Grossett & Dunlap, New York, 1978, 370 pages.

Schwartz sees the discipline of archaeology (within the general frame of anthropology) as at a crossroads in its paradigm-quest for status, with "psychic archaeology" as the only practical route to its salvation. One might quibble with Schwartz over how compelling the latter solution and how imminent the former dilemma, and even as to how amenable the human animal is to logical persuasion—but one cannot blink his facts nor fault his arguments.

Many readers have known of Edgar Cayce's accurate prediction which anticipated the finding of the Dead Sea Scrolls by ten years, and a few have been aware of the ARE's tentative efforts to verify Cayce predictions respecting ancient times in Egypt, Persia, and Bimini; also, some will know slightly of psychic archaeology's first project, the 1907–1921 efforts of Frederick Bligh Bond with automatic writing which gave him a "heavenly blueprint" for his digs at Glastonbury. But Schwartz recounts many more important and fascinating efforts during the brief seventy years of this field's existence—including the semitrance efforts of Ossowiecki (with ethnologist Poniatowski) during the late thirties and war years in Poland, when, inter alia, he located both current and ancient burial sites with equal facility—and including the dowser-General, Scott Elliot of Scotland, Russian scientist Pluzhnikov with a crew of dowsers, and senior Canadian anthropologist Norman Emerson with a staff of light-trance psychics; plus several others. All examples leading, in Schwartz's reconstruction, to papers and symposia at the American Anthropological Association conventions in 1961, 1973, 1974, 1975, 1977, and 1978. Will active archaeologists either tacitly or formally give the psychic a fair try? If they do, Schwartz's last, and best, chapter gives extensive, careful advice on how to avoid psychic pitfalls, and his 54 pages of appendices, notes, bibliography, and index makes this a highly practical—as well as entertaining—volume.

Upton Sinclair, *Mental Radio*. Introduction by William McDougall. Revised second printing, Charles C. Thomas, Springfield, IL, 1962, 237 pages.

A major example of qualitative telepathy research, *Mental Radio* was first published in 1930 and was seen then as a very important piece of work, as indicated by the Preface being written by no less a figure than Albert Einstein. But this is no highly technical, dry study; on the contrary, it is lively and most engrossing. The reader should note especially Mrs. Sinclair's description of her state of mind when attempting telepathy or clairvoyance: this is one of the finest explanations we have of the "psychic mood."

Susy Smith, *The Enigma of Out-of-Body Travel*. New American Library, New York, 1965, 152 pages, index, bibliography.

The style of this, one of several popular accounts of various aspects of psychical research which Miss Smith has produced, is rather informal, and many parapsychologists would not accept all of the evidence adduced as readily as the author appears to do. Nevertheless, this is a good introduction to the kinds of experiences writers mean by "astral travel" or "astral projection," etc., while the bibliography will enable the interested student to read further. The author deals with apparent bilocation, various theories about an "astral," "etheric," "Beta," or "subtle" body, the bearing of out-of-the-body experiences upon survival, whether they are only hallucinatory or objective and veridical in nature, among other topics. She writes clearly and with a sense of humor.

ADDITIONAL READING

J. C. Barker, *Scared to Death: An Examination of Fear, its Causes and Effects*. Muller, London, 1968; paperback: Dell, New York, 1969.

William Barrett and Theodore Besterman, *The Divining Rod: An Experimental and Psychological Investigation*. University Books, New Hyde Park, NY, 1968.

S. Brown, *The Heyday of Spiritualism*. Hawthorn Books, New York, 1970.

Hereward Carrington, *Modern Psychical Phenomena*. Dodd, Mead & Co., New York, 1919.

Robert Crookall, *Case-Book of Astral Projection*. University Books, Secaucus, NJ, 1972; Citadel Press, Secaucus, NJ, 1980.

Robert Crookall, *More Astral Projections*. Aquarian Press, Wellingborough, England, 1964.

Robert Crookall, *The Study and Practice of Astral Projection*. Aquarian Press,Wellingborough, England, 1961.

Martin Ebon, *Beyond Space and Time: An ESP Casebook*. New American Library, New York, 1967.

Martin Ebon, *Prophecy in Our Time*. World Publishing Co., New York, 1968; paperback: New American Library, New York, 1969.

Martin Ebon, *True Experiences in Telepathy*. New American Library, New York, 1967.

Simeon Edmunds, *Hypnotism and the Supernormal*. Wilshire Books, Hollywood, 1969.

Simeon Edmunds, *"Spirit" Photography*. Society for Psychical Research, London, 1965.

Oliver Fox, *Astral Projection: A Record of Out-of-the Body Experiences*. University Books, New Hyde Park, NY, 1963.

Andrew Lang, *The Book of Dreams and Ghosts*. AMS Press, New York, 1970.

Andrew MacKenzie, *Apparitions and Ghosts: A Modern Study*. Barker, London, 1971.

Andrew MacKenzie, *Frontiers of the Unknown*. Barker, London, 1968; paperback: Popular Library, New York, 1970.

Andrew MacKenzie, *Hauntings and Apparitions*. Academy Chicago, Chicago, 1982.

Andrew MacKenzie, *Riddle of the Future: A Modern Study of Precognition*. Taplinger, New York, 1975.

Sylvan Muldoon and Hereward Carrington, *The Phenomena of Astral Projection*. Rider, London, 1951; Samuel Weiser, Inc., York Beach, ME, 1970.

Sylvan Muldoon and Hereward Carrington, *The Projection of the Astral Body*. Rider, London, 1956; Samuel Weiser, Inc., York Beach, ME, 1968.

Frank Podmore, *From Mesmer to Christian Science: A Short History of Mental Healing*. University Books, New Hyde Park, NY, 1965.

John L. Randall, *Psychokinesis: A Study of Paranormal Forces Through the Ages*. Souvenir Press, London, 1982.

William G. Roll, *The Poltergeist.* Scarecrow Press, Metuchen, NJ, 1976.

L. Rose, *Faith Healing.* Gollancz, London, 1968.

Ronald Rose, *Living Magic.* Rand McNally, New York, 1956; paperback edition: *Primitive Psychic Power.* New American Library, New York, 1968.

Herbert Thurston, *Ghosts and Poltergeists.* Regnery, Chicago, 1954.

Herbert Thurston, *The Physical Phenomena of Mysticism.* Burns Oates, London, 1952.

Gordon Turner, *An Ouline of Spiritual Healing.* Max Parrish, London, 1963.

Leslie Weatherhead, *Psychology, Religion, and Healing.* Hodder & Stoughton, London, 1951; paperback: revised edition, Abingdon, New York, 1954.

Donald J. West, *Eleven Lourdes Miracles.* Duckworth, London, 1957.

Ambrose Worrall, *Gift of Healing.* Ariel Press, Columbus, OH, 1965; paperback: *Miracle Healers.* New American Library, New York, 1968.

EXPERIMENTAL AND QUANTITATIVE STUDIES

K. Ramakrishna Rao (Ed.), *The Basic Experiments in Parapsychology.* McFarland, Jefferson, NC, 1984, 264 pages.

In this volume Dr. Rao provides samplings and descriptions of many of the landmark experiments, mostly of early parapsychology, which will easily serve as patterns for readers to perform their own replications. These include all of the variations of card-tests, dream generation and testing, psi-conducive altered states of consciousness, including the hypnotic, meditative and gansfeld states; also, some of the more modern experiments, such as remote viewing, are reported.

J. B. Rhine, *Extrasensory Perception.* Revised edition, Bruce Humphries, Boston, 1964, 240 pages.

Originally published in 1934, Dr. Rhine's first book marked a principal turning point in psychical research, for it provided the first sizeable statistical evidence for psi and led to the laboratory-oriented work which has dominated psychical research since then. Included in this edition is a new chapter sketching the progress during the thirty years between publications. It is an exciting work because it is a pioneer effort, and that sort of commitment, determination to overcome obstacles, and freshness of purpose should enthrall the reader as he learns the astonishing results of those early subjects like Pearce, Linzmayer, Stuart, and others. Essential reading in order to understand modern parapsychology.

J. B. Rhine, *The Reach of the Mind*. Revised edition, Apollo Editions, William Sloane Associates, New York, 1960, 235 pages.

Dr. Rhine's Preface to the revised edition is a useful summary of developments between 1947, when the book first appeared, and 1960. This is a very interesting account of the progress of experimental research which established statistical evidence for the existence of psi, demonstrated that repeatable experiments could be devised and could become increasingly refined and precise. Dr. Rhine postulates some probing ideas about the possible nature of psi based upon the experimental data, and throughout the book demonstrates a remarkably clear and relaxed writing style. An important book which can be usefully compared with Rhine's *Extrasensory Perception* and Soal's work.

Louisa E. Rhine, *Mind Over Matter*. Macmillan, New York, 1970, 390 pages, index, illustrations.

Dr. Rhine presents here the first full discussion of the evidence for PK which has been gathered over a period of thirty-five years both in the United States and elsewhere. She explains the genesis of the research, the first collation after nine years of experimentation, the psychological concomitants of success, various criticisms among parapsychologists and other scientists, discusses possible relationships between ESP and PK, and closes with an outline of the relatively few theoretical frameworks which have been formulated to account for PK. As in her two earlier books, which dealt with spontaneous phenomena, Dr. Rhine has brought together the evidence carefully and she writes simply and clearly. There is, of necessity, a fair amount of statistical material, but its significance is always explained so that the student should have no difficulty in following the argument or understanding the data. The concensus among psychical researchers about PK is not so widespread as that regarding ESP, and the student should be familiar with the evidence so that he can weigh its impact for himself. In no other book has this data been collected and discussed so completely.

S. G. Soal and F. Bateman, *Modern Experiments in Telepathy*. Faber and Faber, London, 1954; Yale University Press, New Haven, 1954, 425 pages, index.

Dr. Soal, for many years a distinguished mathematician at the University of London, is probably the most experienced psychical researcher of quantitative work in Great Britain. Thorough, conscientious, aware of the great need for careful controls, he was fortunate to find two very good subjects who demonstrated remarkable gifts of psi. This book describes his early disappointments in trying to replicate Rhine's work and his later success with Shackleton and Mrs. Stewart. His success in repeating such statistically phenomenal results was of incalculable importance to the progress of psychical research in the laboratory. Both authors write well and explain the conditions and significance of the experiments very clearly.

Robert H. Thouless, *Experimental Psychical Research*. Penguin Books, London, 1963, 148 pages, index, brief bibliography.

Dr. Thouless has been a leader in British psychical research for a good many years. Trained in psychology, he has brought to his work in parapsychology a balanced, open mind together with a freshness and originality of thought which have been very productive. He and Dr. Weisner first suggested the use of the Greek letter "psi" for the psychic faculty, and they have formulated an interesting theoretical framework for psi. In this compact book, Dr. Thouless clearly explains the experimental evidence for psi, how the experiments were conducted, the simple mathematical analysis for extra-chance deviation, the controls needed to obviate criticism, the decline and displacement effects, etc. He also suggests how "amateurs" can devise their own experiments and how parapsychologists might proceed in new directions to learn more about the operation of psi. His chapter on the issue of critics who accuse experimenters of "cheating" is especially noteworthy. Highly readable.

ADDITIONAL READING

L. W. Allison, *Leonard and Soule Experiments*. Boston Society for Psychic Research, Boston, 1929.

Betty Shapin and Lisette Coly (Eds.), *Parapsychology and the Experimental Method*. Parapsychology Foundation, New York, 1982.

PHILOSOPHICAL AND RELIGIOUS IMPLICATIONS OF PSYCHICAL RESEARCH

Edwina Cerutti, *Olga Worrall: Mystic with the Healing Hands*. Harper & Row, New York, 1975, 169 pages.

The greatest virtue and charm of this volume is its intimacy. It brings us an Olga Worrall that many of her public have never seen or suspected—a person of patience and of caring, a Christian totally dedicated to service, a wife and widow brimming with love for her Ambrose. The author, now living in a provincial town only a few miles from Olga's Baltimore residence, has had the advantage of countless days and hours of conversation with her subject, drawing out the latter's views and feelings on myriads of issues. She has also had the advantage of Olga's voluminous files, many of which were loaned to her for extensive study and for quoting. This is a book for the general public. A different author—one with a fair background in the spiritual/psychic field—could have written a book showing a knowledge of and appreciation for the more basic facts and values in this field, and by evaluating and commenting on substantive questions. However, her total lack of background knowledge and her continuing skepticism might provide the very thrust that could carry this well-written and touching story to best-seller ranks, to bring Olga Worrall's story to the whole nation as it deserves.

Raynor C. Johnson, *A Religious Outlook for Modern Man*. McGraw-Hill, New York, 1963, 220 pages, index.

No author has done more to synthesize the data of psychical research with that of science, philosophy, religion, and mysticism into a meaningful pattern than Dr. Johnson. A distinguished physicist by training with an unusual ability to present inherently complex concepts and materials in a straightforward, lucid manner, he is judicious, open-minded, and fascinating. He presents what he views as basic questions thinking persons must ask, draws important inferences about possible answers from the human experiences of different kinds of men who have sought spiritual knowledge, and stimulates the reader to challenge his own thinking. This book is an excellent introduction to Johnson's thought as he has crystallized his main theses for the general reader; it is an equally fine way for the student who has gained some knowledge of psychical research and has reflected upon the significance of such data to broaden his framework of thought with a wise and helpful writer.

Raynor C. Johnson, *The Imprisoned Splendor*. Harper & Row, New York, 1953, 424 pages, index, bibliography.

This work has become one of the most widely read syntheses of science, psychical research, philosophy, and religion yet produced. It is the first of Dr. Johnson's works of this kind; the others are annotated in the following chapter. It is not surprising that this book has become so popular because Dr. Johnson has addressed himself to precisely those issues which intrigue all men. He has the advantage of a first-rate mind, thorough scientific training, many years of teaching, broad and deep interests in psychical research and mysticism, and an almost unique ability to pull disparate strands of data and approaches together into a significant whole. Add to this a freedom from dogmatism and a concern for spirituality which is evident throughout. Here is a highly original mind with exciting insights into life's riddles presented in a lucid, and often eloquent, style.

Michael Perry, *Psychic Studies: A Christian View*. Newcastle Press, North Hollywood, 1984, 224 pages.

The author is Editor of *The Christian Parapsychologist*, London, which is the journal of the (English) Churches' Fellowship for Psychical and Spiritual Studies, while his vocation is as archdeacon of Durham, Church of England. His book takes the position that the Christian church has for too long ignored the psychics among its flock. He urges the Christian establishment to adopt a "non-dismissive attitude toward the paranormal and to open a dialogue with Spiritualists, among others, to find common ground," even though basic differences of fundamental opinion will always remain. He is convinced the psychic realm exists, even though some alleged phenomena at the present are beyond his "boggle threshold," but feels the Church has vacated its responsibility to deal sympathetically with psychically-related problems. For instance, as to troublesome spirits, he sees the proper approach as "trying to reconcile the spirit to God, and not as a kind of spiritual DDT to get rid of them."

Herbert Thurston, S. J., *The Church and Spiritualism*. Bruce Publishing Co., Milwaukee, 1933, 384 pages.

The late Father Thurston was certainly one of the most knowledgeable Roman Catholic students of psychical research, spiritualism, and their relation to Christianity. While he naturally supports the Roman Catholic doctrine that attempts to communicate with the dead are wrong, he disagrees with other Roman Catholic writers who hold that all psychic phenomena are fraudulent and argues that, whatever their source or nature, the impressive evidence of men of great eminence and irreproachable integrity substantiates that such paranormal occurrences do happen. Father Thurston had read widely, had witnessed many phenomena, and had already written a good deal about psychic matters before this book was compiled. It is one of the major works by a Roman Catholic expert; and although unfavorable to spiritualism, it is balanced, carefully reasoned, and avoids impugning the good faith of those who view the phenomena differently. Extremely well written.

ADDITIONAL READING

Louis K. Anspacher, *Challenge of the Unknown*. Current Books, New York, 1947.

Dean Kraft, *Portrait of a Psychic Healer*. Putnam's, New York, 1981.

John Langdon-Davies, *Man: The Known and Unknown*. Secker & Warburg, New York, 1960; paperback: *On the Nature of Man*. New American Library, New York, 1961.

Morton Leeds and Gardner Murphy, *The Paranormal and the Normal: A Historical, Philosophical, and Theoretical Perspective*. Scarecrow Press, Metuchen, NJ, 1980.

Arthur W. Osborn, *The Meaning of Personal Existence*. Theosophical Publishing House, Wheaton, IL, 1966.

James A. Pike, *If This Be Heresy*. Harper & Row, New York, 1967.

J. B. Priestley, *Man and Time*. Doubleday, Garden City, NY, 1964; paperback: Dell, New York, 1968.

Alson J. Smith, *Religion and the New Psychology*. Doubleday, Garden City, NY, 1951.

MEDIUMSHIP

Hugh Lynn Cayce, *Venture Inward*. Harper & Row, New York, 1964; Paperback Library, New York, 1967, 207 pages, good bibliography of writings about Edgar Cayce, and briefer lists of books about other aspects of the paranormal, dreaming, and meditation.

The literature on Edgar Cayce produced during the last decade is vast, and a movement akin to a cult has developed around his views on reincarnation, diet, geological changes, meditation, etc. All sorts of extravagant claims have been made about Cayce and many of the works concerning his undeniable paranormal gift are quite sensationalistic and unsound. This book by his son is probably the best introduction to Cayce. The author, while believing that his father's teachings are true, does discuss them sensibly and judiciously. He warns readers of the inherent dangers in automatic writing, the planchette, Ouija board dabbling, and psychedelic drugs, while outlining some safer means of expanding one's consciousness. He writes well and gives a good cross section from his father's "readings" to enable the reader to judge the kinds of problems—physical, psychical, and philosophical—with which his father dealt while in trance. It is a pity that Cayce was not thoroughly investigated by trained parapsychologists so that we had completely objective data about his work; but from the stenographic records kept over many years, the evidence of his extraordinary psi faculty seems incontestable. The student can begin a study of this remarkable man through this very interesting work.

Arthur Ford, *Nothing So Strange*. Harper & Row, New York, 1958, 246 pages.

The late Arthur Ford was considered by many to be one of the major sensitives of the last fifty years. He was a gentle, religious man with complex personal problems who was interested primarily in establishing evidence for survival of death and in bringing to bear upon Christian faith the findings of psychical research and the spiritualist movement. This autobiography, written in collaboration with Margueritte Harmon Bro, a well-known religious writer, tells of his family background, of the strange awakening of his psychic gift during the First World War, of the encouragement of Sir Arthur Conan Doyle, of his role in the famous Houdini survival test, his study with the great teacher Yogananda, and his own views on the meaning of life and the impact that conviction of survival can have upon a person's life. Ford was one of the moving spirits behind the formation of Spiritual Frontiers Fellowship. He was neither so introspective nor so intellectual as Eileen Garrett, but his observations about mediumship and its significance are worth considering. The book is most readable.

Eileen J. Garrett, *My Life as a Search for the Meaning of Mediumship*. Rider, London, 1939.

Mrs. Garrett was unquestionably one of the greatest mediums of the century. She was also one of the most intelligent, intellectually curious, and psychologically courageous figures in the history of psychical research. She constantly turned the light of investigators upon her own trance state, trying to understand her unusual gifts, determined to unravel a little the mystery of the human mind and its faculties, and thereby come to some fruitful conclusion about the meaning of life and how her mediumship could help others in such a search. Her motto was really "Know thyself." This book recounts her Irish childhood, religious and personal tensions, personal tragedies, her training as a medium, her emerging psychic sensitivity, and her literary and philosophical influences. Extremely well written.

Gladys Osborne Leonard, *My Life in Two Worlds*. Cassell, London, 1931, 300 pages.

One of the finest of all trance mediums, Mrs. Leonard, during a career of about forty years, cooperated fully with numerous researchers of the Society for Psychical Research and produced some of the most impressive evidence for survival in the annals of psychical research. She and her "Control," "Feda," supposedly an Indian ancestor, gave convincing sittings to hundreds of bereaved people following the fame gained through Sir Oliver Lodge's book *Raymond*.

She submitted to various tests, e.g., the book tests and Whately Carington's word association tests, while she was exhaustively investigated over many years by the Rev. Charles Drayton Thomas. Like Mrs. Piper, she was of the utmost integrity, desirous of the fullest cooperation, and there has never been the slightest doubt as to her honesty. In this well-written work, Mrs. Leonard describes how she came to be a medium, various experiences with physical mediumship, the development of her trance work, her own spiritualistic beliefs, and suggestions for psychic development. Whether one accepts all of her personal views, the student will find this book well worth reading for the light it sheds upon the personality and thoughtful conclusions of a very gifted psychic.

Joseph K. Long (Ed.), *Extrasensory Ecology: Parapsychology and Anthropology.* Scarecrow Press, Metuchen, NJ, 1977, 427 pages.

Anthropologist Joseph Long presented a paper to the Association convention in 1973, on his field's relationship to parapsychology. It was the springboard for a full-blown symposium on psi and anthropology at the Association's 1974 meeting, out of which this volume grew. He could hardly have done better than to obtain the participation of anthropologists Margaret Mead and J. N. Emerson—Emerson having pioneered the use of clairvoyants for archaeology fieldwork in Canada. Also participating were physicists Evans Harris Walker, and Charles Musès, psychiatrists Jule Eisenbud and Berthold E. Schwartz, engineer James B. Beal and psychologist Henry Reed—all of whom had been previously involved in parapsychological research with spontaneous psi in life.

Alta Piper, *The Life and Work of Mrs. Piper.* Introduction by Sir Oliver Lodge. Routledge & Keegan Paul, London, 1929, 204 pages.

Mrs. Piper was undoubtedly the most thoroughly investigated medium of all time. Using both trance and automatic writing, she worked with the leading researchers from 1885 until the end of World War I, and occasionally after that. The controls imposed upon her over eighteen years by Richard Hodgson, Sir Oliver Lodge, William James, and Frederick Myers were exhaustive and constricting, including private detectives, anonymous sitters, forbidding her to read the newspapers, etc. To all of this—plus the unpleasant physical tests of the depth of her trance like pins, incisions, and sharp chemicals—Mrs. Piper submitted willingly and with enthusiasm, despite the very considerable annoyance and inconvenience to her personal life. All those who worked with her were unanimous in their conviction that she was a lady of indubitable integrity, unquestionable psychic ability, and had produced the most important evidence for survival of any medium. In this book by her daughter, Mrs. Piper's personal characteristics, her home life, as well as her psychic work are described simply and clearly. It is interesting that neither Mrs. Piper nor her daughter state that they are convinced by her own data of the spiritualistic interpretation. This is a sensitive and balanced account with a good sampling of the most important cases of her career by a daughter who often acted as recorder during her mother's sittings, and had a sound critical faculty of her own.

ADDITIONAL READING

Hereward Carrington, *The Physical Phenomena of Spiritualism: Fraudulent and Genuine*. T. Werner Laurie, London, n.d.

Arthur Ford, *Unknown but Known*. Harper & Row, New York, 1968.

Eileen J. Garrett, *Adventures in the Supernormal*. Creative Age Press, New York, 1948; paperback: Paperback Library, New York, 1968.

Helen Greaves, *The Dissolving Veil*. Churches' Fellowship for Psychical and Spiritual Studies, London, 1967.

Shirley Harrison and Lynn Franklin, *The Psychic Search*. G. Gannett, Portland, ME, 1981.

Mme. Dunglas Home, *D. D. Home: His Life and Mission*. Ayer Press, Salem, NH, 1976.

Grace Rosher, *Beyond the Horizon*. James Clarke, London, 1961.

E. T. Smith, *Psychic People*. Morrow, New York, 1968; paperback: Bantam Books, New York, 1969.

SURVIVAL ISSUE

Paul Beard, *Living On: How Consciousness Continues and Evolves After Death*. Continuum, New York, 1981, 202 pages (Allen & Unwin, London, 1980).

Paul Beard, in his effective role as executive head of the College of Psychical Studies in London, over many years provided patient and sound training for the development of mediums and psychics, such as the late Eileen Garrett, and provided training for SFF's Bob Ashby as a research officer. At the same time, Beard has been a persevering researcher and prolific writer in the field. In this volume, Beard assumes that life after death has been proven, and so is concerned with the meaning of our existence, and the nature of our destiny. He finds evidence for the likelihood that some entity, indentifiable with the person we at present recognize ourselves to be, did exist before our current "births" and will persist after the death of our current bodies. From his research he concludes that "a picture gradually arises of an inner world to which men belong *both* before and after death, and in which the same spiritual laws hold good, there as here," and that death is but an altered state of consciousness, followed by a continuing transformation in which different levels of consciousness represent successive stages of a universal process rather than separate realms of existence. Beard's principal sources are mediumistic communications; however, out-of-body experiences and visions through awakened spiritual perception also are cited, but he points out that these latter "describe only what can be observed from the threshold; they are glimpses into a next world, not journeys into the interior."

Paul Beard, *Survival of Death: For and Against*. Hodder & Stoughton, London, 1966, 177 pages, index, brief bibliography.

Although Beard is himself convinced of survival, this is an attempt to weigh some of the principal objections to the survival hypothesis, such as the extended telepathy or Super ESP concept, erroneous claims of ostensible discarnates who turn out to be fictional or still alive, and subconscious imaginings of mediums. The evidence of survival given here consists of generally familiar cases often cited, and there is no reference to American studies of the problem, which is a pity. The book is possibly more important in terms of the conclusions Beard draws as to the *raison d'être* of ostensible discarnate communications, and their bearing upon a person's view of life. He writes very well and perceptively; and one senses that he is a critical sitter, well aware of many crudities in the simplistic spiritualist viewpoint of survival, and eager to present a more reasoned and balanced case for survival.

Martin Ebon, *The Evidence for Life After Death.* New American Library, New York, 1977, 177 pages.

With characteristic care and conservatism, Mr. Ebon presents a series of case reports and evaluations of studies, phenomena and people that are significantly involved in major categories of the survival question. He reports intimate views, opinions, and conversations with major scientists such as Dr. Raymond A. Moody, Jr., Dr. Elisabeth Kübler-Ross, Dr. Karlis Osis, Dr. J. B. Rhine, and Dr. Robert Crookall and yet keeps his account very readable—exciting reading, in fact. Psychics, too, are interestingly covered, such as the opinions of the opinionated Ingo Swann, and the little-known involvement of Dr. Carl Wickland and his medium/wife, Anna, in the controversial Arther Ford–Houdini–"Margery"–Conan Doyle brouhaha. Although many of the items here reported involve controversy, of one thing we may be sure: Martin Ebon carefully plays the skeptic's role and never seduces the reader with optimistic innuendo beyond the reasonable reach of the evidence in this or any other part of the psychic field.

Hornell Hart, *The Enigma of Survival: The Case for and against an Afterlife.* Charles C. Thomas, Springfield, IL, 1959; Rider, London, 1959.

Hart's book is one of the most important in survival research because it was the first to undertake to examine in an orderly, logical manner both sides of the case, giving fair, accurate representation of the evidence and the difficulties each position entails. Hart was an acknowledged expert in this aspect of psychical research, had established himself as a careful researcher in work at Duke, and played a large part in the census of apparitions in 1956. While he finally plumps for acceptance of survival, his presentation of the contrary case is sound enough that readers may not agree with his conclusion. His "persona theory" to account for mediumistic dramatizations, fictional "spirits," and other such embarrassments of sittings is original and useful. Clearly written in a style that will arrest the attention.

Elisabeth Kübler-Ross, *On Death and Dying*. Macmillan, New York, 1969, 289 pages.

When this book was originally published, it broke new ground and utterly demolished the long-standing and curious American taboo against discussing death. Many have jumped on the bandwagon since, but it was Dr. Ross's basic work that made death and dying a respectable subject for formal study in much the same way that Sigmund Freud freed sex a century ealier. Like Freud, she patiently listened to her subjects and let them teach her about the stages, languages, and problems of the process and psychology of dying. The book states these. Many misguided persons think of death as the proper punishment for sin. But life invented death before the expanding consciousness of man discovered sin and guilt and before theology sought a causal nexus between them. Jesus' revelation of God's forgiving love and his demonstration of life after death repudiate this. This book shows people that death is a natural and inevitable part of life and that its calm acceptance is the key to the completion with dignity of a meaningful life well lived.

Sir Oliver Lodge, *Raymond*. Methuen, London, 1916, 396 pages, index, illustrations.

One of the most famous of all works on survival, this recounts a series of sittings which Sir Oliver, Lady Lodge, and other members of their family held with Mrs. Leonard and Vout Peters at which they received evidential material purporting to come from Lodge's youngest son, Raymond, killed in September, 1915. Coming as it did at the height of British losses during World War I and from such a distinguished family, the book was an immediate best seller, going through many printings and editions, and contributing greatly to the growth of interest in psychical research and in spiritualism at that time. Lodge was an experienced researcher, as well as a pre-eminent scientist and educator, and he took precautions to obviate alternative explanations wherever possible to increase the evidentiality; and the book, although fifty-five years old, is still worth reading to see which kind of details can convince some critical, educated people of the identity of a deceased loved one. The last part of the book contains some views by Sir Oliver about life, survival, God, and the significance of life; and they, too, are enlightening as to the philosophical framework not only of Lodge but of many of his contemporaries. Lucidly written by a great scientist who tried to be fair and critical, despite the great emotional involvement he had in the issue, this is an important book to read.

Craig R. Lundahl (Ed.), *A Collection of Near-Death Research Readings*. Nelson-Hall, Chicago, 1982, 240 pages.

This is an anthology, a NDE reader, if you will. The editor has selected articles (most of them previously published) from all of the leaders of this new science—Osis, Moody, Ring, Sabom, Audette, and Grosso. Although the "deathbed visions" collected by Osis are not technically "near death experiences" of the genre established by Moody's *Life After Life*, they do fill out the spectrum and show the antecedents in psychical research exemplified by the earlier work of William Barrett in England and James H. Hyslop in the United States; the spectrum is what Paul Beard has called "views from the threshold of death."

Two features make this book especially valuable. One is an adaptation from Raymond Moody's classic in which he defines and illustrates the most common facets of the NDE, viz., ineffability, hearing the news, peace and quiet, the noise, the dark tunnel, out of the body, meeting others, the being of light, the review, the border, coming back, telling others, effects on lives, and a new attitude toward death. Also valuable is Michael Grosso's attempt to explain the NDE phenomena, emphasizing the consistency and universality, the psi aspects, and the NDE's power to modify attitudes and behavior.

James A. Pike with Diane Kennedy, *The Other Side: An Account of My Experiences with Psychic Phenomena*. Doubleday, Garden City, NY, 1968, 396 pages, excellent bibliography.

This is the account written by the late Bishop Pike of the seemingly paranormal occurrences which followed his son Jim's suicide, and of the Bishop's attempts to learn about paranormal phenomena. In the course of the book there are lengthy sections quoted of records of mediumistic sittings, including the famous television session with the late American medium Arthur Ford. Possibly because of the pressure from the tremendous publicity which attended that television encounter and his desire to present his own, as opposed to the press's, conclusions about his experiences, the book seems to have been written very hastily. It is wordy and awkward in many places, and is not of the same quality of organization and style, with the careful reasoning and prudent presentation of substantive material, as that of Pike's other works. Then, too, he is dealing with a field in which he was still a neophyte. Nevertheless, it is an interesting account by a controversial, able, and courageous man who tried honestly "to tell it as it is." Useful for the student as an instance of first-hand, subjective material to be contrasted with collected, objectives studies as seen in Hart's book.

Kenneth Richmond, *Evidence of Identity*. G. Bell & Sons, London, 1939, 111 pages, glossary.

This is one of the best discussions we have of the problem of identity, the role of the trivial in evidence of identity, the difficulties inherent in the impact of vicarious evidence as opposed to personal experience, the distinction between "conviction" and "proof," demonstrated with clarity of expression which the student will find most helpful. The cases are taken from SPR's records and have been carefully vetted by Richmond. Many famous instances are included while the student is given annotations as to where he may find the full accounts. Since the issue of identity is at the heart of the survival issue, this volume is an excellent introduction to this thorny problem.

Zoë Richmond, *Evidence of Purpose*. G. Bell & Sons, London, 1938, 112 pages, glossary.

Another volume in the Bell series, although thirty years old, this is an excellent introduction to an important facet of survival research. Mrs. Richmond gives twelve cases of spontaneous apparitions, five of "compulsive impressions," and seven of mediumistic messages, all twenty-four cases having evidence of some purpose behind them, rather than pure randomness or chance coincidence. The cases are well attested, and while not every reader may agree with Mrs. Richmond's assessment of the cause or *modus operandi* resulting in the phenomena, the book is very clearly written, easy to read, with full annotations for those who wish to study the original reports.

Edward W. Ryall, *Born Twice: Total Recall of a Seventeenth-Century Life*. Harper & Row, New York, 1974, 214 pages.

This fascinating and excellent book is greatly enhanced by an outstanding introduction and appendix by Dr. Ian Stevenson, who is without doubt the world's greatest scientific authority on reincarnation memories. Most of his cases have involved children who were Asians, Brazilians, and Amerindians. Conversely, Mr. Ryall is an Englishman in his mid-seventies, whose memory of a life 300 years ago has remained clear and constant throughout this life. The details and broad scope respecting seventeenth century life recorded in this book boggle the mind. Painstaking research has verified customs, costumes, military campaigns, and astronomical anomalies to such an extent that "memory" becomes the most plausible explanation. This is certainly a *must* book for scientists, skeptics, and reincarnationists.

H. F. Saltmarsh, *Evidence of Personal Survival From Cross Correspondences*. G. Bell & Sons, London, 1938, 159 pages, glossary, excellent bibliography of cross correspondence materials from the *SPR Proceedings*.

The "cross correspondences" comprise a long series of highly complex automatic writings which many consider the most impressive evidence for survival yet obtained. Saltmarsh was very well versed in the records and had consulted the leading scholars who had explored the intricacies of the puzzles. He has produced an excellent introduction to one of the most important sets of materials in psychical research and has succeeded in demonstrating the complicated designs, subtle allusions to erudite classical motifs, and careful clues which finally led to the solving of some of the problems. He is balanced and considers the various alternative explanations as to the possible sources of the cross correspondences, leaving to the reader his own conclusions as he pursues his studies. Very clearly presented, this is essential reading.

Alson J. Smith, *Immortality: The Scientific Evidence*. New American Library, New York, 1967, 168 pages, index.

Originally published in 1954, this is an attempt by a minister to weigh the evidence which supports the survival hypothesis, the philosophical and religious aspects of the problem, the bearing of precognition and apparent retrocognition upon the issue, what he views as the growing disenchantment with materialism among eminent scientists, and an overall assessment of the impact which parapsychology has had upon modern man's view of himself and his destiny. Smith wrote well, even eloquently, and the student will find this a sound survey of survival evidence and pertinent matters. Some may feel that the author makes generalizations which are dubious and finds more significance in some instances than may be warranted. While this is not the balanced weighing of pro's and con's one finds in Hart, it is a readable and reasonably thorough account which is easily obtained; as such, it can provide a suitable introduction to the issue.

ADDITIONAL READING

A. T. Baird (Ed.), *One Hundred Cases for Survival after Death*. Bernard Ackerman, 1944.

Laurence Bendit and Phoebe Payne, *This World and That*. Faber & Faber, London, 1950.

David Christie-Murray, *Reincarnation: Ancient Beliefs and Modern Evidence*. David & Charles, North Pomfret, VT, 1982.

Robert Crookall, *The Supreme Adventure: Analyses of Psychic Communications*. James Clarke, London, 1961.

C. J. Ducasse, *Paranormal Phenomena, Science, and Life after Death*. Parapsychological Monographs No. 8, Parapsychology Foundation, New York, 1969.

Eileen J. Garrett, Editor, *Does Man Survive Death? A Symposium*. Helix Press, New York, 1957.

Bruce Greyson and Charles P. Flynn, *The Near-Death Experience: Problems, Prospects, Perspectives*. C. C. Thomas, Springfield, IL, 1984.

Arthur Guirdham, *The Cathars and Reincarnation*. Neville Spearman, Saffron Walden, England, 1970.

S. Ralph Harlow, *A Life after Death*. Doubleday, Garden City, 1961.

J. Head and S. L. Cranston (Eds.), *Reincarnation: An East-West Anthology*. Theosophical Publishing House, Wheaton, IL, 1968.

J. Head and S. L. Cranston (Eds.), *Reincarnation in World Thought*. Julian, New York, 1967.

J. B. Hutton, *Healing Hands*. Allen & Unwin London, 1966.

James H. Hyslop, *Contact with the Other World*. The Century Co., New York, 1919.

Rosamund Lehmann, *The Swan in the Evening*. Harcourt, Brace & Jovanovich, San Diego, CA, 1967.

Sir Oliver Lodge, *Why I Believe in Personal Immortality*. Doubleday, Doran & Co., Garden City, NY, 1929.

Jane Sherwood, *The Country Beyond*. Neville Spearman, Saffron Walden, England, 1969.

C. Drayton Thomas, *Life Beyond Death With Evidence*. William Collins, London, 1928.

C. Drayton Thomas, *Some New Evidence for Human Survival*. William Collins, London, 1922.

SELF-HELP AND DEVELOPMENT

Hal N. Banks, *An Introduction To Psychic Studies*. Self-published, 1976, 248 pages mimeographed on soft 8½x11 paper with plastic binding. (P.O. Box 2151, Roswell, NM 88201)

This home study course for individual or group is quite comprehensive (23 chapters), but the title, "Introduction," might be misleading; "Outline" would be more accurate, as the text is rather sketchy. However, each chapter is followed by a suggested reading list. At six intervals in the course a list of 13 "test" questions is included; the author promises to evaluate and return the student's answers. If you want merely a framework or an overview, perhaps this course is for you. The author is a Presbyterian minister.

Pat and Bud Hayes, *Our First Thousand Groups*. 1971, 74 pages. Self-published; distributed by Spiritual Frontiers Fellowship, 10819 Winner Road, Independence, MO 64052.

If your social or religious group is interested in the psychic but doesn't know what to do about it, this booklet is for you. With simple, easy–to–follow instructions, a wide variety of interesting and exciting exercises that work are explained. Detailed guidance is in one-two-three order and can be followed without any long preparatory periods. How to meditate usefully; how to perform spiritual healing that is often spectacularly successful; how to see and interpret auras; how to read basic character and "see" homey activities in your friends' lives; and much more.

Harold Sherman, *How To Picture What You Want*. Fawcett, New York, 1978, 224 pages.

This book title is somewhat misleading for it gives the impression of a naïve "how to" book for the gullible masses. Nothing could be further from the truth. Octogenarian Harold Sherman—who has written more than one hundred books—has been a life-long psychical researcher, especially of his own strong psychic abilities. In 1938, while writing stories for *Boy's Life*, the Boy Scouts' magazine, Harold arranged with Arctic explorer Sir Hubert Wilkins to link up once a day for a mind-reading session during Wilkins' trek; these spectacular communications from the North Pole to New York City were later published in *Thoughts Through Space*, Sherman's first book on the psychic scene. His current effort focuses on the "power of imagery" in its broadest and deepest senses; some of the chapter headings give an idea of its scope: all existence starts with imagery; the influence of childhood imagery; the power of imagery in healing, sex, ESP, mass-consciousness, dreams, spirit communications, sports, creativity, to get rid of wrong images; image your future; create a better self-image; images of an afterlife.

ADDITIONAL READING

Hereward Carrington, *Your Psychic Powers and How to Develop Them*. Newcastle Publishers, Hollywood, 1975.
Patricia Hayes, *Know Yourself*; 1974. Self-published; distributed by Spiritual Frontiers Fellowship, 10819 Winner Road, Independence, MO 64052.
Harold Sherman, *How to Make ESP Work for You*. Fawcett, New York, 1978.
Harold Sherman, *How to Take Yourself Apart and Put Yourself Together Again*. Fawcett, New York, 1977.
Mark Thurston, *Understand and Develop Your ESP*. A.R.E. Press, Virginia Beach, 1977.

Textbooks

Norma Bowles and Fran Hynds, with Joan Maxwell, *PSI Search*. Harper & Row, San Francisco, 1978, 168 pages.

Concerned with the lack of authentic popular information on parapsychology, the authors initially created the "PSI Search" travelling exhibit, from which this book was a natural spin-off. A part of their concern resulted from the popular confusion they saw, much of which was caused by the public's inability to distinguish valid knowledge from pseudoscience and occult areas. Separate chapters summarize laboratory experimental research, field investigation of spontaneous phenomena, and the authors' reflections. Added, also, are several resource listings.

Louisa E. Rhine, *PSI, What Is It?—The Story of ESP and PK*. Harper & Row, New York, 1975, 248 pages.

This book is dedicated by Mrs. Rhine "to my grandson, Ronnie, who, at age eleven, wished for a book about psi 'without all those big words,'—and to all the other young and older people who feel a similar need." But this is not a kiddy-book and Dr. Rhine does not talk down to her readers. This book surveys and explains the world of psi in life and lab, and ends by showing how simple experiments can be performed and evaluated, as well as how interested persons can get into work in the psi field.

ADDITIONAL READING

Louisa E. Rhine, *Manual for Introductory Experiments in Parapsychology*. Parapsychology Press, Durham, NC, 1977.
Betty Shapin and Lisette Coly (Eds.), *Education in Parapsychology*. Parapsychology Foundation, New York, 1976.

CHAPTER FOUR

BIBLIOGRAPHY
FOR THE ADVANCED STUDENT

THE DISTINCTION BETWEEN THE bibliography presented in this chapter and that in the previous is not hard and fast, but it did seem desirable to indicate to the student that some books would be appreciably more difficult and subtle than others and that certain works presuppose a considerable knowledge of the field in order to be grasped. The division is, however, only a guideline, and each student must decide which works can be by-passed and which are too advanced at the moment.

GENERAL SURVEYS AND INTRODUCTIONS
TO PSYCHICAL RESEARCH

Denis Brian, *The Enchanted Voyager: The Life of J. B. Rhine.* Prentice-Hall, Englewood Cliffs, NJ, 1982.

Brian reports that for the period from 1930 to 1960 a biography of Rhine was inextricably entwined with a history of experimental parapsycholgy; neither was viable without the other. From the 1960's onward, however, numbers of competent parapsychologists, many of whom had been trained by Rhine, began to operate elsewhere, mostly in academia. This, the first of several biographies of Rhine, is based in large part of many extensive interviews Brian had with Rhine over a period of ten years (1968-1978) regarding his work in parapsychology. Then, for the two years before Rhine's death in 1980, Brian concentrated on Rhine the man, in his interviews, which were capped by unrestricted access to Rhine's monumental files of correspondence. It would be hard to visualize a more adequate background and source for a writer.

C. D. Broad, *Lectures on Psychical Research*. Routledge & Kegan Paul, London, 1962; Humanities Press, New York, 1962, 450 pages, indices.

This collection of the late Professor Broad's most important lectures covers a wide variety of topics from the quantitative work of Soal, Rhine, and Tyrrell to mediumistic studies and the question of survival. Longtime Professor of Philosophy at Trinity College, Cambridge, Broad was one of the most eminent academic figures of his time, a President of the SPR, and a cautious expert in psychical research. His writing is unusually clear and compact, and his philosophic erudition evident in the careful definitions and the logical, balanced consideration of every alternative explanation. This is one of psychical research's most distinguished books full of profound insights. It is a work to study and to refer to repeatedly.

Whately Carington, *Telepathy: An Outline of its Facts, Theory, and Implications*. Methuen, London, 1945, 170 pages, good bibliography, index.

Carington had one of the finest minds ever brought to psychical research. His work with qualitative telepathic experiments, mediumistic word association testing, discovery of the displacement effect and its subsequent use to Soal, thoughts on survival—all were important. In this book, he has brought all of his experience, knowledge, and originality of thought to bear upon telepathy in order to construct a theoretical framework to account for its occurrence and thereby, in his view, to answer tentatively at least many of the most perplexing questions posed by paranormal occurrences of various sorts. His association theory of "psychons" or clusters of ideas has been fruitful both by its insights and by the criticisms it has encouraged. Carington had a trenchant wit and a wry sense of humor which make this one of the most entertaining books of real consequence in the field. Essential reading for the advanced student.

Jule Eisenbud, *Paranormal Foreknowledge*. Human Sciences Press, New York, 1982, 312 pages.

Dr. Eisenbud has for four decades been one of the more practical researchers and at the same time one of the most innovative theorists in parapsychology. Italy's premier parapsychologist, Emilio Servado, calls this volume one of the most important and original contributions so far written on the controversial problem of precognition—a problem which seems in contradiction to everything science has come to represent; Eisenbud states categorically that precognition seems to fly in the face of "the laws of thermodynamics, of entropy, of physical reality, *en bloc.*" When theory and phenomena joust with one another, we could not ask for a better play-by-play announcer than Jule Eisenbud.

C. E. M. Hansel, *ESP: A Scientific Evaluation.* Charles Scribner's Sons, New York, 1966, 263 pages, index, bibliography.

Professor Hansel is perhaps the most vociferous antagonist of parapsychology today and this book brings together his strongest criticisms of not only the procedures but the conclusions of parapsychology in their entirety. He argues that since parapsychologists have purported to establish the reality of ESP by so-called "conclusive" experiments which rule out all alternative explanations for the data, these specific experiments must be examined thoroughly and critically to see if this claim is valid. He concludes that it is totally invalid, for in none of these experiments can *only* ESP be the possible explanation; and in many, if not all, the most likely cause for any above–chance results is fraud on the part of the subjects or experimenters or both. He, therefore, finds both Rhine's and Soal's groups guilty of slipshod methods, gross neglect, and spurious results. ESP is not established and all the notions to the contrary are moonshine. This is an important book to read after one is familiar with the field in order to see what some of the principal objections of skeptical scientists are to parapsychology, what light upon improving experiments they can make, and how free of the bias they lay at the door of parapsychologists they themselves are. It would also be useful to read the reviews of this book by Dr. Ian Stevenson in the July, 1967 issue of the *ASPR Journal,* and that by the late R. G. Medhurst in the March, 1968 issue of the *SPR Journal.* Hansel writes clearly and well.

Renée Haynes, *The Hidden Springs: An Enquiry into Extra-Sensory Perception.* Hollis & Carter, London, 1961; The Devin-Adair Co., New York, 1961, 264 pages, index.

This is a highly original treatment of psi, considering its manifestations, operation, and significance from various viewpoints: biological, anthropological, sociological, psychological, and religious. Ms. Haynes, currently Editor of the *SPR Journal*, is a leader of the SPR, a cautious student of psi, and a devout Roman Catholic. She has discussed the relationship of psi phenomena with basic tenets of Catholicism and finds the relationship largely sympathetic. Her concepts are unusual and cogently argued; but the book requires very careful reading, for her style is recondite, compressed, and full of erudite nuances which the casual reader will miss. The book is difficult to access judiciously until one is well-read in psychical research and somewhat cognizant of the ancillary fields she brings to bear upon psi.

Rosalind Heywood, *The Infinite Hive.* Pan Books, London, 1966; U.S. edition: *ESP—A Personal Memoir.* E. P. Dutton, New York, 1963, 252 pages.

Mrs. Heywood is one of Great Britain's most distinguished authorities on psychical research and this is an unusual type of autobiography by a highly gifted woman who is also psychic; she weaves together her personal experiences of a varied kind in many parts of the world, and adds to this pattern in her own psychic perceptions together with her intellectual musings upon them and upon the entire range of paranormal phenomena. The work is especially noted for her remarkable balance, her frankness about her own psychic gift, and her intellectual—as opposed to subjective—views about that gift. Exceptionally well written.

Arthur Koestler, *The Roots of Coincidence.* Century-Hutchinson, London, 1972, 142 pages, postscript by Renée Haynes, bibliography, index.

This work is one the most impressive syntheses of parapsychology's discoveries and purview with those of physics yet to appear. Mr. Koestler presents in a lucid and captivating fashion the concepts with which the theoretical physicist constantly works and which seem perverse and "impossible" in terms of our ordinary system of sense perception. He discusses Kammerer's "seriality" and Jung's "synchronicity"; proposes his own "holon" schemata to explain the warp and woof of nature, and brings together in an intriguing and persuasive way the various strands of psychical research, mysticism, biology, physics, and philosophy. Essential reading for the advanced student.

Stanley Krippner, *Human Possibilities: Mind Exploration in the USSR and Eastern Europe*. Doubleday/Anchor, New York, 1980, 384 pages.

No one of the western world is more knowledgeable about parapsychology in the Soviet orbit than Stanley Krippner. He was one of the first western parapsychologists permitted to travel in the USSR to talk with Russian parapsychologists, and no western psi specialist has made more return trips to Soviet dominated countries to exchange data with scientists involved in psychic studies; in addition to the USSR, he has made repeated visits to Bulgaria, Czechoslovakia, East Germany, Hungary, Poland, and Romania. Dr. Krippner's credentials are impeccable; director of the first Dream Laboratory (Maimonides Medical Center) devoted exclusively to the psi research, editor of the international journal, *Psycho-energetic Systems*, past president of the Parapsychological Association, past president of the Association of Humanistic Psychology, trustee of the Academy of Religion and Psychical Research, an organizer of the Kirlian Research Association, and presently director of the Saybook Institute in San Francisco (successor to the Humanistic Psychology Institute).

The range of subject matter covered in this volume is exceedingly broad, and includes ESP, psychokinesis, creativity through hypnosis, suggestopedia, Kirlian photography, acupuncture with laser beams, holographic patterns, bioplasma, electromagnetic behavior modification, and psychic self-regulation (the Soviet variety of biofeedback). The great value of this book lies in the fact that it has first-hand knowledge, obtained through extensive interviews with the scientists and experimenters behind the iron curtain, and through the observation of many of their activities and techniques.

Elizabeth E. Mintz (with Gertrude R. Schmeidler), *The Psychic Thread: Paranormal and Transpersonal Aspects of Psychotherapy*. Human Sciences Press, New York, 1983, 232 pages.

Therapists who want to be aware of the psychic dimension in their practice cannot find better guidance than this volume. Dr. Mintz writes from a background of thirty years of practice as a psychotherapist with a conventional grounding in clinical psychology and psychoanalysis, and considerable exposure to the Gestalt approach as well as other contemporary viewpoints. She reports that among her patients she finds a great hunger for experiences that transcend the materialistic and mechanistic, and she tells how she has tried to satisfy that hunger in practical ways. But this book doesn't prove psychic phenomena nor provide theories to explain such—that's not what the book is about.

F. W. H. Myers, *Human Personality and its Survival of Bodily Death*. Two volumes. Introduction by Gardner Murphy, Longmans & Green, New York, 1954. Volume I, 660 pages; Volume II, 700 pages, index, glossary.

Myers's book is unquestionably the most famous, most original, and most important single work in psychical research. Some might argue that this should be one of the very first books a student should read, but I have placed it in the second bibliography because I feel that the student will benefit much more from Myers's ideas if he is already well-read in the field. The length alone is daunting, and it is a very complex work, the cap-stone of Myers's research, study, and pondering over several decades. Gardner Murphy's introduction makes an essential point: it is both foolish and unjust to read Murphy's theories without constant referrals to his substantiating material in the appendices. Myers's death left the work unfinished, and it was collated into its final form by co-workers at the SPR. It is truly a monumental synthesis of analytical data from the new psychology and psychiatry, physiology, philosophy, and, of course, psychical research. Here one finds for the first time the concepts of the "subliminal self" as Myers termed it, together with a theoretical framework for exploring its operation and its bearing upon paranormal phenomena. The entire question of the body-mind relationship, the issue of what constitutes a personality—such central matters are at the core of psychical research and their serious consideration begins with this most remarkable book.

F. W. H. Myers, *Human Personality and its Survival of Bodily Death.*
Foreword by Aldous Huxley. One volume, abridged by Susy Smith.
University Books, New Hyde Park, NY, 1961, 416 pages, index.

For this one volume version of Myers's classic, Miss Smith has culled
out much of the substantiating material from the large appendices,
and has placed what she considers the most important of the support-
ive data within the text itself, so that the book is much more easily
handled and read. The central theories are, of course, retained, and
there is sufficient corroborative material left to show that Myers had
a sound basis for a given point. For some, this presentation may be
the best introduction to Myers, leaving the original, full work for a
later stage of study. Any abridgement, especially by more than half,
changes the impact of a work; but Miss Smith has been judicious in
her retentions, and the reader can certainly follow Myers's thought
and appreciate the range of his mind. Myers, of course, would be the
last to insist that what he wrote at the turn of the century would be
equally valid today, as knowledge in psychical research and psychology has greatly advanced; and the issue of survival has proven a
much more difficult and complex one than he envisaged. Whatever
its drawbacks, however, this is the most essential single work the student can read.

Eugene Osty, *Supernormal Faculties in Man.* Methuen & Co., London, 1923, 242 pages, index, numerous bibliographical references in
the notes.

Osty was a leading French researcher who directed the Institut Métapsychique International in Paris for a number of years, collaborated
with many prominent investigators, and wrote widely upon psychical
research. In the course of this volume, he examines the mechanism
of sensitives, or "metagnomes" as frequently termed by European
students in the 1920's and 30's, and postulates various theories as
to the psychological makeup, processes, and affective factors in the
paranormal information produced. Osty was a physician and very
interested in the physiological as well as psychological aspects of the
subject. There is a wealth of data, hundreds of instances drawn principally from his own experiences, and many references to other European, especially French, work which will be of great value to the
student. The style is rather turgid and repetitive, for Osty was trying
for clarity and precision; but it will repay study.

Charles Richet, *Thirty Years of Psychical Research*. W. Collins Sons
& Co., London, 1923, 626 pages, index.

Richet, winner of a Nobel Prize, was one of the leading physiologists
of his day, and although at first rejecting the reality of paranormal
phenomena in the 1870's, he came to accept both mental and physical
phenomena of various types. He coined the term "ectoplasm" for the
quasiphysical substance ostensibly extruded from physical mediums;
he investigated many of the most prominent mediums; expecially
Eusapia Palladino and Eva C., and he was adamant that all such
phenomena must meet scientific standards while avoiding all trap-
pings of occultism, spiritualism, and religious overtones. This is a
major work by one of the great scientists of France, and it is in sharp
contrast to the writings of nearly all British and American psychical
researchers who have felt that the evidence for physical phenomena,
especially ectoplasmic materializations, falls far short of that needed
for acceptance. While he examines all types of phenomena, the bulk
of the book deals with the four kinds he is convinced of:
"cryptaesthesia," his term for General Extrasensory Perception,
"telekinesis," or psychokinesis, precognition, and ectoplasmic manifestations. His firm rejection of the survivalist hypothesis, despite his
conviction of the paranormal phenomena, was unusual among his
generation. He was a man of vast erudition, a wry sense of humor,
and a Gallic lucidity of style. No student can afford to ignore this
summary of Richet's decades of painstaking experimentation, keen
observation, and courageous stand in defiance of his orthodox scientific brethren.

Gertrude Schmeidler (Ed.), *Extrasensory Perception*. Atherton
Press, New York, 1969, 166 pages.

Dr. Schmeidler is one of the leading American parapsychologists,
and in this volume she has collected nine papers—all previously published—and has made perceptive comments about each, as well as
providing an overall context for them with an excellent introductory
essay. The papers include Hansel's attack on the Pearce-Pratt series,
the rejoinders of Pratt and Rhine, the Anderson-White study on the
bearing the relationship between students and teachers had on clairvoyance tests, and interesting aspects of ESP stimulation—social and
personal predilections—different variance factors in ESP phenomena and assessments, and dream studies. The selection is overall of

a high quality and is representative of the really sound research being carried on in the discipline. As such, it presents the advanced student with a fine opportunity for conveniently studying current research.

J. R. Smythies, (Ed.), *Science and ESP*. Routledge & Kegan Paul, London, 1967; Humanities Press, New York, 1967, 306 pages.

This volume consists of thirteen essays by distinguished scholars from the disciplines of psychiatry, philosophy, physics, anthropology, biology, and psychology, as well as psychical research. Among the contributors are such well–known figures as Sir Cyril Burt, C. D. Broad, Sir Alister Hardy, Rosalind Heywood, Francis Huxley, H. H. Price, and Emilio Servadio. The papers are of varying quality and pertinence, but the student will find it worthwhile to compare the different attempts to account for ESP in terms of the writer's own discipline with some interdisciplinary viewpoints. C. D. Broad's essays stands out for its usual lucidity and severity of logic while Burt's lengthy essay is brilliant. The appendix by Dr. Beloff on "A Guide to the Experimental Evidence for ESP" is a very useful item for the student and the general reader.

René Sudre, *Parapsychology*. Citadel Press, New York, 1960, 401 pages, index, numerous bibliographical references in notes.

Sudre in his youth knew the principal French researchers such as Geley, Richet, and Osty, and is in the tradition of these figures in being strongly anti-spiritualistic, highly critical of the British and American investigators for ignoring or rejecting what he feels is indisputable evidence for the reality of physical or "teleplastic" phenomena, while constructing needless and complex theories of hallucination to avoid the objective nature of such occurrences. Furthermore, he resolutely deprecates the great emphasis upon the quantitative approach: "Decimals have never convinced anyone." Sudre gives a very interesting account of the historical development of research into the paranormal, with special attention to the European work. The student will find his style clear, if often acerbic toward those with whom he disagrees (and they seem legion). At a time when physical phenomena (with the exception of some PK experiments) seem virtually non-existent in the English literature, it is certainly worthwhile to study a very different viewpoint.

G. N. M. Tyrrell, *The Nature of Human Personality*. Allen & Unwin, London, 1954, 120 pages, index.

The last of Tyrell's books, this represents the author's most mature reflections about the overall significance of psychical research, man's innate faculties, his difficulties in overcoming his evolutionized common sense outlook to recognize the reality of psychic phenomena, the bearing of paranormal occurrences upon religion, and other philosophical and psychological discussions. It would be helpful to have read Tyrrell's *The Personality of Man* before undertaking this book, since it is, in a sense, a sequel to the earlier work; but it can perfectly well be read on its own. As in all of Tyrrell's writings, his style is lucid, his arguments cogent, his erudition deep and wide, covering not only psychical research but many ancillary fields as well.

G. N. M. Tyrrell, *Science and Psychical Phenomena* and *Apparitions*. University Books, New Hyde Park, NY, 1961, with a foreword by Laura A. Dale to *Science and Psychical Phenomena*, and a preface by Professor H. H. Price to *Apparitions*. *Science*, 371 pages, index; *Apparitions*, 168 pages, appendix of cases.

Science and Psychical Research was first published in 1938, as a general treatment of the entire discipline. As such, it was one of the earliest in English and remains one of the best. By the time he wrote the book, Tyrrell had thirty years of experience in psychical research and over fifteen of full time work at it; he was a highy trained engineer, fully versed in the quantitative approach, an acute student of the qualitative aspect, and a widely read and original thinker. Add to this his excellence of style, balanced viewpoint, and sense of humor and the student will find that thirty-five years after it was written, this is a splendid overall view of the field, which will pique him to study further and to think for himself about the underlying significance of the whole.

    Apparitions is generally conceded to be the most original work yet produced about this phenomenon and the greatest single contribution to psychical research of Tyrrell. Professor Price's Preface gives a clear and useful summary of Tyrrell's thesis so that the student can have the general framework in mind before studying the author's theories. Like all of Tyrrell's work, this is carefully thought out, painstakingly substantiated, and lucidly presented. Essential for all students of psychical research, after they have a sound understanding of the basic data.

L. L. Vasiliev, *Mysterious Phenomena of the Human Psyche.* University Books, New Hyde Park, NY, 1965, 204 pages, illustrations, index.

Vasiliev was a highly regarded Russian physiologist before he became involved in the first parapsychological research at Leningrad University, and his work aroused both interest and controversy on both sides of the Iron Curtain. He examines the evidence for psychokinesis, telepathy, clairvoyance, the role of sleep and dreams in possible paranormal phenomena, the use of psychedelic drugs in such experimentation, and theories about the nature of extrasensory perception. Naturally, he rejects any dualistic, much less any spiritualistic, explanations about survival or mediumship; instead, he discusses a new Russian science, "thanatology"—the study of nature of death. He seems to have felt that in ESP some form of energy from the brain was utilized and that it was essential to discover this energy so as to confute the occult, mystical, and other superstitious leanings which "pollute" western parapsychology on occasion. This is an important book for an understanding of Russian research and the current interest in their work.

D. J. West, *Psychical Research Today.* Penguin Books, London, 1962, 224 pages, index, bibliography in references, eight photographs.

This is a highly skeptical account by a former Research Officer of the SPR and a trained psychiatrist. West considers that the evidence for paranormal faculties among mediums, physical phenomena, apparitions, haunts, poltergeists, spiritual healing, etc., is so scanty and so plagued with fraud and credulity as to warrant little acceptance. There is, however, he holds, enough evidence for the presence of ESP from the laboratory experiments, even though confirmation by frequent replication has not been so far possible. He suggests various new attacks, discusses some of the most important exploratory theoretical views, and urges more experiments by trained researchers. West is one of the most cautious and critical of all writers on psi phenomena, and it is useful to compare his explanations as a psychiatrist who accepts the existence of ESP with those of Hansel as a psychologist who rejects ESP. The book is clearly written.

ADDITIONAL READING

Allan Angoff (Ed.), *Parapsychology and the Sciences*. Parapsychology Foundation, New York, 1974.

Allan Angoff (Ed.), *The Psychic Force: Essays in Modern Psychical Research from the International Journal of Parapsychology*. Putnam's, New York, 1970.

Allan Angoff and B. Shaplin (Eds.), *Proceedings of an International Conference: PSI Factors in Creativity*. Parapsychology Foundation, New York, 1970.

Maurice Barbanell, *Spiritualism Today*. Herbert Jenkins, London, 1969.

Theordore Besterman, *Collected Papers on the Paranormal*. Helix Press, New York, 1968.

George Devereux (Ed.), *Psychoanalysis and the Occult*. International Universities Press, New York, 1971; paperback: International Universities Press, New York, 1971.

Simeon Edmunds, *Spiritualism: A Critical Survey*. Aquarian Press, Wellingborough, UK, 1966.

Jule Eisenbud, *PSI and Psychoanalysis*. Grune & Stratton, New York, 1970.

Nandor Fodor, *Between Two Worlds*. Paperback Library, New York, 1969.

Nandor Fodor, *Encyclopedia of Psychic Science*. University Books, New Hyde Park, NY, 1966.

Sigmund Freud, *Studies in Parapsychology*. Collier-Macmillan, New York, 1963.

Eileen J. Garrett, *Awareness*. Garrett Publications, New York, 1943.

Eileen J. Garrett, (Ed.), *Behind the Five Senses*. J. B. Lippincott, New York, 1957.

Eileen J. Garrett, *Telepathy*. Garrett Publications, New York, 1968.

Trevor H. Hall, *The Spiritualists*. Duckworth, London, 1962; Helix Press, New York; 1963.

J. Hettinger, *Exploring the Ultra-Perceptive Faculty*. Rider, London, 1941.

J. Hettinger, *The Ultra-Perceptive Faculty*. Rider, London, 1940.

J. Arthur Hill, *Psychical Investigations*. Cassell, London, 1917.

J. Arthur Hill, *Spiritualism: Its History, Phenomena, and Doctrine*. George H. Doran Co., New York, 1919.

A. C. Holms, *The Facts of Psychic Science and Philosophy*. University Books, New Hyde Park, NY, 1969.

Robert G. Jahn, *The Role of Consciousness in the Physical World*. Westview Press (AAAS), Boulder, 1981.

Shafica Karagulla, *Breakthrough to Creativity*. De Vorss & Co., Marina Del Rey, CA, 1956.

Andrew Lang, *Cock Lane and Common Sense*. AMS Press, New York, 1970.

R. C. LeClair, Editor, *The Letters of William James and Theodore Flournoy*. University of Wisconsin Press, Madison, 1966.

G. K. Nelson, *Spiritualism and Society*. Schocken, New York, 1969.

Arthur W. Osborn, *The Superphysical*. Ivor Nicholson & Watson, London, 1937.

Frank Podmore, *Modern Spiritualism*. Methuen, London, 1902; recent edition: *Mediums of the 19th Century*. University Books, New Hyde Park, NY, 1963.

K. Ramakrishna Rao, *J. B. Rhine: On the Frontiers of Science*. McFarland, Jefferson, NC, 1982.

D. H. Rawcliffe, *The Psychology of the Occult*. Ridgeway, New York, 1952; paperback: *Occult and Supernatural Phenomena*. Dover, New York, 1971.

J. B. Rhine, *New World of the Mind*. William Sloane & Associates, New York, 1953.

J. B. Rhine and Robert Brier, *Parapsychology Today*. Citadel Press, New York, 1968.

Joseph F. Rinn, *Searchlight on Psychical Research*. Rider, London, 1954.

Betty Shapin and Lisette Coly (Eds.), *Concepts and Theories of Parapsychology*. Parapsychology Foundation, New York, 1981.

Betty Shapin and Lisette Coly (Eds.), *The Philosophy of Parapsychology*. The Parapsychology Foundation, New York, 1977.

L. Spence, *An Encyclopedia of Occultism*. University Books, New Hyde Park, NY, 1960.

Raymond Van Over and Laura Oteri (Eds.), *William McDougall, Explorer of the Mind: Studies in Psychical Research*. Helix Press, New York, 1967.

G. E. Wolstenholme and E. C. P. Millar, (Eds.), Ciba Foundation, *Extrasensory Perception.* Little, Brown, New York, 1956; paperback: Citadel, New York, 1966.

SPONTANEOUS PHENOMENA

Barbara Brown, *Supermind: The Ultimate Energy.* Harper & Row, New York, 1980, 286 pages.

Supermind is a feast. It represents the latest thinking of one of the boldest researchers in the field of mind-body relationships. Brown, a pioneer in biofeedback, author of the best-selling *New Mind, New Body*, has integrated a number of intriguing theories and observations in this current volume. Among the topics she addresses: the primitive nature of the physical self, the human capacity for what she calls "biological awareness," inadequate information as a cause of stress-related illnesses, the "second illness" caused by anxiety over having an illness in the first place, the "intellect of the unconscious," dissociation, idiot savants, hypnosis, imagery, and mystical states ("quintessential consciousness"). On one level the book also lets us look at the author's own creative process—wrong turns, insights, changes of mind. With a candor rare among scientists, Brown offers detailed accounts of her personal adventures in consciousness: an experience with mescaline, a state of dissociation when she had to give a lecture while suffering from an excruciating headache, a childhood out–of–body experience, perceptual distortions due to "rumination" over imagined wrongs. "None of the theories about the origin or essence of mind is defensible," Brown writes, "and none can account for the outreachings of mind we call awareness and images and insights."

Everard Feilding, W. W. Baggally, and Hereward Carrington, *Sittings with Eusapia Palladino and Other Studies.* Introduction by E. J. Dingwall. University Books, New Hyde Park, NY, 1963, 324 pages.

This very important volume contains the full account of about fifteen sittings undertaken with the famous—or infamous, depending on one's point of view—Italian physical medium Eusapia Palladino, together with several other significant reports on other mediums and physical phenomena. Everard Feilding was an extraordinarily acute and experienced investigator, while Hereward Carrington was an expert on physical phenomena and an excellent amateur magician, and W. W. Baggally cooperated in many investigations for the SPR. Probably no other physical medium, except "Margery," has aroused such controversy as Palladino, an earthy, erotic Italian who cheated whenever she could, and yet seemed on occasion to produce most remarkable phenomena under stringently controlled conditions. The student will benefit from Dr. Dingwall's notes and comments, for he is noted as one of the most knowledgeable and critical investigators in the field. The complexity of psi and the difficulties and perserverance required of the dedicated psychical researcher are nowhere more vividly presented than in the studies contained in this book.

Alan Gauld and A. D. Cornell, *Poltergeists*. Routledge & Kegan Paul, Boston and London, 1979, 406 pages.

No other book on this subject has the broad scope or number of cases to be found within its pages. Over 500 cases are reviewed, dating from the year 530 A.D. until 1975, occurring in many countries, and including over fifty cases investigated by the authors themselves. The cases are analyzed in numerous ways, including even computer analysis. Their mulifaceted approach clearly shows the fallacy of attempting to distinguish between poltergeists, hauntings and apparitions, because in truth they overlap and partake of characteristics conventionally applied to one "type" only. All conventional theories of parapsychologists attempting to "explain" the poltergeist are found wanting by these authors, but unfortunately, the authors do not spell out a comprehensive explanation or theory of their own. This is the first time that a parapsychologist has flatly proposed in a major writing that, in addition to *psychic power* from a subject living person, poltergeists in many instances seem to (and perhaps *must*) involve a spirit entity to provide the intelligent direction and the specific control of the weird phenomena that result. In their final chapter the authors state that "there are some poltergeist cases, and some hauntings too, in which the phenomena sometimes appear as if controlled by an intelligent agency." We can then ask: "Whose is the intelligence concerned, and what kind of intelligence is it?" In resolving these questions they find it *not* particularly significant or helpful to note that there frequently is "*some* connection between the emotional or personal problems of the various (living) agents and the outbreaks of the phenomena." But after subdividing and evaluating their hundreds of cases they concluded that "There are a few cases . . . which fulfill our proposed criteria for accepting the intelligence at work as that of a discarnate entity"—and yet they find it impossible with present data "to decide whether or not the supposed discarnate entities are to be identified with surviving portions of formerly incarnate human beings."

Edmund Gurney, Frederick W. H. Myers, and Frank Podmore, *Phantasms of the Living*. Trubner & Co., London, 1886; abridged edition prepared by Mrs. Henry Sidgwick, Kegan Paul, London, 1918; E. P. Dutton, New York, 1918, *Phantasms of the Living* and *On Hindrances and Complications in Telepathic Communication*, abridged and edited by Eleanor Sidgwick, University Books, New Hyde Park, NY, 1962. The edition annotated is the 1918 version. lx plus 520 pages, table of cases, lengthy synopsis of each sub-heading in each chapter.

The original version of this classic work, in 1886, was in two enormous volumes, containing over seven hundred cases with discussion and theoretical postulations. The abridged version has retained slightly less than two hundred of these, omitting all but first-hand accounts. Thus, as Mrs. Sidgwick notes in the Preface, the cases retained must be taken "as typical cases, not as exhibiting the mass of evidence obtainable at the time." More than enough remains, both of cases and of the original discussion, to indicate the strong case for telepathy which Myers and Gurney made, and to show the brilliance of these two early experts in psychical research. The rolling majesty of their writing is arresting, if foreign to the clipped style of today. In recent years, there has been a tendency in some quarters to make light of the work of the early researchers, a suggestion that they were less than critical and too much concerned with possible religious overtones or paranormal phenomena. From a close reading of this book—together with Myers's classic *Human Personality* and early volumes of the *SPR Proceedings*—the student will find that such modern strictures are largely invalid. In Myers's eloquent Introduction to this book, for example, he is most cautious about the bearing upon the survival issue of the infant psychical research discipline. More years of research convinced him of survival, but it is a capital error to suppose that he, or his distinguished colleagues, desperately twisted the data to fit their own philosophical predilections or religious yearnings. This monumental study is essential for the advanced student; here one can find the seedtime for those canons of evidence and strict standards of scholarship which only the critics of psychical research ignore.

Jeffrey Mishlove, *The Roots of Consciousness*. Random House, New York, 1975, 348 pages.

This book is both irritating and rewarding. It rambles far and wide and is a survey of almost anything, including astrology and magic, which falls under the broad theme of the paranormal. Its weakness is also its strength, however, because one must appreciate the book's encyclopaedic scope, even if it doesn't neatly fit under one subject. The first section quickly touches upon shamanism and the ancient religious backgrounds of the occult in Mesopotamia, Egypt, India, China, Greece, Rome, Israel, and Arabia, and comes up through modern times in the Western world. Its best section by far is the second. It gives an excellent summary of the history of parapsychology, although Mishlove describes it all as scientific approaches to consciousness. The final section is partly devoted to certain people (including Arthur M. Young and the *reflexive universe*) and their theories about the universe which attempt to make sense of both the objective and subjective worlds, and partly on the practical applications of PSI. This massive book is interesting and easy to read.

Walter Franklin Prince, *The Case of Patience Worth*. University Books, New Hyde Park, NY, 1964, 509 pages.

No single case has been more carefully and thoroughly investigated, analyzed, and presented than that of Mrs. Curran, a middle-class St. Louis housewife who, beginning in 1913, with a Ouija board, produced remarkable literary works: poems, novels, epigrams, which displayed not only unusual creative power and originality, but unparalleled spontaneity of production. The ostensible source was the spirit of "Patience Worth" who claimed to have lived in the seventeenth century. Dr. Prince spent ten months investigating Mrs. Curran, her family, education, friends, and literary abilities and presents this painstaking research in one of the classic books of psychical research. As puzzling today as when it was exhaustively examined in

1927, the case poses important questions, as yet unanswered, about the nature and extent of the subconscious, innate histrionic abilities, and the range of imagination and subliminal information-gathering which must be postulated to vitiate the spiritist hypothesis. Essential reading.

Stephen A. Schwartz, *The Alexandria Project*. Delacorte Press, New York, 1983, 274 pages.

Stephen Schwartz, a fellow of the Royal Geographic Society (London) and a member of the Explorers Club of New York, has been one of the first in the United States to promote and write about psychic archaeology, and his first book on the subject, *Secret Vaults of Time*, is still the definitive book on the subject. Since then, Schwartz has created and been the president of a unique research team called the Mobius Group, based in Los Angeles, which sponsored the project of psychical research described in *The Alexandria Project*. The Mobius Group is an international association of scientists from many disciplines that utilizes a team of carefully selected and tested psychics on its projects of field research. The psychics of the Mobius Group honed their skills initially in the Los Angeles area by locating homocide victims, buried ruins, and even located an ancient sunken ship off the California coast. And before leaving for Egypt, eleven of them separately recorded their "remote viewing" of a buried city under the deserts of Egypt, using a map covering forty square miles, by which they accurately pin-pointed, within inches, the specific areas to be explored. These advance "readings" were proved so extremely accurate by subsequent digging, that Egyptian archaeological authorities readily gave permission for the balance of the project. Subsequent discoveries on this expedition included the ruins of Marc Antony's palace and a palace probably belonging to Cleopatra, the ancient lighthouse of Pharos, the probable site of Alexander's tomb and the actual finding of what may be his bones, plus the probable remains of the famed Library of Alexandria. This book is a scientific journal of an archaeological dig that reads like a psychic detective story.

Stewart Wavell, Audrey Butt, and Nine Epton, *Trances*. E. P. Dutton and Co., New York, 1967, 253 pages, 24 illustrations, bibliography, index.

Far too little work has been done among primitive peoples and their beliefs and practices which are ostensibly paranormal in nature. This book by Butt, an Oxford anthropologist, Wavell, an explorer who has lived much of his life in the Orient, and Epton, a travel writer who has had many experiences with such cultures, is, therefore, very welcome. The trio of authors apparently came together as a consequence of a BBC broadcast, and while the book is not a scholarly anthropological study, it is a sound work, exceedingly well written, with much of interest to the student of psi. Butt has studied the Akawaio Indians in the Amazon jungles for some years and the chapters on the "shamans" are intriguing. Other groups dealt with include the Gnaoua of Morocco, the Temers of Malaya, the Bali Barong performances with deadly "kris" daggers, various mystical groups of Algeria, Sumatra tribes, etc. Since we know so little about mediumistic trance, the interesting features which seem common among such divergent cultures in the inducement of trance are significant to psychical research. Healing and communication with spirits are important functions of the trance state among the peoples studied here, and the student will find much of importance in this book, not least the useful bibliography to anthropological studies.

ADDITIONAL READING

Theodore Besterman, *Crystal-Gazing: A Study in the History, Distribution, Theory, and Practice of Scrying.* University Books, New Hyde Park. NY, 1965.

Robert Crookall, *The Techniques of Astral Projection.* Samuel Weiser, Inc., York Beach, ME, 1975.

Sir William Crookes, *Researches in the Phenomena of Spiritualism.* Psychic Book Club, London, 1953.

Eric J. Dingwall, (Ed.), *Abnormal Hypnotic Phenomena: A Survey of Nineteenth Century Cases.* J. & A. Churchill, London, 1967; Barnes & Noble, New York, 1968, 4 volumes.

Eric J. Dingwall and Trevor H. Hall, *Four Modern Ghosts.* London, 1958.

Eric J. Dingwall, K. M. Goldney, and Trevor H. Hall, *The Haunting of Borley Rectory.* Duckworth, London, 1956,.

Jan Ehrenwald, *Telepathy and Medical Psychology.* W. W. Norton, New York, 1948.

T. Fukurai, *Clairvoyance and Thoughtography*. Rider, London, 1931.

Alan Gauld and Anthony D. Cornell, *Poltergeists*. Routledge & Kegan Paul, London and Boston, 1979.

Gustave Geley, *Clairvoyance and Materialization*. Fisher Unwin, London, 1927.

Celia Green, *Lucid Dreams*. Institute of Psychological Research, Oxford, Eng. 1968.

Celia Green, *Out-of-the-Body Experiences*. Institute of Psychological Research, Oxford, Eng., 1968.

Trevor H. Hall, *New Light on Old Ghosts*. Duckworth, London, 1965; Transatlantic, Hollywood-by-the-Sea, FL, 1965.

Robert H. Hastings, "An Examination of the Borley Report," *Proceedings of the Society for Psychical Research*. Volume 55, Part 201, New York, March, 1969.

Janet Mitchell, *Out-of-Body-Experiences: A Handbook*. McFarland, Jefferson, NC, 1981.

Frederick W. H. Myers, *The Subliminal Consciousness*. Ayer Press, Salem, NY, 1976.

Harry Price, *The End of Borley Rectory*. London, 1946.

Harry Price, *Rudi Schneider: A Scientific Examination of his Mediumship*. London, 1930.

William G. Roll, *The Investigation of RSPK Phenomena*. Psychical Research Foundation, Durham, NC, 1963.

Betty Shapin and Lisette Coly (Eds.), *Psi and States of Awareness*. Parapsychology Foundation, New York, 1978.

Ian Stevenson, *Telepathic Impressions*. University of Virginia Press, Charlottesville, VA, 1970.

E. Z. Vogt and R. Hyman, *Water Witching*. University of Chicago Press, Chicago, 1959.

Albert von Schrenk-Notzing, *Phenomena of Materialization*. Dutton, New York, 1920.

EXPERIMENTAL AND QUANTITATIVE STUDIES

C. Maxwell Cade and Nona Coxhead, *The Awakened Mind*. Delacorte Press, New York, 1979.

This is the story of the "Mind Mirror"—the superelectroencephalogram that simultaneously reads right and left brain hemispheres in all four brain-wave categories (beta, alpha, theta, and delta), and presents the entire data visually on a scanning screen; numerical values are available, but the pictorial presentation is said to be most meaningful. Dr. Cade, a fellow of the Royal Society of Medicine in Britain where the Mind Mirror was developed, has used the device to test over 4,000 people, including some fifty spiritual healers. With the latter, he has tested both healer and healee side-by-side on two machines, and finds that miraculous healings frequently take place when the healer can achieve near-duplicate pictures on the two machines—sometimes achieved by experimentally moving his hands to different parts of the healee's body (and the patient's will to be cured is said to be a possible factor in achieving near-duplicate pictures).

Haakon Forwald, *Mind, Matter and Gravitation: A Theoretical and Experimental Study.* Parapsychological Monographs No. 11, Parapsychology Foundation, New York, 1970, 72 pages.

Mr. Forwald has written a fine summary of twenty years of research into PK effects with dice of varying size and weight. A very able and careful Swedish electrical engineer, Forwald has written several articles for the *Journal of Parapsychology* about his findings and computations regarding the physical aspects of PK, but this pamphlet is an easy way for the student to learn about his research and his theoretical explanations. There have been several criticisms directed at Forwald by parapsychologists: first, the most of his work has been done alone, while he acted as both subject and investigator, so that there is no witnessed substantiation for many of his results (some, however, were gained at Rhine's laboratory); secondly, that his predilection for a gravitational explanation due to his professional training may have led him to ignore or seriously to underestimate the psychological causative factors in PK. Nevertheless, this small but important monograph is a key work in the growing literature about PK.

K. Ramakrishna Rao, *Experimental Parapsychology: A Review and Interpretation.* Charles C. Thomas, Springfield, IL, 1966, 255 pages, index, glossary, exhaustive bibliography of over 1200 items, mostly articles pertaining to experimental work.

Rao has set out to summarize the experimental development of parapsychology since Rhine wrote his book *Psychical Research After Sixty*

Years, in 1940. Much of great importance has occurred in that quarter of a century and, Rao, for some years associated with Rhine at Duke University and now pursuing research at an Indian university, is an experienced researcher. His interest lies almost solely with laboratory, quantitative work, as he feels that only in such data can "proof" of the psi faculty be attained. Included in this work are accounts of all significant experiments during a twenty-five-year period, plus a critical examination of various theories of psi by Rhine, Roll, Murphy, Broad, Flew, Price, Carington, Tyrrell, and others. Rao's style is rather academic and sometimes even ponderous; but he has a keen mind, ideas of his own, and uncompromising evidential standards of a quantitative nature.

J. B. Rhine and J. G. Pratt, *Parapsychology: Frontier Science of the Mind.* Charles C. Thomas, Springfield, IL, revised edition, 1962, 224 pages, bibliography, index.

Intended as "a survey of the field, the methods, and the results of ESP and PK research," this volume, co-authored by two of the most experienced and respected parapsychologists, is a straightforward, carefully written account, emphasizing the objective, experimental work performed over the last forty years. An excellent glossary and long bibliographies of both books and articles covering the entire range of paranormal phenomena, data, and theories are included. This work is recommended following some familiarity with the experimental material of psychical research. It is very readable.

Gertrude R. Schmeidler and R. A. McConnell, *ESP and Personality Patterns.* Yale University Press, New Haven, 1958, 110 pages, appendices, bibliographical references, index. Preface by Gardner Murphy.

Dr. Schmeidler is best known for her "sheep" and "goat" experiments, and they are the major basis for this book, the statistical work for which was done by Dr. McConnell, a biophysicist as well as an experienced parapsychologist. The authors have aimed at satisfying the professional scientist without bewildering the interested layman, and have succeeded admirably. The statistical tables are clear, the statistical terminology is remarkably well explained and sections of a very technical nature can easily be skipped. The material dealing with the ESP subjects' response to Rorschach and other psychological testing, the experimentation with concussion patients, and the discussion of new areas of research needing attack are fascinating. Both write extremely well; this is scholarly parapsychology at its best and most readable.

Charles T. Tart, Editor, *Altered States of Consciousness: A Book of Readings*. Wiley, New York, 1969, 575 pages.

This is the best introduction to this important topic yet published. While the work is not directed at the layman, the writing is generally so clear that the advanced student should not find undue difficulty with the material, especially as it has been subdivided into useful sections dealing with hypnosis, psychedelic drugs, meditation, the "hypnagogic state" between sleeping and waking, dreams, etc. There are experimental and theoretical discussions of the various states which may shed a good deal of light upon the workings of the psi faculty. There is a massive bibliographical reference section which the student wishing to explore further will find invaluable, although much more has been published since this volume was prepared. While only two of the papers are directly concerned with psi phenomena, there seems a growing interest among parapsychologists about altered states of consciousness as they may bear upon conditions favorable to psi, and the advanced student should be aware of this aspect of work.

René Warcollier, *Experimental Telepathy*. Boston Society for Psychic Research, Inc., Boston, 1938, edited and abridged by Gardner Murphy, 294 pages, glossary.

A most useful collection of sixteen papers by a thoughtful, thorough, and imaginative French researcher, this volume contains a mine of speculative concepts as well as valuable experimental work illustrated by many drawings of the telepathic targets and attempts. Warcollier was a chemical engineer who brought to psychical research a sound scientific background, rigid standards of work, and a fertile mind. The student will find his ideas refreshing and germinal, his stance open minded and frank. Although some of the articles are fifty years old, they remain well worth studying both for the quality of the experimental work in telepathy they represent and for the shrewd observations and the problems of experimentation in telepathy and other paranormal fields.

ADDITIONAL READING

Allan Angoff and Betty Shapin (Eds.), *A Century of Psychical Research: The Continuing Doubts and Affirmations*. Parapsychology Foundation, New York, 1971.

Roberto Cavanna (Ed.), *Proceedings of an International Conference on Methodology in Psi Research: PSI Favorable States of Consciousness*. Parapsychology Foundation, New York, 1970.

Roberto Cavanna and Montague Ullman (Eds.), *Proceedings of an International Conference on Hypnosis, Drugs, Dreams, and PSI: PSI and Altered States of Consciousness*. Parapsychology Foundation, New York, 1968.

Martin Ebon (Ed.), *Test Your ESP*. World Publishing Co., New York, 1970; paperback: New American Library, New York, 1971.

J. G. Pratt, *On the Evaluation of Verbal Material in Parapsychology*, *Parapsychological Monographs No. 10*. Parapsychology Foundation, New York, 1969.

J. B. Rhine (Ed.), *Progress in Parapsychology*. Parapsychology Press, Durham, NC, 1971.

L. E. Rhine, *Manual for Introductory Experiments in Parapsychology*. Parapsychology Press, Durham, NC, 1966.

J. H. Rush, *New Directions in Parapsychological Research, Parapsychological Monographs No. 4*. Parapsychology Foundation, New York, 1964.

Gertrude Schmeidler, *ESP in Relation to Rorschach Test Evaluation, Parapsychological Monographs No. 2*. Parapsychology Foundation, New York, 1960.

Gertrude R. Schmeidler, *Parapsychology: Its Relation to Physics, Biology, Psychology and Psychiatry*. Scarecrow Press, Metuchen, NJ, 1976.

Harold Sherman, *Thoughts through Space*. Creative Age Press, New York, 1942.

S. G. Soal, *The Experimental Situation in Psychical Research*. F. W. H. Myers Memorial Lecture, Society for Psychical Research, London, 1947.

S. G. Soal and H. T. Bowden, *The Mind Readers*. Faber, London, 1959.

Montague Ullman and Stanley Krippner, *Dream Studies and Telepathy: An Experimental Approach, Parapsychological Monographs No. 12*. Parapsychology Foundation, New York, 1970.

L. L. Vasiliev, *Experiments in Mental Suggestion*. Institute for the Study of Mental Images, Church Crookham, Hampshire, Eng., 1963.

René Warcollier, *Mind to Mind*. Creative Age Press, New York, 1948; paperback: Collier-Macmillan, New York, 1963.

D. J. West, *Tests for Extrasensory Perception: An Introductory Guide*. Revised edition. Society for Psychical Research, London, 1954.

PHILOSOPHICAL AND RELIGIOUS IMPLICATIONS

A. G. N. Flew, *A New Approach to Psychical Research*. Watts, London, 1953, 158 pages, index, bibliography, two appendices.

Professor Flew is a highly skeptical student of psychical research who is principally concerned with the problems of language, precision in concepts, philosophical issues, and the nature of requisite evidence to establish the reality of psi phenomena. He argues that the qualitative evidence is so dubious because of the notorious inaccuracy of human testimony that it can be given little credence. We are left, therefore, with the statistical evidence, which is also suspect in some respect because of loose experimentation controls. He, however, feels that there is sufficient basis for the hypothesis of psi on statistical grounds, but rejects utterly the philosophical implications of the mind-body, religious and survivalist overtones, and what he deems are widely improbable and unwarranted assumptions about the undermining of physicalistic or materialistic views of man's nature by the psi evidence. This is a very stimulating book by a professional philosopher who has read the evidence, has a keen mind, an incisive and amusing style, and original ideas. His approach is similar to D. J. West's, but with a philosophical rather than a psychological bent. An important book to read and compare with critical works like Hansel's, Lamont's , and Rinn's.

Margaret Lewis Furse, *Mysticism: Window on a World View*. Abingdon, Nashville, 1977, 220 pages.

This book is a valuable contribution to the analysis of mysticism. To appreciate its import and to learn from it the reader needs some acquaintance with philosophical and theological terminology and also with the questions and positions which have given rise to this terminology. Yet Furse writes clearly, and any reader who initially lacks such preparation but who is willing to do some supplementary reference work is sure to find the careful reading of her book a valuable experience. She provides material on Eastern mysticism—i.e., the mysticism of Taoism, Hinduism, Buddhism, and Zen Buddhism. And there is a great deal on Christian mysticism, and Christian mystics such as Teresa of Avila and Meister Eckhart, and on commentaries on mysticism worked out by Evelyn Underhill, William Ralph Inge, and Friederich von Hügel. Unfortunately, however, Sufism and the several varieties of Jewish mysticism are omitted altogether. It is not only the person who is a novice at these studies who will profit from this book. The author does the student of mysticism a service by calling attention to the roles in Western mysticism of Greek, Syrian, and Egyptian mystery schools and to the mysticism of Plato. Her inclusion of these is noteworthy because the mystery schools are often ignored in studies of mysticism, and it is often denied that Plato is a mystic at all. Yet Platonism has roots in the mystery traditions, and much Jewish and Christian mysticism is really Jewish Platonism and Christian Platonism.

Sir Alister Hardy, *The Divine Flame*. Collins, London, 1966, 254 pages.

This is the second series of Gifford Lectures at the University of Aberdeen, and in this volume, Sir Alister is concerned less with biology and evolution than with psychology, anthropology, parapsychology, and theology. Because he is dealing with issues not so directly within the purview of his own scholarly expertise, these lectures, while preserving the same splendid quality of writing, are upon possibly less sure ground; or at least open to a wider variety of interpretation and criticism. The central points the author makes are that the evidence of physical science does not contravene the possibility of a divine order or divine being, as materialists have argued; that psychological, especially Freudian, interpretations of myths and primitive magical rites may well be only partial explanations; that the testimony of outstanding mystics as well as ordinary people bear evidence to the divine reality; that psychical research has suggested, if not definitely demonstrated, that a dualistic view of man is highly plausible, i.e., that brain and mind may well be distinct; and that, consequently, the fashionable view that the concept of a God is merely and exteriorized psychological construct to meet deep-seated human needs is not necessarily valid. There is strong empirical evidence to merit the belief in a "divine flame" pervading the universe, open to the questing human being, and giving to existence meaning and dignity. Like the first volume, this is exciting and inspiring reading.

Sir Alister Hardy, *The Living Stream: A Restatement of Evolution Theory and its Relation to the Spirit of Man*. Collins, London, 1965, 292 pages.

This collection of the first series of the Gifford Lectures at the University of Aberdeen is an important synthesis of the author's ideas. One of Great Britain's most distinguished zoologists, a former President of the Society for Psychical Research and thus a highly qualified expert in psychical research, Hardy combines his knowledge of biology and parapsychology with his philosophical and religious thoughts. His treatment of the evolutionary theory as it has developed since Darwin is fascinating, for he writes superbly, and as the lectures were given for a non-specialist audience, he has aimed at the layman in his account. Hardy believes that the evolutionary schemata is far less deterministic in an environmental sense than has been generally understood, and postulates an idea of "organic selection" through which species engage in environmental selection and develop organic changes to meet the needs of the new environment. But it is in the final lectures that the relation of the work with psychical research is most apparent. Hardy argues that psychical research bears upon the materialist dominance in thought about human personality and demonstrates that this viewpoint is not so impressive as many think. Rather, he holds that telepathy demonstrates that mind is something else or more than brain and possibly more than individual mind; if so, he feels that this might explain some of the problems of evolutionary development. Finally, in his lecture on "Natural Theology in the Evolutionary Scheme," Sir Alister eloquently presents his belief in a pervasive force—a Divine Power—which while not synonymous with the traditional personalized God, is nevertheless within extrasensory reach by prayer. There are few scientists who combine the knowledge of their own specialty with that of psychical research and possess such a deft literary ability as Sir Alister. This book is an exciting excursion with a wise and thoughtful scholar.

John J. Heaney, *The Sacred and the Psychic: Parapsychology and Christian Theology.* Paulist Press, Ramsey, NJ, 1984, 186 pages.

John J. Heaney, writing from a background as a professor of theology in a Catholic institution has done an extraordinarily fine job of surveying the field of parapsychology and relating its insights to Christian doctrine. For anyone who is not well read in the field of parapsychology here in this one book is an opportunity to become quickly acquainted with the most respected leaders and their particular observations. In his thirteen chapters Heaney carefully explains practically all the different kinds of psychic manifestations, and then discusses their implications for Christian theology. The book does not attempt to deal with the major world religions but does give them brief comment. Such subjects as telepathy, psychokinesis, demonic possession, healing, precognition and prophecy are ably dealt with. Out-of-the-body experiences and recent studies of "Near Death" are taken under careful consideration. As further examples of the breadth of his work he discusses mediums and reincarnation. Some of his best work is done in relating near-death observations to traditional ideas of heaven and hell. Important implications on the resurrection of Jesus, and our after-life come from study of apparitions.

Raynor C. Johnson, *The Light and the Gate.* Hodder and Stoughton, London, 1964, 312 pages, index.

Dr. Johnson writes about four men who have greatly influenced his thinking about the meaning of life: the Irish poet and mystic A. E. (George Russel), the Australian novelist and diplomat, Ambrose Pratt, the American-born Buddhist sage, Venerable Sumangalo, and the British preacher and writer, Dr. Leslie Weatherhead. Included are four essays which connect each figure's principal concerns. As with all of Johnson's works, this is mind-stretching, superbly written, and challenging. For the student who has reached that point where he ponders the significance of the expanded world view which psi phenomena present, this book will suggest new vistas; for each of these men is remarkable in his own way, and each has sought to find "the light and the gate" in his own manner.

Raynor C. Johnson, *Nurslings of Immortality*. Hodder and Stoughton, London, 1957; Harper & Row, New York, 1957, 279 pages, index.

In this, his second synthesis of philosophical, religious, mystical, scientific, and parapsychological data, Johnson presents the case for Douglas Fawcett's philosophy of Imaginism, and discusses how well it seems to answer the riddles of man's existence, God's nature, purpose in human life, the existence of evil, etc. Because Fawcett's basic concept is quite different from our normal philosophical frame of reference, parts of the work are quite difficult to grasp, despite Dr. Johnson's usual lucid style and careful analogies. It gives the thoughtful reader much to ponder; but it would be helpful to have read Johnson's *The Imprisoned Splendour and A Religious Outlook for Modern Man* first, and to have a firm grasp of psychical research before undertaking this work.

Lawrence LeShan, *Toward a General Theory of the Paranormal: A Report of Work in Progress*. Parapsychology Foundation, Inc., New York, 1969, 112 pages, index.

This brief, very clear monograph is one of the most important theoretical works to appear in parapsychology for some time. Dr. LeShan has presented a hypothesis that each individual has his own reality within which he operates and that there are various types of Individual Realities or IR's: common sense, scientific, mystical, and clairvoyant. He discusses how congruent the theoretical-scientific, the S–IR, and the mystic-clairvoyant, the C–IR, have become with the new physics and quantum theory, and how incongruent these are with the common sense IR. He examines the hypothesis through the experiences of mystics and sensitives, expecially Mrs. Eileen Garrett, and through the writings of scientific theorists like Planck, Heisenberg, and Eddington. It is a fascinating and encouraging small book which requires careful study, based on a very thorough knowledge of both the data and theories of psychical research. Essential reading for the advanced student.

Frank C. Tribbe, *Portrait of Jesus?—The Illustrated Story of the Shroud of Turin*. Stein & Day, New York, 1983, 281 pages.

This is, as of now, the definitive book on the Shroud of Turin. The Shroud has become the focus of intense religio-scientific attention and inquiry, centering on tests undertaken by an international team from October 8 to 13, 1978. Crucial questions facing the investigators were these: Is this cloth, which appears to bear the imprint of a man crucified, authentic? To what degree can we regard it as the shroud that enveloped the body of Jesus? But far beyond purely technical matters that concerned the team of scientists who joined in research on the Shroud of Turin, vital historical and spiritual considerations have been prompted by this Shroud. In his foreword, Dr. Edward W. Bauman, director of Bauman Bible Telecasts, notes that the facts concerning the Shroud have significance "for all faiths and hope for all people." This ecumenical concept is reflected throughout the book, representing, as the author puts it, a "nondenominational viewpoint." This book is encyclopedic in nature. It includes a report and analysis of what is known or conjectured concerning the history of the Shroud, through more than a thousand years of relative obscurity, and, in fascinating detail, since its reemergence in the fourteenth century. Tribbe is cautious in dealing with undocumented claims, but does not hesitate to support certain historical hypotheses, such as the assumption that the Shroud was held for some time by persons associated with the Knights Templar. Ultimately, however, he notes, it is not the more or less well documented history of this unique relic but its enigmatic, awesome reality that makes us pause.

G. N. M. Tyrrell, *Grades of Significance*. Rider, London, Second Edition, 1947, 221 pages.

First written in 1930, Tyrrell in his Preface to the Second Edition, terms the essay "not an attempt to condense a system of philosophy, but only a parable intended to encourage a peculiar orientation of thought in the reader's mind." This orientation is found in his concept of "aspects" of reality and the varying significance to be attached to them depending upon one's presuppositions, personality stance, and the level of spiritual awareness. The discussion of psychical research, its connection with spiritualism, religion, scientific materialism and determinism, and Tyrrell's illustrating comments on mysticism are all most stimulating and thought-provoking. A germinal work, not only for Tyrrell himself, but for any student of the paranormal.

John White (Ed.), *What is Enlightenment?—Exploring the Goal of the Spiritual Path*. J. P. Tarcher, Los Angeles, 1984, 226 pages.

This is White's thirteenth book in the consciousness field; he describes it as "a kind of sequel" to his first book, *The Highest State of Consciousness*, published thirteen years ago. Both are anthologies; *Highest State* contained thirty-three selections, of which three are reprinted in the current volume, including a chapter from the classic, *Cosmic Consciousness* by Richard M. Bucke, with which this book opens. In its fifteen chapters, the other contributors are Alan Watts, Aldous Huxley, Evelyn Underhill, Huston Smith, Allan Cohen, Satprem, Lex Hixon, Roger Walsh, Gopi Krishna, Dane Rudhyar, Da Free John, Ken Wilber, and White, himself. An eight-page appendix lists seventy-four items for further reading with a one-sentence description of each; twenty-five of those titles are books about women.

ADDITIONAL READING

Donald H. Andrews, *The Symphony of Life*. Unity Books, Lee's Summit, MO, 1966.

Henri Bergson, *Matter and Memory*. Macmillan, New York, 1911.

C. D. Broad, *The Mind and its Place in Nature*. Harcourt Brace Jovanovich, San Diego, CA, 1949.

Richard M. Bucke, *Cosmic Consciousness*. Revised edition. University Books, New Hyde Park, NY, 1961; paperback: Dutton, New York, 1969; Citadel, New York, 1970.

Sir Cyril Burt, *Psychology and Psychical Research*. Seventeenth F. W. H. Myers Memorial Lecture, Society for Psychical Research, London, 1968.

Whately Carington, *Matter, Mind, and Meaning*. Methuen, London, 1949; Books for Libraries, Freeport, NY, 1970.

Alexis Carrel, *Man: The Unknown*. Harper & Row, New York, 1935.

W. H. Clark, *Chemical Ecstasy: Psychedelic Drugs and Religion*. Sheed and Ward, New York, 1969.

Robert Crookall, *The Interpretation of Cosmic and Mystical Experiences*. Attic Press, Greenwood, SC, 1969.

J. W. Dunne, *An Experiment With Time*. Third edition. Hillery, New York, 1958; paperback: Princeton, 1955.

Anthony Flew (Ed.), *Body, Mind, and Death*. Macmillan, New York, 1964.

Gustave Geley, *From the Unconscious to the Conscious*. William Collins, London, 1920.

David Harvey, *The Power to Heal: An Investigation of Healing and the Healing Experience*. Aquarian Press, Wellingborough, Eng., 1983.

Paul L. Higgins, *Encountering the Unseen*. T. W. Denison, Minneapolis, 1966.

Thomson J. Hudson, *The Law of Psychic Phenomena: A Working Hypothesis for the Systematic Study of Hypnotism, Spiritism, Mental Therapeutics*. Hudson–Cohan, Chicago, 1970.

Raynor C. Johnson, *Watcher on the Hills*. Hodder & Stoughton, London, 1959.

C. G. Jung, *The Interpretation of Nature and the Psyche*. Princeton University Press, Princeton, 1955.

Lawrence LeShan, *From Newton to ESP: Parapsychology and the Challenge of Modern Science*. Turnstone Press, Wellingborough, England, 1984.

Lawrence LeShan, *The Medium, the Mystic and the Psysicist*. Ballantine, New York, 1982.

R. E. L. Masters and J. Houston, *The Varieties of Psychedelic Experience*. Holt, Rinehart, and Winston, New York, 1966; paperback: Dell, New York, 1967.

Arthur W. Osborn, *The Future is Now: The Significance of Precognition*. University Books, New Hyde Park, NY, 1962.

Laura Oteri (Ed.), *Quantum Physics and Parapsychology*. Parapsychology Foundation, New York, 1975.

J. B. Rhine, *Telepathy and Human Personality*. The Tenth F. W. H. Myers Memorial Lecture, Society for Psychical Research, London, 1950.

John Rossner, *Toward Recovery of the Primordial Tradition: Ancient Insights and Modern Discoveries*. University Press of America, Lanham, MD, 1979-1984. Volume I: *Toward a Parapsychology of Religion;* Book One: *From Ancient Magic to Future Technology.* Book Two: *From Ancient Religion to Future Science,* Volume II: *The Primordial Tradition in Contemporary Experience— Explorations in Psyche, Sacrament and Spirit;* Book One: *Religion, Psyche and Science.* Book Two: *Spirits and Cosmic Paradigms.* Book Three: *The Psychic Roots of Ancient Wisdom and Primitive Christian Gnosis.*

J. R. Smythies (Ed.), *Brain and Mind: Modern Concepts of the Nature of Mind*. Routledge & Kegan Paul, London, 1967.

E. Bruce Taub-Bynum, *The Family Unconscious: An Invisible Bond*. Foreword by Stanley Krippner. Theosophical Publishing House, Wheaton, IL, 1984.

Wilson Van Dusen, *The Natural Depth in Man*. Harper & Row, New York, 1972.

J. H. M. Whiteman, *The Mystical Life*. Faber & Faber, London, 1961.

MEDIUMSHIP

Eileen J. Garrett, *Many Voices: The Autobiography of a Medium*. G. P. Putnam's Sons, New York, 1968, 242 pages, index.

This is the last of Mrs. Garrett's books to be published, and while there is of necessity some repetition of experiences to be found in her *Adventures in the Supernormal* and *My Life as a Search for the Meaning of Mediumship*, in *Many Voices* she has presented her most mature and concerned views upon matters psychic. She was acknowledged as one of the greatest of all mediums, quick-witted, a shrewd businesswoman and administrator, with Celtic wit and charm. During her long life she came into contact with a host of remarkable people and her reminiscences bristle with literary figures like Joyce, Hardy, A. E., and Conan Doyle, as well as noted pyschical researchers. Her chief monument is the Parapsychology Foundation which has generously supported psychical research for many years, and she recounts its inception and aims. Ever seeking, always questioning, probing, never satisfied with the facile or simplistic answer, this book shows the thoughts and experiences of one of the most remarkable women of our time.

Geraldine Cummins, *Swan on a Black Sea: A Study in Automatic Writing: The Cummins-Willett Scripts*. Introduction by C. D. Broad, autobiographical note by Geraldine Cummins. Samuel Weiser, Inc., York Beach, ME, 1970, 168 pages.

This is a compilation of scripts automatically written by the well-known Irish sensitive, Geraldine Cummins, and purporting to be dictated by the late Mrs. Coombe-Tennat who, under the pseudonym of Mrs. Willett, played a key role in the famous "cross-correspondences" in the first two decades of this century. Not until after her death in 1956, was it publicly known that she was "Mrs. Willett." The value and quality of these scripts has been assessed quite differently by various parapsychologists, but they are clearly the most important mediumistic materials to be published for quite some time; and whatever their true origin, they reveal the extraordinary sense of personality, identity, and the highly veridical information which such materials, at their very rare best, can present. Professor Broad's introduction is most perceptive and valuable. Essential reading.

Susy Smith, *The Mediumship of Mrs. Leonard*. University Books, New Hyde Park, NY, 1964, 260 pages, bibliography.

This volume is a sound, if rather favorable, study of Mrs. Leonard, certainly one of the greatest mediums in history. Like many such biographical works, it can be somewhat misleading in that it naturally concentrates upon the "hits"—and there were a great many most impressive cases in this category—and says little about the "misses," the inaccuracies, the inevitable "padding," etc. Still, it is one of the better and more comprehensive books about mediumship, and the author had the opportunity of coming to know Mrs. Leonard, a remarkably cultured, kind, and honest lady, so that her bias may be understood. Among other matters, the discussion of the Word Association Tests of Whately Carington is especially noteworthy, as are the questions of the book tests, occasional direct voice phenomena, newspaper precognition tests, and the famous Bobbie Newlove case which caused such a controversy in the mid-thirties. Since everyone who dealt with Mrs. Leonard was agreed upon her complete integrity and constant cooperation with all investigations, this volume is an important one to study. It can profitably be compared with Mrs. Leonard's own books about her mediumistic gift and with Alta Piper's work about her mother.

Charles C. Wise, Jr., *Thus Saith the Lord: The Autobiography of God*. The Magian Press, Penn Laird, VA, 1984, 292 pages.

Charles C. Wise, Jr., in this latest of his books, has given us a panoply of New Age thinking in what amounts to a series of essays on an extraordinary variety of themes. The book is held together on the premise that Mr. Wise is a channel for those thoughts which God wishes expressed to humanity as we enter the Aquarian Age. Speaking for God is the ultimate presumption, and lest some gullible persons be swept along with every line in this book we do well to heed this admonition from the book itself: "Listen to teachers, but give blind obedience to none. Don't look for salvation from space-people, 'walk-ins,' or a heavenly hierarchy . . . anything that purports to be God's Will or God's Plan should be given a careful and critical going-over." Hundreds of writers have attempted to describe, interpret or speak for God. For twenty years in his writings, Dr. Wise has attempted to see intimate and realistic aspects of deity; two of his major efforts concerned the personality and experiences of Jesus the Christ: *Picture Windows on the Christ* and *The Magian Gospel of Brother Yeshua*, both from the Magian Press. But what are we to make of such an audacious book? Should we swallow it whole, like so much celestial pablum? Those who think as they read are certain to be shocked and even outraged by some of the statements so blithely recorded in this volume. But, what is your God like? What would he say on various subjects if you could tune to celestial wavelengths? Inevitably literature of this type purporting to come from God or higher planes far above the mind of the writer will at points reflect the humanity and prejudices of the channel. In *Thus Saith the Lord*, Charles Wise has written a book of extraordinary breadth filled with much to simulate the mind.

ADDITIONAL READING

M. Bouisseau, *The Life of a Sensitive*. Sidgwick & Jackson, London, 1955.

Geraldine Cummins, *Unseen Adventures*. Rider, London, 1951.

Eric J. Dingwall and Harry Price, *Revelations of a Spirit Medium*. London, 1922.

Theodore Flournoy, *From India to the Planet Mars*. University Books, New Hyde Park, NY, 1963.

E. W. Fornell, *The Unhappy Medium: Spiritualism and the Life of Margaret Fox*. University of Texas Press, Austin, 1964.

Alan Gauld, *Mediumship and Survival: A Century of Investigations*. David & Charles, North Pomfret, VT, 1983.

Emma Hardinge, *Modern American Spiritualism: A Twenty Years' Record of the Communion between Earth and the World of Spirits*. University Books, New Hyde Park, NY, 1970.

Peter Hurkos, *Psychic: The Story of Peter Hurkos*. Bobbs–Merrill, Indianapolis, 1961.

J. Leasor, *The Millioneth Chance: The Story of the R 101*. Hamish Hamilton, London, 1957.

Gladys Osborne Leonard, *Brief Darkness*. Cassel & Co., London, 1931.

Gladys Osborne Leonard, *The Last Crossing*. Cassel & Co., London, 1937.

A. Muhl, *Automatic Writing*. Helix Press, New York, 1964.

Ira Progoff, *The Image of an Oracle*. Helix Press, New York, 1964.

W. H. Salter, *Trance Mediumship*. Society for Psychical Research, London, 1950.

SURVIVAL ISSUE

Robert Crookall, *What Happens When You Die*. Colin Smythe, London, 1978, 196 pages.

Dr. Crookall had been studying out-of-the-body experiences (OBE) for over twelve years, and this is his fourteenth book on the subject. It differs from the preceding books in being a gallant attempt to construct a framework of thought bringing together the accounts of several hundred people who have attempted to describe what it feels like to be temporarily or permanently out of the physical body, the latter corresponding to biological death. The book is a direct sequel to two previous ones: *The Supreme Adventure* and *Events on the Threshold of the After Life*. Without having read these, or at any rate some of the others, this latest book will prove hard going. And even with the advantage of having read his previous studies the style of *What Happens When You Die* is difficult. For instance, on two consecutive pages taken at random (130-1) there are no fewer than twenty-eight notes in parentheses, making it difficult to follow the main sentence. But the persistent reader will be well rewarded. Dr. Crookall does not flinch from taking Professor McDougall's advice, which he quotes, to be bold in grasping a vast range of converging evidence, and convincing those who are open to conviction—by no means all of us—that it *does* converge.

Briefly, his conclusions are that every one of us has three temporary bodies and one eternal body, all of them interpenetrating in some way the only body we are normally conscious of. This conclusion has already won considerable acceptance among those who have studied the subject, having been advanced by several research workers in recent decades, and being consistent with the conventional wisdom of past ages. But Dr. Crookall carries the matter further than anyone else.

C. J. Ducasse, *A Critical Examination of the Belief in a Life After Death*. Charles C. Thomas, Springfield, IL, 1961, 318 pages, index.

A major treatment of the survival problem by one of America's most distinguished academic philosophers, the late Professor Ducasse, longtime professor at Brown University. He was renowned for his excellent grasp of psychical research, his remarkably lucid style, and the brilliant logic of his examination of philosophical matters. He brings all these talents to bear upon this vital question, and critically discusses virtually every facet, from the mind–body dualism to reincarnation. The entire work is so closely and cogently reasoned that it is imperative to read it with the greatest scrutiny; it cannot be skimmed profitably. Ducasse's work, with that of James, Broad, and Price, comprises a major part of the intellectual and philosophical capstone of psychical research, and should be undertaken only after sound and thorough preparation.

Corliss Lamont, *The Illusion of Immortality*. Introduction by John Dewey. Third Edition. Philosophical Library, New York, 1959, 278 pages, index, excellent bibliography available from the numerous footnotes.

Dr. Lamont's purpose is straightforward and unequivocal: " . . . this whole book is intended precisely to show that to believe in immortality means to *trample reason under foot* (sic)." This is possibly the most clearly presented of all anti-survivalist works. Every facet of the question is examined. Lamont argues for a monistic, humanistic viewpoint based upon the physiological and psychological findings of science which demonstrate beyond doubt, he feels, the complete unity of body, mind, and personality, hence rendering any survivable facet of man impossible. His knowledge of psychical research and spiritualism, both of which he attacks—the latter more strongly than the former—is rather sparse, and like many anti-survivalists he finds himself dubious about telepathy but forced to invoke it as an alternative in explaining the most impressive mediumistic evidence. Dr. Lamont is a very able protagonist, knowledgeable about philosophy, religion, science, and their interaction with reference to this vital issue. He writes exceedingly well, with sympathy, and without a sense of intellectual arrogance towards those who accept immortality. This is an essential book for the student concerned with survival to study in order to balance his stance. It is useful to consult Ducasse's *A Critical Examination of the Belief in a Life After Death* for his criticisms of various of Lamont's arguments.

Gardner Murphy, *Three Papers on the Survival Problem*. American Society for Psychical Research, New York, 1970, 90 pages.

This pamplet contains reprints of three important papers first published in 1945. They are: "An Outline of Survival Evidence" in which he gives examples of the different types of evidence so far adduced; "Difficulties Confronting the Survival Hypothesis," in which Dr. Murphy considers the various loopholes—including Super ESP—in veridical information which ostensibly supports the survivalist hypothesis; and "Field Theory and Survival," in which the complex concept of field theory is considered as it might pertain to paranormal phenomena, human personality, and possible survival. These are major essays in survival research and theory which should be studied by the advanced student.

Karlis Osis and Erlendur Haraldsson, *At the Hour of Death*. Avon Books, New York, 1977, 244 pages.

In the late 1950's Dr. Osis began the investigation and recording of paranormal deathbed observations while he was Research Officer for the great psychic, Eileen Garrett, at her Parapsychology Foundation. This work culminated in 1961 in a scientific monograph, "Deathbed Observations of Physicians and Nurses." Very little professional or popular interest in this facet of psychical research was evidenced until 1969, when psychiatrist Elisabeth Kübler-Ross published *On Death and Dying*, in an effort to change our attitudes toward the dying patient and his interests. Nevertheless, death, and its study (known as thanatology) was still a taboo subject that was being revalued but slowly in our American civilization until the dawn of the "Moody phenomena," as several have labeled the surprising popularity of M.D.-philosopher Raymond A. Moody, Jr., whose book, *Life After Life* (1975), stood America on its collective ear with low-key, understated data of "clinical death" cases, where experient after experient returned to life and reported some fifteen phases of the death-cum-paradise experience—even including identical descriptive phrases. So, with such encouragement, Dr. Osis, now director of research at the American Society for Psychical Research, and his associate, Dr. Haraldsson of Iceland, decided to update the American statistics (reported in the 1961 monograph) with a new survey, and to follow it with a companion study in India, in order that cross-cultural patterns might be studied. The primary results in all three studies are substantially identical, as reported in this book, though a few cultural variables do appear. The overwhelming conclusion the reader surely must reach is that deathbed visions do happen and are relevant to the death transition experience; they are not "hallucinations," not caused by drugs, and not the result of senility; transition is usually pleasant and there usually is a "greeter" to help one across. Appropriately, Elisabeth Kübler-Ross provides the introduction for this volume.

Kenneth Ring, *Heading toward Omega.* Morrow, New York, 1984, 348 pages.

Ever since Raymond Moody and Elisabeth Kübler-Ross drew attention to the phenomena called the near-death experience (NDE), there has been enormous public fascination with the how and why of it. Religion, science and the public have asked: Is the phenomena of clinical death-and-revival real and, if so, what does it mean? Ring's first book, *Life At Death*, was the first truly scientific study of NDEs. With his current book he breaks new ground and builds upon the scientific foundation of *Life At Death* by considering the social and evolutionary dimensions of the NDE. *Heading toward Omega* has profound implications for every field of human endeavor and knowledge—for physical, psychological and social factors, and through intellectual history and politics to education, philosophy and religion.

Kenneth Ring, *Life at Death: A Scientific Investigation of the Near-Death Experience.* Coward, McCann & Geoghegan, New York, 1980, 310 pages.

Dr. Kenneth Ring is a professor of psychology at the University of Connecticut, one of the founders of the Association for the Scientific Study of Near-Death Phenomena, and a trustee of the Academy of Religion and Physical Research. Ring's work is the first to be published which systematizes and evaluates data on the Near-Death Experience (NDE), which was initially brought to the public's attention by the anecdotal reports of Dr. Raymond Moody in his book, *Life After Life* (Mockingbird, 1975). In an introduction to this volume Moody says: "The finding of a common pattern of experiences occurring at or near death is unusual enough in itself; we can only guess at its significance. . . . The facts about the near-death experiences are in themselves fantastic enough. Any exaggerations on our part could only succeed in making the case for their importance less plausible than it in fact is." But, cautiously and without exaggeration, Ring does indeed search for the *significance* of the commonality in the NDE. He says, "What to make of this common set of elements associated with the onset of death is the central challenge of this book." The bulk of this book is given over to the first-person reports of those who returned from a NDE, and to scientific evaluations of them. Ring concludes his book with this provocative thought: "There is indeed a higher spiritual dimension that pervades our lives and that we will discover for ourselves in the moment of our death. The question is, however—will we discover it in the moments of our lives?" The book is supplemented by five appendices, notes, bibliography, and an index.

Michael Sabom, *Recollections of Death: A Medical Investigation.* Harper & Row, New York, 1982, 224 pages.

This book on the "near-death experience" might well have been subtitled, "The Conversion of a Skeptic." When Dr. Sabom, cardiologist and professor of medicine, was told of Moody's book, *Life After Life*, his response was, "I don't believe it," which he considered to be the kindest thing he could say. Having participated in over a hundred resuscitation efforts with cardiac patients, he was satisfied that the Moody NDE was *not* happening. An associate inquired, "But, did you ask them?" When Sabom was finally challenged to make his own preliminary survey, he got a positive response from the third patient he questioned and the story told him fitted the Moody pattern perfectly. Ultimately, Sabom found that people who almost die, but don't, and then recover to describe the experience, never mention anguish or pain, or even despair; rather, they recall a strange, unfamiliar feeling of tranquillity and peace. Some considered this experience to be a privileged glimpse of another realm of existence. The formal study reported in this book was conducted with an entire population of patients who were medically judged to have been "near death." Of these, Sabom found that 43 percent had the classic "near-death experience" (NDE). His findings extend and are fully consistent with the findings of Raymond Moody, Kenneth Ring, and John Audette. Especially valuable were his efforts that tend to establish the true objective nature of the experience—that it was *real* and independent of the subject's mind and brain states. Many of the patients were able to describe accurately and in detail the cardiopulmonary resuscitation (CPR) procedures and related activity that they "saw and heard." This is by far the most scientifically useful report yet published in the NDE field.

W. H. Salter, *Zoar: The Evidence of Psychical Research Concerning Survival.* Sidgwick and Jackson, London, 1961, 238 pages, index.

The late W. H. Salter was for over thirty years Hon. Secretary of the SPR; he knew most of the early group of stalwarts; he had a highly developed critical faculty and a remarkable style of writing. Added to these qualities was a strict standard of evidentiality together with a sage grasp of the limitations of quantification attempts of qualitative materials such as mediumistic communications. Based upon almost half a century of research and constant discussions with the most acute leaders in psychical research, this work is one of the most important in the field. In order to follow its argument in its subtleties and to appreciate its impact, however, one really must have a firm understanding of the principal survival evidence and the alternative explanations evinced for that evidence. Like Ducasse's work, this is a book to study and ponder.

Ian Stevenson, *Twenty Cases Suggestive of Reincarnation.* Proceedings of the American Society for Psychical Research, Volume XXVI, New York, September, 1966, 362 pages. Foreword by C. J. Ducasse.

In this scholarly study, Dr. Stevenson has presented a representative sample of the many cases whose data incline towards a reincarnationist interpretation. They are principally Oriental in origin, and this raises a very important question as to the role which cultural tendency may play in paranormal phenomena, an issue which Dr. Stevenson discusses, and which other parapsychologists, especially Gardner Murphy, have also written about. Dr. Stevenson is one of America's most eminent parapsychologists, a trained psychiatrist, and a leader in what we might term the "revival" of interest in the question of survival among psychical researchers. This work is the most significant study of reincarnation, as opposed to "discarnate survival," produced in recent years. Dr. Stevenson carries his erudition lightly and the volume is highly readable.

Ian Stevenson, *Unlearned Language: New Studies in Xenoglossy.* University Press of Virginia, Charlottesville, 1984, 223 pages.

This is an update and expansion of Dr. Stevenson's xenoglossy philosophy as contained in his earlier volume, *Xenoglossy* (on the "Jensen" personality case), which was published in 1974 as Volume 31 of *A.S.P.R. Proceedings*, and by the University Press of Virginia. Involved here are two extensively developed additional cases of responsive xenoglossy. The earlier volume covered a case developed under hypnosis, as does the first case in this volume; the second case reported here occurred as spontaneous, involuntary alterations of personality, during which periods the "new" personality (Sharada) could open her eyes and move about as she conversed freely in the "foreign" language. The first case in this volume (the "Gretchen" personality) was the subject of a brief preliminary report by Stevenson in 1976 (Journal of the American Society for Psychical Research 70: 65-77). *Glossolalia* is, by definition, the speaking of a non-language which, by rhythm, tone, alliteration and other phonic characteristics, only mimics language, even though there may in some cases be religious or metaphysical claims of "interpretation." *Recitative xenoglossy* is the parroting or reciting of words, phrases, or brief passages of an identified (or identifiable) foreign language not known to the speaker, but which words were possibly "memorized" at a forgotten previous time; a person speaking recitative xenoglossy cannot understand or respond to speech in that foreign language. In *responsive xenoglossy* the subject engages in intelligible conversation in the foreign language which was never learned by the subject in this life-time. Needless to say, Stevenson has gone to great lengths in both of these cases, as he previously had done in the Jensen case, to establish with great certainty that the subjects have never had an opportunity to truly learn the foreign language in question.

ADDITIONAL READING

C. D. Broad, *Human Identity and Survival*. F. W. H. Myers Memorial Lecture, Society for Psychical Reseach, London, 1958.

Hereward Carrington, *The Case for Psychic Survival*. Citadel Press, New York, 1957.

Jacques Choron, *Modern Man and Mortality*. Macmillan, New York, 1964.

Geraldine Cummins, *Beyond Human Personality*. Psychic Press, London, 1952.

Geraldine Cummins, *The Road to Immortality*, L. S. A. Publications, London, 1947.

E. R. Dodds, "Why I do not believe in Survival," *Proceedings* of The Society for Psychical Research. Volume XLII: pp. 147-72, London, 1934.

C. J. Ducasse, *A Critical Examination of the Belief in a Life After Death*. C. C. Thomas, Springfield, IL, 1974.

C. J. Ducasse, *Nature, Mind, and Death*. Open Court Publishing Co., La Salle, IL, 1951.

Herman Feifel (Ed.), *The Meaning of Death*. McGraw–Hill, New York, 1959.

Camille Flammarion, *Death and Its Mystery*, London, 1922.

John Hick, *Death and Eternal Life*. Harper & Row, New York, 1980.

Sir Oliver Lodge, *The Survival of Man*, Methuen, London, 1927.

T. K. Oesterreich, *Obsession and Possession by Spirits Both Good and Evil*. University Books, Secaucus, NJ, 1985.

Karlis Osis, *Deathbed Observations by Physicians and Nurses, Parapsychological Monographs No. 3*. Parapsychology Foundation, New York, 1961.

Kenneth Ring, *Life At Death: A Scientific Investigation of the Near-Death Experience*. Coward, McCann, Geoghegan, New York, 1982.

Ian Stevenson, *Cases of the Reincarnation Type: Volume I, Ten Cases in India*. University Press of Virginia, Charlottesville, 1975.

Ian Stevenson, *Cases of the Reincarnation Type: Volume II, Ten Cases in Sri Lanka.* University Press of Virginia, 1977.

Ian Stevenson, *Cases of the Reincarnation Type: Volume III, Twelve Cases in Lebanon and Turkey,* University Press of Virginia, 1980.

Ian Stevenson, *Cases of the Reincarnation Type: Volume IV, Twelve Cases in Thailand and Burma.* University Press of Virginia, 1983.

C. Drayton Thomas, *In the Dawn Beyond Death.* Lectures Universal, Ltd., London, 1959.

John F. Thomas, *Beyond Normal Cognition: An Evaluative and Methodological Study of the Mental Content of Certain Trance Phenomena.* Ayer Company, Salem, NH, 1975.

Arnold Toynbee *et al., Man's Concern with Death.* Hodder & Stoughton, London, 1968.

Una, Lady Troubridge, *The Life and Death of Radclyffe-Hall.* Hammond, London, 1961.

Nea Walker, *The Bridge.* Cassell, London, 1927.

Nea Walker, *Through a Stranger's Hands.* Hutchinson, London, 1935.

Leslie D. Weatherhead, *The Manner of the Resurrection in the Light of Modern Science and Psychical Research.* Abingdon Press, New York, 1959.

Stewart Edward White and Harwood White, *Across the Unknown.* E. P. Dutton, New York, 1939.

Stewart Edward White, *The Betty Book.* E. P. Dutton, New York, 1937.

Stewart Edward White, *The Unobstructed Universe.* E. P. Dutton, New York, 1940.

Carl Wickland, *Thirty Years among the Dead.* Spiritualist Press, London, 1949.

SELF-HELP AND DEVELOPMENT

Anonymous, *A Course in Miracles.* Three volumes. Foundation for Inner Peace (P.O. Box 635-HS), Tiburon, CA, 94920; 1975; 1,232 pages; $40. postpaid.

This material was received clairaudiently by one person, now identified to be the late (Dr.) Helen Schucman, a research psychologist in the Department of Psychiatry, Presbyterian Hospital, New York. She had been raised completely without religious orientation, though her father was of Jewish heritage and she professed to be an atheist; yet, soon after "the Voice" began speaking in her head, dictating the *Course*, he identified himself as Jesus the Christ. Schucman took this spirit-dictation in shorthand and read it to an associate for typing, *only* for the purpose of completing the manuscript and thus to stop the Voice and be finished with the experience; to the day of her death she did not accept her mediumship. Nevertheless, the Text, Workbook for Students, and Manual for Teachers, that make up the set, have been praised by hundreds of religious leaders as of importance only second to the Bible. It could have been titled, "How to Explicitly Orient Your Life to God."

ADDITIONAL READING

Hans J. Eysenck and Carl Sargent, *Know Your Own Psi-Q: Probe Your ESP Powers*. Ballantine, New York, 1984.

Jeffery Mishlove, *Psi Development Systems*. McFarland, Jefferson, NC, 1983.

Harold Sherman, *Know Your Own Mind*. Fawcett, New York, 1982.

Robert Skutch, *Journey Without Distance: The Story Behind A Course in Miracles*. Celestial Arts, Berkeley, 1984.

Shirl Solomon, *How to Really Know Yourself through Your Handwriting*. Taplinger, New York, 1973.

Charles T. Tart, *Learning to Use Extrasensory Perception*. University of Chicago Press, Chicago, 1976.

TEXTBOOKS

Stanley Krippner (Ed.), *Advances in Parapsychological Research*, Vols. 1 to 4 (continuing). Plenum Press, New York, 1977-1984.

These biennial reviews identify, explicate, and evaluate the findings in the field of parapsychology that are likely to endure and to be in turn a foundation for future work and study. And it would be hard to find a better researcher-editor to do this job than Stanley Krippner, whose work as an investigator, experimenter and educator has spanned the broadest reaches of the psychic world. Though not topically confined, the volumes of the series have, so far, tended to focus on one broad category: Volume 1—psychokinesis; Volume 2—ESP; Volume 3—survival of consciousness beyond bodily death; and Volume 4—healing, imaging and gansfeld sensing. The forewords and introductions also provide real substance; for example, in Volume 3, Sally Ann Drucker's foreword is a life history of Eileen Garrett. Robert L. Van de Castle's introduction pays homage to the "big three"— Murphy, Pratt and Rhine. Highly recommended.

ADDITIONAL READING

Stephen E. Braude, *ESP and Psychokinesis: A Philosophical Examination*. Temple University Press, Philadelphia, 1975.
Carroll B. Nash, *Science of Psi: ESP and PK*. C. C. Thomas, Springfield, IL, 1978.
James M. O. Wheatley and Hoyt L. Edge (Eds.), *Philosophical Dimensions of Parapsychology*. C. C. Thomas, Springfield, IL, 1976.
B. B. Wolman (Ed.), *Handbook of Parapsychology*. Van Nostrand, Reinhold, New York, 1977.

CHAPTER FIVE

RESOURCES AVAILABLE TO THE STUDENT

IN THIS CHAPTER STUDENTS will find information about research societies and foundations, other organizations related to psychical research, libraries with strong holdings in the discipline's literature, publications of importance, and a note about bookshops. All of the information was determined to be as accurate as possible at the time of the compilation. Subscription rates and membership dues have not been included because they constantly change. You should direct your inquiries to the appropriate organization at the address given for full details. All of the organizations listed welcome those who are seriously interested in psychical research and students should not hesitate to investigate membership possibilities; indeed, they should support the research and information activities by membership in the societies and any related groups in which they are interested.

RESEARCH ORGANIZATIONS IN THE UNITED STATES

The American Society for Psychical Research, 5 West 73rd St., New York, NY 10023

First formed in 1885, the ASPR is one of the major research bodies in the world dealing with paranormal phenomena. It collects and investigates reports of spontaneous phenomena, supports research into experimentation and quantitative analysis, has studied the claims of numerous mediums, and is concerned with any and all aspects of psychical research. The Society's standards in research are most rigorous and scientific, as befits a group of scholars devoted to critical investigation and analysis. It maintains one of the finest libraries in the field, the use of which is open to Members, Fellows, and bonafide scholars. It presents lectures and cooperates with similar bodies in other countries. The annual membership fee entitles a member to a free copy of the *Journal* and *Proceedings*.

The *Journal* is published in January, April, July, and October. *Proceedings* are published irregularly and contain reports of greater length and of special interest. The *Newsletter* is published four times a year and deals with brief news items of general information about research, lectures, and other activities of the ASPR and its members.

For any information about membership, publications, and activities of the ASPR, direct inquiries to the ASPR at the above address. Since the ASPR is the leading research society in the United States, serious students of psychical research should find it very advantageous to join and will, furthermore, by their membership, help increase the much needed support for the continuation and expansion of psychical research.

Foundation for Research on the Nature of Man, Box 6846, College Station, Durham, NC 27708

The FRNM was established by Dr. J. B. Rhine when he retired from Duke University. There are two aspects to the Foundation so far: The Institute for Parapsychology which continues the research of the Parapsychology Laboratory at Duke University which Dr. Rhine directed for so many years; and the Parapsychology Press which publishes *The Journal of Parapsychology* as well as monographs from time to time.

The Journal of Parapsychology is published in March, June, September, and December. One of the principal scholarly journals in the field, especially in terms of quantitative work, the advanced student in particular should be familiar with it.

The Parapsychological Association

This is an international society of professional parapsychologists founded in 1957 to enable them to hold annual meetings and exchange views. Its membership is not open to the general public. The Parapsychological Association was accepted as an Affiliate of The American Association for the Advancement of Science in 1969 which indicated that its standards of scholarship met the highest criteria. This step has greatly enhanced not only this particular Association's prestige, but that of the discipline which it presents, and is one of the most encouraging signs of changing public and scientific attitudes towards psychical research.

The annual Proceedings of the Parapsychological Association are titled *Research In Parapsychology-(year)* and are abbreviated as RIP-(year). Publication is approximately one year after the annual August convention, and volumes are available from Scarecrow Press, 52 Liberty Street, Metuchen, NJ 08840, and London. These volumes are well worth purchasing for the advanced student and are essential for anyone who wishes to build a sound personal library in psychical research.

The Parapsychological Foundation, Inc., 228 E. 71st St., New York, NY 10021

Established in 1951 by the late Mrs. Eileen Garrett, the Foundation has aimed to support research into all facets of ESP and paranormal phenomena. It has held international conferences of scholars from many different disciplines such as psychology, psychiatry, physics, pharmacology, medicine, religion, and physiology, as well as parapsychology. It has published important monographs covering research it has supported—the series of *Parapsychological Monographs*; for ten years it published the *International Journal of Parapsychology:* its *Proceedings* cover material presented at its international conferences; its bimonthly *Parapsychology Review* (which replaced the *Newsletter* in 1970) keeps researchers and interested laymen abreast of work and activities around the world; it has published books, and for several years, the Foundation published a popular magazine, *Tomorrow*, dealing with matters of psychical research. It has maintained one of the leading libraries in parapsychological materials open to bona fide students; and it has periodically supported publications of very different types in Great Britain, France, Switzerland, and Italy. Its own Division of Research also undertook important work upon the survival issue, mediumistic phenomena, the use of certain drugs to stimulate ESP, etc. If students are interested further, they should write the Foundation for information about its current activities and subscription to the *Parapsychology Review*.

Psychical Research Foundation, Inc., Psychology Dept., West Georgia College, Carrollton, GA 30118

The Foundation was established for the purpose of investigating evidence for survival, and Mr. W. G. Roll is Project Director. The personnel and facilities of the Foundation have recently been expanded, and it is anticipated that it will be feasible to investigate more cases and launch more experimentation bearing upon its prime purpose. The Foundation publishes a quarterly bulletin, *Theta*, dealing with current research on the survival problem and book reviews of pertinent works. This is an excellent and inexpensive manner in which to keep abreast of survival research, which is rapidly expanding.

Academy of Religion and Psychical Research, P.O. Box 614, Bloomfield, CT 06002.

The Academy was created in 1972 to serve as academic affiliate of Spiritual Frontiers Fellowship and to focus its interests upon the interface between science (including parapsychology) and religion. Its purpose is to provide a forum to encourage dialogue and educational exchanges between academics of religion, philosophy, the historic sciences and disciplines, and the clergy, parapsychologists, psychical researchers, new disciplines, and laity (and the general public). Annual conferences are held conjunctively with SFF each year, while academically sponsored special conferences are held at irregular intervals. A quarterly journal and annual Proceedings are published. A Research Division sponsors and funds appropriate projects. Both academic and supporting memberships are available.

Central Premonitions Registry, Box 482, Times Square Station, New York, NY 10036

Accepts and records precognitive impressions and experiences.

Institute of Noetic Sciences, 475 Gate Five Rd., Suite 300, Sausalito, CA 94965.

Founded in 1973 by Apollo-14 astronaut Edgar D. Mitchell, IONS is a foundation dedicated to research and education on the subject of human consciousness. It publishes a Newsletter and occasional books; it funds research, holds special research conferences, and conducts a travel program. The organization is headed by president Willis Harman and executive secretary Brendan O'Regan; three membership categories are available.

International Association for Near-Death Studies. Box U-20, University of Connecticut, Storrs, CT 06268

Developed by the personal research and books of Elisabeth Kübler-Ross, Raymond A. Moody, Jr., Kenneth Ring, and Michael Sabom, this discipline has now solidly established the Near-Death Experience (NDE) as a discrete phenomenological experience that occurs in some cases of clinical death and other near-death cases, followed by artificial or natural resuscitation. IANDS sponsors conferences, encourages research, publishes a newsletter (*Vital Signs*) and a journal (*Anabiosis*). Membership categories are available.

Mind-Science Foundation, 8301 Broadway, Suite 100, San Antonio, TX 78206

With a small professional staff, this group conducts a program of experimental parapsychological research.

Parapsychological Sources of Information (P.S.I.) Center, 2 Plane Tree Lane, Dix Hills, NY 11746

The Center is a unique and unparalleled research resource, since its shelves, files and computer storage are fully comprehensive and almost totally exhaustive as to parapsychological data in periodical literature and published papers. The Center accepts contract research assignments and provides live-in facilities for researchers. The Center publishes *Parapsychology Abstracts International*.

Psychophysical Research Laboratory, 301 College Rd. East, Princeton, NJ 08540

With a small professional staff under the direction of Charles Honorton, this group conducts a program of experimental parapsychological research.

Survival Research Foundation, P.O. Box 8565, Pembroke Pines, FL 33084

This organization conducts special research which attempts to record incontrovertible scientific proof of spirit survival of bodily death by using ciphers and other technical tests for spirit communication.

LIBRARIES IN THE UNITED STATES

Students interested in using any of the libraries listed should inquire at the library regarding permission and the regulations covering such use. They will find the personnel connected with these libraries most cooperative and helpful. This listing is not necessarily exhaustive of significant collections.

The American Society for Psychical Research, 5 W. 73rd St., New York, NY 10023

Approximately 6,000 volumes. This is one of the best collections of materials on psychical research in the world. It is open to members and to bona fide researchers.

Parapsychology Foundation, 228 E. 71st St., New York, NY 10021

Approximately 7,500 volumes. The Eileen J. Garrett Library is especially strong in post-1930 literature. A periodical index covering articles since 1966 is in progress of being compiled. There is a very full collection of learned periodicals from many countries. The Library is for reference only and no volumes may be removed from the premises. It is open to the public from 9 A.M. to 5 P.M. Monday through Friday.

Spiritual Frontiers Fellowship, Inc., 10819 Winner Rd., Independence, MO 64052

Approximately 5,000 volumes. This library's holdings include many works on psychical research, but it is especially strong upon the religious and philosophical aspects, healing, prayer, and mysticism. Most of its books are available through mail to members of SFF.

P.S.I. Center Research Library, 2 Plane Tree Lane, Dix Hills, NY 11746

This library is unique in its exhaustive periodical holdings in the PSI field, inlcuding copies of articles on this subject in all periodicals. Its book holdings are less than 2,000.

PUBLICATIONS IN THE UNITED STATES

Details about subscription rates may be obtained from the offices of the publication or of the organization which produces the publication. These organizations also occasionally publish pamphlets, lectures, and monographs which may be of interest to the student.

Journal of the American Society for Psychical Research. Published in January, April, July and October. A larger publication than the SPR's *Journal*, this is equally erudite and a principal source of information about current research, theories, and controversies in parapsychology, as well as containing excellent book reviews.

Journal of Religion and Psychical Research (issued quarterly) and *Proceedings of the Academy of Religion and Psychical Research* (issued annually). See Academy, in Section 2, above. Address inquiries to The Academy of Religion and Psychical Research, P.O. Box 614, Bloomfield, CT 06002.

Journal of Parapsychology. Published in March, June, September, and December. This journal specializes in quantitative experimental articles, although many others are also printed, together with fine book reviews. This is a vital source of data about research in the laboratory. Address inquiries to The Editor, *Journal of Parapsychology*, Foundation for Research on the Nature of Man, Box 6846, College Station, Durham, NC 27708.

New Realities. (Previously titled *Psychic.*) Published bimonthly. A popular magazine designed to present sound information about psychical research, its ancillary fields and its ramifications in a manner easily read and grasped by the man in the street. During the three years it has been published, it has maintained a high level of material and of production. Its aim seems similar to that of Mrs. Eileen Garrett's now defunct *Tomorrow*. Address inquiries to *New Realities*, The Bolen Company, 680 Beach St., San Francisco, CA 94109.

Parapsychology Abstracts International. Issued semi-annually by the Parapsychology Sources of Information Center, beginning in 1983. Over one hundred journals of parapsychology and related areas will be the sources drawn upon, and each issue, ranging from 50 to 150 pages, will provide approximately 250 abstracts per issue. This series will summarize the literature of parapsychology from earliest times to date; each issue will balance the presentation of new material with data from earlier periods. P.A.I. is truly international and presently includes English abstracts translated from Spanish, Portuguese, German, Japanese and French. Each abstract carries full citation, permitting one's local library to obtain referenced publications for the reader. Inquire from P.S.I. Center, 2 Plane Tree Lane, Dix Hills, NY 11746.

Parapsychology Review. Published bimonthly. This contains some larger articles, but much of its material is in the form of news items about a wide variety of activities in psychical research around the world, recent library acquisitions at the Eileen J. Garrett Library, and book reviews. Probably the best manner of keeping abreast of the manifold facets of the growing discipline internationally is through this publication. Address inquiries to The Parapsychology Foundation, Inc., 228 E. 71st St., New York, NY 10021.

Proceedings of the American Society for Psychical Research. Published irregularly, these volumes contain more lengthy artricles and studies than the *Journal* could accommodate, but with as high a standard. Address inquiries about these publications, as well as the pamphlets the ASPR has available, to The American Society for Psychical Research, 5 West 73rd St., New York, NY 10023.

Psi Research is published by Washington Research Center, 3101 Washington St., San Francisco, CA 94115. It includes articles, reviews and notes by both Eastern and Western researchers, with emphasis on studies in the USSR, Eastern Europe and China.

Research In Parapsychology (R.I.P.) consists of papers, abridgments and abstracts from the annual conventions of the Parapsychological Association, and serves in lieu of a proceedings. R.I.P. is issued about one year after each convention. It is published by and may be purchased from Scarecrow Press, 52 Liberty Street, Metuchen, NJ 08840.

Spiritual Frontiers. Journal of Spiritual Frontiers Fellowship, published quarterly, and now thirty years old (in three successive editions). The journal encompasses a wide range of topics and includes articles by and about parapsychologists, among others, and about parapsychological experiments, but is written expressly for the general reader. Its primary emphasis is upon the religious and philosophical significance of psychical research within the Christian context. Space is especially provided for first-person accounts of psychic and mystical experience, and regular columns are devoted to new age interests such as dream evaluation, mediumship, astrology, Shroud of Turin data, archaeological impact on theology, and the like; book reviews and letters are regular features. Address inquiries to SFF, 10819 Winner Rd., Independence, MO 64052.

Theta. Published quarterly. Deals with recent research, evaluation, scholarly papers and books bearing upon the issues of consciousness survival of bodily death. It is an excellent way to keep up with survival research. Address inquiries to Psychical Research Foundation, Psychology Dept., West Georgia College, Carrollton, GA 30118.

Vital Signs is a quarterly news digest and *Anabiosis* is the semi-annual journal of the International Association for Near-Death Studies, U-20, University of Connecticut, Storrs, CT 06268. Both are concerned with reports and evaluation of the near-death experience (NDE).

ORGANIZATIONS RELATED TO PSYCHICAL RESEARCH IN THE UNITED STATES

There are dozens of occult and esoteric groups which have interest in psi phenomena in one fashion or another, but as indicated earlier, this work does not deal with the occult traditions. The spiritualist movement does not have the strong centralization in the United

States as it does with the SAGB in London. Consequently, the student does not have the same opportunity for observation of many mediums in one location unless he attends one of the spiritualist camps held mostly during the summer in various parts of the country; but some of these camps have, on occasion, been plagued with exposures of fraudulent mediums so that great care must be exercised.

Spiritual Frontiers Fellowship, 10819 Winner Rd., Independence, MO 64052. Established in 1956 by a group of clergymen and laymen encouraged by the formation of the Churches' Fellowship for Psychical and Spiritual Studies in Great Britain, the aims of SFF include investigation of the relationship between the paranormal and Christianity, the religious significance of the findings of psychical research, the mystical tradition, prayer, spiritual healing, and the issue of survival. There are a large number of groups for study throughout the country, an annual meeting, library and book services, and a periodic newsletter. Membership is open to anyone concerned with these aims, and details may be obtained by writing the Executive Secretary at the address above.

RESEARCH ORGANIZATIONS IN THE UNITED KINGDOM

The Society for Psychical Research, 1 Adam & Eve Mews, London, W8 6UG

Formed in 1882 under the leadership of Sir William Barrett, F. W. H. Myers, Henry Sidgwick, and other leading scholars, the SPR has as its purposes: "to examine without prejudice or prepossession and in a scientific spirit those faculties of man, real or supposed, which appear to be inexplicable on any generally recognized hypothesis." During ninety years, the Society has done precisely that with a level of scholarship, critical standards of evidence, and integrity which will stand comparison with any research organization of whatever discipline. Its *Journal* and *Proceedings*, together with monographs and significant lectures which it reproduces, are possibly the most important sources in English of raw material for the student of psychical research. The Society, in order to maintain its utter impartiality, does not hold any "corporate views," but publishes material of contradictory opinions, so long as they are scholarly.

An annual membership subscription entitles the member to the use of the excellent library, admission to the monthly lectures, and copies of the *Journal* and *Proceedings*. The SPR welcomes members from any country, and since its publications are essential reading for the serious student, one will find it well worthwhile to join, thereby obtaining them and further strengthening the support for psychical research. All inquiries regarding membership or publications should be directed to the Secretary at the above address.

LIBRARIES IN THE UNITED KINGDOM

Students interested in using any of the libraries listed should enquire at the library regarding permission and the regulations covering such use. They will find the personnel connected with these libraries most cooperative and helpful. This listing is not necessarily exhaustive of significant collections.

The Churches' Fellowship for Psychical and Spiritual Studies, St. Mary Abchurch, Abchurch Lane, London EC4N 7BA

Approximately 2,000 volumes. Strongest in the Christian approach to psychical research, healing, prayer, and mysticism. Phone 01-636 3469 for information about the use of the library.

The College of Psychic Studies, 16 Queensberry Place, London, SW7 2EB

Approximately 11,000 volumes. Especially strong on all phases of spiritualism, the religious aspects of psi, healing, meditation, etc., as well as in esoteric traditions. A fairly good section on psychical research is being steadily built up. The principal research publications are subscribed to, although not all back issues are available.

The Greater World Christian Spiritualist League, 5 Lansdowne Rd., London, W11 3AL

Approximately 2,000 volumes, mostly upon spiritualist topics.

The Harry Price Collection, London University, Senate House Library, London, WC1

15,000 volumes left to the University by the late researcher and writer. Access is by permission of the librarian in charge of the collection. Very strong in legerdemain, witchcraft, and physical phenomena studies. Few additions since the later 1930's.

The Society for Psychical Research, 1 Adam & Eve Mews, London, W8 6UG

Approximately 10,000 volumes. One of the principal libraries of the world on psychical research as a discipline, mediumistic studies and files of primary materials, plus coverage of European research and publications. Open to members and to bona fide researchers.

The Spiritualist Association of Great Britain, 33 Belgrave Square, London, SW1 8QB

Approximately 4,000 volumes, mostly on spiritualist matters.

The Theosophical Society, 50 Gloucester Place, London, W1

About 13,000 volumes. Excellent coverage of the general field, with special strengths in theosophy, occultism, and eastern philosophy.

PUBLICATIONS IN THE UNITED KINGDOM

Details about subscription rates may be obtained from the offices of the organization producing the publication. These organizations also occasionally publish pamphlets, lectures, and monographs which may be of interest to the student.

The Churches' Fellowship for Psychical and Spiritual Studies publications. The long-time *Quarterly Review* was discontinued and in its place is issued the excellent journal, *The Christian Parapsychologist*; the founding editor was Leslie Price and the current editor is the Venerable Michael Perry. This journal is issued six times a year, and includes timely and substantive articles, book reviews, letters, and news notes. Highly recommended. Subscription information available from the CFPSS, St. Mary Abchurch, Abchurch Lane, London, EC4N 2EB, England.

Light, A Journal of Psychic Studies. Published in March, June, September, and December. *Light* is concerned with any and all aspects of psychical studies, from the experimental to the religious significance of psi, but its emphasis is upon the latter. Founded in 1881, *Light* was for many years a spiritualist journal, but its viewpoints are much wider now, although by no means of the scientific nature to be found in the *SPR Journal*. Address enquiries to The College of Psychic Studies, 16 Queensberry Place, London, SW7 2EB, England.

Journal of the Society for Psychical Research. Published in March, June, September, and December. Probably the most prestigious of all journals in the field, its approach is highly critical, scholarly, and erudite. Articles concern experimentation, reports of spontaneous phenomena, theoretical discussions, and re-assessments of earlier works. The book reviews are of a very high quality.

Proceedings of the Society for Psychical Research. Published irregularly, these volumes contain more lengthy articles and studies than the *Journal* could accommodate, but with as high a standard. Address enquiries about these publications, as well as the numerous pamphlets the SPR has available to The Secretary, The Society for Psychical Research, 1 Adam & Eve Mews, London, W8 6UG, England.

ORGANIZATIONS RELATED TO PSYCHICAL RESEARCH IN THE UNITED KINGDOM

There are a great many occult and esoteric groups interested in psi phenomena in connection with certain traditions or approaches; but this volume does not deal with the occult and they are not, therefore, listed.

The Churches' Fellowship for Psychical and Spiritual Studies, St. Mary Abchurch, Abchurch Lane, London, EC4N 7BA. Founded in 1954 by clergy and laymen to study the paranormal and ESP in relation to church teaching, it numbers among its patrons twenty-one Anglican Bishops and many leading members of the Free Churches. While full membership is restricted to those who belong to a church affiliated with the World Council of Churches, associate membership is open to all those genuinely seeking a deeper knowledge of paranormal phenomena. The Fellowship has specialist research groups in psychical phenomena, healing, mysticism, meditation, and mental health, approximately one hundred study groups throughout the country, yearly conferences, a library with postal service, and a journal. For further information, write the General Secretary at the above address.

The College of Psychic Studies, 16 Queensberry Place, London, SW7 2EB. Established in 1884 as the London Spiritualist Alliance, the College is now a body without any corporate viewpoint, welcoming to membership anyone interested in psychical research or related fields. It has a large library, holds weekly lectures upon a wide variety of subjects, arranges sittings with approved mediums, holds courses dealing with many topics, is concerned with healing, meditation, etc. Recently, it has become involved in some research projects as well. While it is not a research–oriented organization like the SPR, the College is interested in all activities which shed light upon psychical matters. It welcomes members from overseas. Advantages of membership include the use of all College facilities, a free subscription to *Light*, and reduced fees for sittings with mediums, lectures, and courses. Full information may be obtained from the General Secretary of the College at the above address.

Spiritualist Association of Great Britain, 33 Belgrave Square, London, SW1 8QB. The SAGB holds daily sittings of mediums, both individually and in groups, demonstrations of clairvoyance, healing sessions, circles for development of mediumship, etc. There are various kinds of membership available, including daily membership for visitors—one must be a member of SAGB in order to use the facilities or attend sittings with mediums. There is a library and a bookshop. Information may be obtained from the SAGB at the address given above.

BOOKSHOPS FOR WORKS IN PSYCHICAL RESEARCH

While many bookshops have some works dealing with psychical research, most are either general bookshops or tend to specialize in occult and esoteric books rather than in psychical research literature. Consequently, the personnel may not be fully conversant with the field. As noted earlier, some of the organizations offer book purchasing services for their members. Probably the best source for books dealing with psychical research in the United Kingdom is Watkins Bookshop, 19–21 Cecil Court, Charing Cross Road, London, WC2N 4EZ. Watkins has been a specialist shop in books of this kind, as well as in occult and mystical works, for many years, and there is a mail order service not only within the United Kingdom but overseas as well.

In the United States, the leading bookshop in this field is Weiser's Bookstore, 132 E. 24th St., New York, NY 10010. Weiser has a very large stock of works in psychical research, a knowledgeable staff to assist students with their needs, and a mail service for books both for the United States and abroad. Yes! Bookshop, 1035 31st St. NW, Washington, DC 20007, has an extensive collection of psychical research and general psychic books, as well as those dealing with religion, new age, occult and esoteric subjects. Catalogs are issued from time to time (available for a nominal charge) to facilitate sales by mail.

On the west coast there is the Bodhi Tree Bookstore, located at 8585 Melrose Avenue, Los Angeles, CA 90069. They have one of the largest selections in southern California on subjects of astrology, occult, psychology and religions of the world. In northern California there is Fields Book Store, located at 1419 Polk Street, San Francisco, CA 94109. This is the place to shop for psychical research and parapsychology books and the whole range of writings on the paranormal. Also in the area is Shambhala Bookstore, at 2482 Telegraph Avenue, Berkeley, CA 94704. Here you'll find over ten thousand titles, ranging from Christian mysticism and yoga to nutrition and music.

Films and Videotapes

Films for a New Age, from Hartley Film Foundation, Cat Rock Rd., Cos Cob, CT 06807. No finer films and videotapes are to be found than those produced, sold, and rented by the Hartley Foundation on subjects of parapsychology, psychical research, the historical and experimental dimensions of spiritual and mystical experience, and holistic health. Films have been narrated by Edgar Mitchell and other prominent scientists. Catalog available upon request.

CHAPTER SIX

IMPORTANT FIGURES IN PSYCHICAL RESEARCH

THIS CHAPTER IS DEVOTED to brief biographical sketches of some of the major figures in the development and continuation of psychical research in various countries. It is by no means exhaustive, and only a few of the most significant facts about each person have been given. The aim is to enable students to place the figure within the chronology of developments in the discipline and to have a ready reference for names they may encounter in their studies. For fuller treatment of these and other key people, students should consult, for earlier ones only, Nandor Fodor's *Encyclopedia of Psychic Science* (University Books, New Hyde Park, NY, 1966), which is a reprint of the original 1933 edition, with some additions and corrections, and Helene Pleasants, editor, *Biographical Dictionary of Parapsychology,* (Helix Press, New York, 1964).

Arthur James Balfour, first Earl of Balfour, 1848-1930. Brother of Mrs. Eleanor Sidgwick and Gerald William Balfour, President of SPR, 1893. Prime Minister of Great Britain, 1902-05, and member of various governments in other capacities. While he took great interest in psychical research, outside of his Presidential Address in the SPR (*Proceedings*, Volume 10, Part 26, 1894), he did not contribute to the literature. The important "Palm Sunday Case" dealing with his belief that his sweetheart, Mary Lyttleton (who died in 1875) had communicated, especially through "Mrs. Willett," was not published until 1960 (SPR *Proceedings*, Volume 52, Part 189). This is the most significant cross-correspondence of recent years.

Gerald William Balfour, second Earl of Balfour, 1853-1945. Brother of Mrs. Eleanor Sidgwick and Arthur James Balfour, President of

SPR, 1906, 1907. Best known as a leading expert upon the cross-correspondences, in the investigation of which his deep classical erudition stood him in good stead, he came to accept survival and communication between discarnates and the living. His papers on the "Ear of Dionysius" case are major contributions to survival literature and one of the most exhaustive studies of cross-correspondence scripts. He was also much interested in the mechanics of mediumship and of the techniques used by purported discarnates to communicate.

Sir William F. Barrett, 1844-1925. Leader in the foundation of the Society for Psychical Research in 1882, and of the American Society for Psychical Research in 1885. Professor of Physics at the Royal College of Science, Dublin, 1873-1910. A leading physicist of his time, he was instrumental in establishing the high standards of evidence which have characterized the work of the SPR ever since. He wrote several books, including a large work on dowsing, which were widely read. He became convinced of survival.

John Beloff, Lecturer in Psychology, University of Edinburgh. A leader in experimental work in Great Britain, especially in attempts to learn whether subjects can be taught to improve their psi abilities. He has published numerous articles and book reviews in the *Journals* of both the British and the American SPR and in the *Journal of Parapsychology*. Author of *The Existence of Mind*, 1962.

Hans Bender, born 1907. Professor of Psychology. University of Freiburg, West Germany; Director of the Institute for the Study of Borderland Areas of Psychology and Mental Health, University of Freiburg since 1950. He has studied and written upon a wide variety of parapsychological topics and has translated some English works into German, but has been especially interested in poltergeist phenomena.

Lawrence J. Bendit, born 1898. A psychiatrist, Dr. Bendit received his M.D. Degree from Cambridge University with a thesis upon "Paranormal Cognition," the first such degree to be awarded. His special interests are the relationships of paranormal occurrences with psychiatric conditions and the development of psychic faculties. His wife, Phoebe Payne Bendit, was a gifted clairvoyant, and together they have written several books, most widely read of which are *The Psychic Sense* and *This World and That*.

Henri Bergson, 1859-1951. One of the major French philosophers of the twentieth century; Nobel Prize winner; President of the SPR, 1913. A leading dualist, Bergson saw a clear dichotomy between the *élan vital*, the creative life force as expressed in thought, and matter. Consequently, the paranormal phenomena which suggested strongly this dualistic nature of existence fit into his scheme well. He was convinced of survival, since thought is in no way dependent upon the material brain, but utilizes the brain. His presidential address to the SPR (SPR *Proceedings*, Volume 27, 1914) delineates most clearly his views on psychical research.

Theodore Besterman, born 1904. Former research officer and librarian of the SPR, distinguished librarian and bibliographer. Although he has not been active in psychical research since the late 1930's, his contributions in the 1920's and early 1930's are important. He assisted Sir William Barrett in his work on the divining rod, and later wrote his own book on the same topic, investigated several leading European mediums and reported his findings in *Some Modern Mediums*, participated in the impressive tests with the Polish medium Ossowiecki, and in those of the physical medium, Rudi Schneider.

C. D. Broad, 1887-1971. Professor of Philosophy and Fellow of Trinity Church, Cambridge University; President of the Society for Psychical Research, 1935, 1958-60. Professor Broad, one of the most distinguished academic figures of his time, published numerous studies of the philosophical and evidential problems connected with psi phenomena, especially mediumistic data, precognition, and the survival hypothesis. Especially important are his *Religion, Philosophy, and Psychical Research,* and *Lectures on Psychical Research.*

Sir Cyril Burt, 1883-1971. Professor of psychology, emeritus, London University. Sir Cyril, regarded as the dean of British psychologists, specializing in the psychology of education and problem children's learning processes, pursued research into mediumship, telepathy among children, and co-operated in some of Dr. Soal's telepathic experiments. He has written about the relationship between psychical phenomena and psychology. His Myers Memorial Lecture for

1968, "Psychology and Psychical Research," is one of the most important syntheses of the two disciplines in recent years.

W. Whately Carington, 1884-1947. British psychical researcher and writer; editor of *Psyche*, 1921-37; author of many articles and books upon various aspects of psychical research. Noted especially for the use of "free materials" in telepathy tests, Carington discovered the "displacement effect" in these experiments, and suggested to S. G. Soal that he re-examine Soal's disappointing attempts to replicate J. B. Rhine's early card-guessing successful results. This led to Soal's important work with Shackleton and Mrs. Stewart. Carington also introduced the word-association tests with mediums, experimented with PK, and postulated his telepathic theory of "psychons" associated in various patterns. His book *Telepathy: An Outline of Its Facts, Theory, and Implications* is a major contribution to the field.

Hereward Carrington, 1880-1958. Leading psychical researcher and author. A highly trained amateur magician and shrewd observer, Dr. Carrington specialized early in his career in exposing physical mediums, investigated Eusapia Palladino exhaustively, sat on the *Scientific American* committee which examined "Margery's" mediumship, and wrote dozens of books, the most important of which deal with physical mediumship and phenomena.

Edgar Cayce, 1877-1945. American sensitive. Over a long period, while "asleep" in a dissociated state, he apparently could diagnose the illnesses of people not present and clairvoyantly prescribe treatment which the patients often claimed proved efficacious. The Association for Research and Enlightenment at Virginia Beach, Virginia is devoted to the study of Edgar Cayce's work and teachings regarding health, reincarnation, the significance of dreams, and the geological changes he forecast during the last four decades of the twentieth century.

C. T. K. Chari, born 1909. Professor and Chairman of the Department of Philosophy and Psychology, Madras Christian College, India. Professor Chari has written articles concerning the mathematical, scientific, psychological, and philosophical problems and issues connected with psychical research in American, British, and Indian publications.

Florence Cook, 1856-1904. Controversial medium whose ostensible materializations of a full figure claiming to be "Katie King" were observed and supported by Sir William Crookes. Trevor Hall has argued that Crookes lied to maintain the secrecy of his affair with Florence Cook, and this has thrown further doubt into the veracity of the phenomena reported.

Winifred Coombe-Tennant ("Mrs. Willett"), 1874-1956. One of the "SPR group" of mediums involved in the cross-correspondences, Mrs. Coombe-Tennant maintained her anonymity under the pseudonym of "Mrs. Willett." One of the most gifted automatists in the history of psychical research, she was a socially prominent woman of great intellectual gifts, and a delegate to the League of Nations. She co-operated with many investigators, especially Sir Oliver Lodge and Gerald Balfour, in the production of automatic writing as well as spoken material, referred to as "Daylight Impressions." The paranormal content of her material is considered impressive and is among the strongest evidentially for survival yet produced. Mrs. Coombe-Tennant became once again prominent in psychical research with the publication of *Swan on a Black Sea* by Geraldine Cummins (1965), which purports to be scripts dictated by the discarnate Mrs. Coombe-Tennant to the Irish automatist. Professor C. D. Broad considered this work the most important survival evidence produced for many years.

Mina Crandon, "Margery," died 1941. Physical and direct voice medium, wife of a member of the Harvard Medical School faculty, she claimed to be under the control of her deceased brother "Walter." The "Margery" case was probably the most controversial in the history of psychical research. Some investigators were convinced of the reality of paranormal phenomena, but a majority held that they were fraudulent. The latter view was greatly strengthened after the discovery of the striking similarity between a "materialized" thumbprint of "Walter" and that of Crandon's dentist. There is a great deal of literature, with photographs, about the case, which attracted the *Scientific American*'s attention as well as that of Harry Houdini, in both the British and the American societies' publications.

Sir William Crookes, 1832-1919. President of the SPR 1896-99; physicist and early pioneer in psychical research. One of the 19th century's greatest scientists, Crookes' investigations of D. D. Home's mediumship convinced him of the reality of his phenomena, and the publication of his findings led to strong attacks upon him in scientific circles. His lengthy experiments with Florence Cook and "Katie King," together with photographs taken by Crookes which purported to show the medium and the materialized "spirit" side by side, aroused a tremendous controversy still unresolved. While in his later life, he undertook little research, he continued his interest in mediumship, became convinced of survival through sittings which gave evidential material purporting to come from his deceased wife, and said shortly before his death that he remained utterly certain of the reality of psychic phenomena and materialization.

Geraldine Cummins, died 1970. Irish automatist, writer. One of the most important automatists of the century, she produced some remarkable scripts. Beginning in 1923 and continuing until her death, these scripts included some purporting to originate from Frederic Myers, brought together in *The Road to Immortality*, and a long series, *The Scripts of Cleophas*, which deal with Biblical times and which some distinguished Biblical scholars pronounced as accurate and shedding light upon puzzling aspects of the New Testament. Her final work of great moment was *Swan on a Black Sea* (1965, new edition 1970), consisting of scripts purportedly from "Mrs. Willett" or Mrs. Coombe-Tennant, the famous cross-correspondence automatist. This is the book that C. D. Broad considered the most important survival evidence produced for many years, but which was criticized in some quarters.

Mrs. John H. Curran, died 1936. The sensitive through whom the works of "Patience Worth" were produced. Beginning with the ouija board in 1913, for over twenty years Mrs. Curran wrote automatically and dictated poems, epigrams, and several novels pronounced remarkable literary works by experts. Her material indicated an uncanny knowledge about Biblical and medieval times. She also had a very unusual philological consistency in keeping with the insistence of "Patience Worth" that she was the spirit of a woman who had lived in the mid-seventeenth century. Walter Franklin Prince made an exhaustive ten month study of Mrs. Curran, and published his results in 1927, in one of the principal works of psychical research, *The Case of Patience Worth*.

Douglas Dean, born 1916. Chemist; parapsychologist. While he has conducted experiments dealing with PK, dowsing, homing pigeons, and other facets of psi, possibly his most significant work has been done with the plethysmograph. This instrument records changes in blood supply to part of the body, such as a finger or ear lobe, depending upon the emotional response to a mental stimulus. With this, Dean has experimented on volunteers to determine if telepathy or clairvoyance can be detected under laboratory conditions between agent and subject. His results have been encouraging, and have led to other attempts at instrumentalization of experiments in parapsychology. Dr. Dean was founder and first president of the Kirlian Research Association. He has done extensive research with spiritual healers to establish various physical effects which the healer can cause, and that can be scientifically recorded, which help to better understand the healing process. He is a past-president of the Parapsychological Association.

Eric J. Dingwall. Psychical researcher; anthropologist; author; librarian. Formerly research officer for the Society for Psychical Research, his knowledge of psychical research's development and the vast literature connected with its history is probably unrivalled. A highly critical and astute investigator, he has been involved in many of the most significant cases, such as that of Ossowiecki, "Eva C.," "Margery," Rudi and Willi Schneider, and the re-examination of the Borely Rectory haunting reported by Harry Price.

E. R. Dodds, born 1893, Professor of Greek, emeritus, Oxford University; President of the SPR 1961-1962. Professor Dodds has been especially interested in the paranormal among ancient peoples and has written several excellent treatises upon this topic. Doubtless his most significant contribution to psychical research, however, is his most perceptive and cogent article, "Why I Do Not Believe in Survival," *Proceedings*, Volume XLII: 147-72, 1934. This summarizes in a brilliant manner the objections to the spiritist hypothesis, while taking full notice of mediumistic evidence, by emphasizing the alternative explanations.

Hans Driesch, 1867-1941. Philosopher and embryologist; President of the SPR, 1926-1927. He espoused the philosophy of "vitalism" which held that cells have an innate characteristic of purposefully struggling for the development of the entire organism of which it is a part;

hence, he rejected the blind determinism of current materialism. He co-operated with researchers in Britain, America, and Europe and participated in investigations of some of the outstanding physical and mental mediums of the period, such as the Schneider brothers and Mrs. Leonard. He was doubtful about physical phenomena, but was more impressed with telepathy, precognition, and clairvoyance.

C. J. Ducasse, 1881-1969. Professor of Philosophy at Brown University. One of America's most esteemed philosophers, Dr. Ducasse was noted for the lucidity of his thought and writing. While he concerned himself with all aspects of psychical research, his greatest interests were in precognition, mediumship, survival, and the construction of an undergirding theoretical framework for psi. His articles on survival and his book, *A Critical Examination of the Belief in a Life After Death* are vital contributions to the study of the survival problem.

J. W. Dunne, 1875-1949. Aeronautical engineer; writer. Dunne is best known for his book, *An Experiment with Time*, in which he described his numerous precognitive dreams and postulated a concept of "serialism." This theory held that there is an infinite regression of "times," each observed by a different facet of the personality, so that "time" is a dimension with an infinite number of subdivisions within it. His views have not won acceptance and have been sharply criticized by many philosophers and scientists, but the precognitive aspects of his works remain most arresting.

Martin Ebon, born 1917. After wartime government service in foreign language work, Mr. Ebon became administrative secretary to Eileen Garrett's Parapsychology Foundation, and served as editor of her periodicals, *Tomorrow* and the *International Journal of Parapsychology*. For a short time he also edited the journal for Spiritual Frontiers Fellowship. From the middle 1960s onward, Ebon has devoted himself to writing and editing books on a wide variety of subjects, although his more than sixty titles have been predominantly on parapsychological subjects. Recent books have included the *Signet Handbook of Parapsychology* (1978), and *Psychic Warfare* (1983). Lectures and workshops on psychic subjects also account for a part of his present activity.

Simeon Edmunds, born 1917. Former research secretary of the College of Psychic Science (now Studies) in London; psychical researcher; writer; hypnotist. A highly critical student of paranormal phenomena, his study of "spirit photography" published by the Society for Psychical Research dismisses as fraudulent all such claims, while his study of spiritualism, *Spiritualism: A Critical Survey*, is a strong attack upon the movement's credulity, widespread fraud, and self-delusion.

Harry Edwards, 1893-1976. Spiritual healer. Probably the most famous of such healers, Edwards believed that the healing which took place, and to which letters from patients attested, was performed by discarnates working through him, rather than by means of any healing power he possessed himself. Medical authorities have remained highly dubious of Edwards' statistics and of the claims of patients, although some doctors have indicated interest in healing. In recent years, there has been considerable increase in medical attention to spiritual healing, although medical figures tend to attribute improvement to psychosomatic causes and not to discarnate or other paranormal sources.

F. H. Everard Feilding, 1867-1936. Barrister; psychical researcher; secretary of the SPR 1903-1920. An exceedingly acute investigator whose articles demonstrated his care of detail, control in experiments, and painstaking thoroughness. Feilding's most significant contribution is his study, with Hereward Carrington and William Baggally, of Eusapia Palladino in 1908, which remains a classic in psychical research, and which convinced him of the reality of physical phenomena.

Camille Flammarion, 1842-1925. Astronomer; President of the SPR 1923. A very distinguished astronomer, Flammarion early in his career became involved in paranormal investigations and spiritualism through reading Allan Kardec's works. He attended a great many seances of both mental and physical mediums, invited Eusapia Palladino to Paris for experiments, and after fifty years, became convinced of survival, the reality of hauntings, physical phenomena, and virtually the entire range of psychic occurrences. His most widely read work is his three volume treatise *Death and Its Mysteries*.

Alice Kipling Fleming, "Mrs. Holland," 1868-1948. Automatist; sister of Rudyard Kipling; longtime resident of India. While Mrs. Fleming had had some success with automatic writing for her own amusement, she became seriously interested following her reading of Myers: *Human Personality and Its Survival of Bodily Death*, and this led to her participation as a member of the "SPR group" in the cross-correspondences during the first decade of this century. Messages purportedly from Myers, Gurney, and Sidgwick were produced and some were found to correspond strikingly with other scripts ostensibly from the same sources obtained by other automatists in Britain and America with whom Mrs. Fleming had no contact.

Antony G. N. Flew, born 1923. Professor of Philosophy at Keele University. Professor Flew is concerned principally with the precise use of language, measurement, and concepts in psychical research. He has been highly critical of much of the work produced, both qualitative and quantitative, and of the philosophical deductions based upon that work. A humanist and atheist, he feels that only the statistical evidence of repeatable experiments can firmly establish psi phenomena, and that while sufficient evidence for psi has already been gathered to warrant utilizing its existence as a hypothesis, there is nothing in such phenomena to warrant religious, survivalistic, or dualistic constructions. His book, *A New Approach to Psychical Research*, discusses his views.

Theodore Flournoy, 1854-1920. Dr. Flournoy was an eminent Swiss psychologist, friend of William James, and best known for his important study of Hélène Smith in *From India to the Planet Mars*. From his lengthy and exhaustive research upon the ostensible discarnate control "Leopold" and the medium's two former "incarnations," Marie Antoinette and an Indian princess, Flournoy concluded that the language of "Mars" was an intricate subconscious construction upon French roots, that "Marie Antoinette" was a subconscious dramatization, but that the veridical information about the Hindu princess was truly paranormal, although not of a discarnate source. Having also investigated Eusapia Palladino and surveyed apparitions and hauntings, Flournoy was convinced of PK, telepathy, clairvoyance, and possible survival, although he doubted that communication with the dead took place. *From India to the Planet Mars* remains one of the most extraordinary studies in the annals of psychical research.

Nandor Fodor, 1895-1964. Psychical researcher; psychologist; writer. Fodor was especially interested in the relationship between psychoanalysis and the paranormal. In his varied career, Fodor changed his views on spiritualism, beginning as rather credulous, swinging to highly critical, and in his later years veering towards a mid-point. He had a wide experience with all types of mediums, engaged in highly publicized feuds, and was a very colorful and knowledgeable man. His *Encyclopedia of Psychic Science*, first published in 1933, shows an astonishing knowledge of the field together with his youthful tendency to editorialize his own views. His later books were more sober and gave some perceptive insights into the possible connections between psychological disturbances, analysis, and psi faculties and manifestations.

Haakon Gabriel Forwald, born 1897. Electrical engineer; inventor. Forwald concerned himself with experiments upon PK for over twenty years. He pursued this interest not only in his native Sweden, but in America as well. Convinced that he demonstrated statistically the reality of PK, he postulated a theory to account for the direction and final placement of the dice used in the experiments. He has probably undertaken more experiments in PK research than any other investigator; the principal criticism directed towards his work by other parapsychologists is that most of it has been conducted by Forwald alone, thus robbing it of verifiability by witnesses.

Eileen J. Garrett, 1893-1970. One of the major trance mediums of the century, Mrs. Garrett also was highly gifted as a writer, businesswoman, administrator, and editor. She retained an unusually critical viewpoint about her own mediumship, and was eager to co-operate in any scientific investigations which would throw light upon mediumship and all other types of psi faculties and phenomena. To this end, she was involved in many experiments with leading psychical researchers in Great Britain, America, and Europe. She founded the Parapsychology Foundation in 1951 to further research through financial grants, conferences, and publications. She was a prolific writer with perceptive views and rewarding insights into life which her varied experiences had provided. Her three autobiographical works are especially important: *My Life in Search for the Meaning of Mediumship* (1938), *Adventures in the Supernormal* (1943), *and Many Voices* (1968).

Gustave Geley, 1868-1924. Psychical researcher; physician; Director of the Institut Métapsychique International 1919-1924. Geley was a leading student of physical phenomena. He participated in investigations of Eva C., and obtained the famous plaster casts produced by the Polish medium Kluski which pointed to materialization under laboratory conditions. He co-operated in much of his research with the distinguished French physiologist Charles Richet. The most significant work Geley wrote is *From the Unconscious to the Conscious,* one of the principal books produced by European psychical research.

Kathleen M. H. Goldney. Psychical researcher; Council member SPR 1943-present; Organizing Secretary SPR 1949-1957. Mrs. Goldney has long been a prominent and highly respected figure in British research. She has studied mediumship extensively and written about the work of Mrs. Hughes and Mrs. Garrett. She collaborated in the famous Shackleton tests with Dr. Soal. She was involved in the Borely Rectory case both with Harry Price and since his death, for she was joint author (with Dr. Dingwall and Mr. Hall) of the critical study of Price's investigation of Borely, *The Haunting of Borley Rectory,* in which doubt is cast upon a sizeable part of Price's evidence and conclusions.

Edmund Gurney, 1847-1888. Psychical researcher; psychologist. One of the Trinity College, Cambridge group, he was a founder of the Society for Psychical Research. An indefatigable investigator, with a brilliant mind, deep knowledge of many fields including hypnotism, in which he was an acknowledged authority. Gurney did as much as anyone to establish the high standards of evidentiality thorough scrutiny of cases. His distinguished level of literary style has characterized the best work of the SPR. He collaborated with Frederic Myers in the classic work, *Phantasms of the Living* (1886), which remains an essential book in psychical research.

C. E. M. Hansel, born 1917. Psychologist. Possibly the most vociferous and prolific critic of contemporary parapsychology, Professor Hansel published several articles analyzing statistical experiments which have been cited by leading investigators as establishing psi as a reality, and found major flaws in all such results and claims. His major work is *ESP: A Scientific Evaluation* (1966), in which he argues that ESP is highly unlikely, has not been verified by the canons of scientific evidentiality due to the absence of a truly repeatable experiment, and can be explained by the hypothesis of trickery on the part of subjects or psychical researchers or both. This latter hypothesis he proposes as the most likely answer. The book has been vigorously attacked by parasychologists in many countries.

Sir Alister C. Hardy, 1896-1985. Professor of Zoology, emeritus, Oxford University; President of the SPR 1965-1969. A distinguished scientist, Fellow of the Royal Society, renowned oceanographer, Sir Alister founded the Religious Experience Research Unit at Oxford upon his retirement. There he and his staff were undertaking the collection of accounts of religious experiences and analysis of the common denominators to be found in various types of such accounts. He had been especially concerned with the revolutionary implications of psychical research for theories of biology, religion, and philosophy. He brought together his views regarding these matters in two major works, the product of his Gifford Lectures, *The Living Stream* (1965), and *The Divine Flame* (1966).

Hornell Hart, 1888-1967. Sociologist; psychical researcher. Dr. Hart was a member of the faculty at Duke University for almost twenty years, and during that period he became involved in psi research, and continued his work after leaving Duke. Especially interested in apparitions and a leading scholar upon this subject, his article "Six Theories About Apparitions" (*SPR Journal*, May, 1956) is a very important contribution. He was also concerned with out-of-the-body experiences and the survival issue. His book, *The Engima of Survival: The Case For and Against an Afterlife* (1959), is a significant addition to the literature.

Renée Haynes (Mrs. Jerrard Tickell), born 1906. Writer; psychical researcher; editor of *The Journal* of the SPR. Miss Haynes has long been interested in the paranormal and has been involved in numerous investigations, as well as contributing to the *SPR Journal*, before assuming her position as editor. She is the author of several books, including a very original treatment of psi, *The Hidden Springs*, and a biographical study of the 18th century Pope Benedict XIV, who evinced interest in the paranormal, *The Philosopher Pope* (1971).

Rosalind Heywood, 1895-1980. Psychical researcher; writer; sensitive. Mrs. Heywood, for many years a member of the Council of the Society for Psychical Research, was a leading figure in psychical research in Great Britain. She combined a natural sensitivity to psi with a rare critical acumen and literary gift for elucidating the evidence and significance of psi for the layman. Her experimental work as a subject and her study as an investigator placed her in an unusually sound position to judge both the subjective and the objective aspects of research. Her two books, *The Sixth Sense* (1959; American title: *Beyond the Reach of Sense)*, and her autobiographical study: *The Infinite Hive* (1964; American title: *ESP: A Personal Memoir)*, are among the finest general treatments of psi yet produced.

Richard Hodgson, 1855-1905. Psychical researcher official of the American Society for Psychical Research 1887-1905. A brilliant Australian psychologist who came under the influence of Henry Sidgwick at Cambridge, Hodgson became a leader in the SPR at its inception, and was sent to India to investigate the claims of Madame Blavatsky and her Theosophical Society. His report was strongly critical, accusing Madame Blavatsky and others of fraudulent phenomena. Highly skeptical, he demonstrated the role of conjuring in producing ostensible psychic phenomena, showed the low observational skills of participants in seances, and was interested in secondary personalities. When William James was impressed with Mrs. Piper's mediumship, Hodgson came to Boston to investigate her with a strong predilection that she was fraudulent. After the most stringent precautions, and over a period of years, he became convinced not only of her psi faculty but of the discarnate source for much of her information. His conversion to the survivalist position appreciably strengthened that school of thought in the early stages of psychical research due to the high regard in which he was held. He contributed many articles to the *SPR Proceedings* and helped edit Myers' monumental study for publication after Myers' death.

Daniel Dunglas Home, 1833-1886. The most famous of physical mediums, Home produced a wide range of phenomena including levitation, partial materialization, psychokinetic effects, bodily elongation, and imperviousness to fire, all generally demonstrated in full light in contrast to virtually every other physical medium's requirement for darkness. He was a celebrity, entertained by the royalty of European courts, lavished with gifts (he never accepted fees for his demonstrations), investigated by such distinguished scientists as Crookes in Great Britain and Hare in America, and he convinced many outstanding figures of the reality of his phenomena. Despite numerous attempts to discover fraud in his mediumship, Home was probably alone among principal physical mediums in never having been found using trickery or devices. Those who remained skeptical of his gift claimed mass hypnosis as the explanation for the conviction of witnesses. While there were some unsavory, or at best, unpleasant, aspects to his personal life, including expulsion from Rome as a wizard and a highly publicized trial over money, his mediumship remains the most impressive instance of physical phenomena on record.

William James, 1842-1910. Professor of Philosophy and of Psychology at Harvard University; founder of the American Society for Psychical Research; President of the SPR 1894-1895. One of the most famous and influential figures of his day, James was a pioneer in the infant discipline of psychology, formulated his pragmatic philosophy, contributed to the study of religion with his classic *The Varieties of Religious Experience*, became a chief protagonist of psychical research, and discovered one of the most important of mediums, Mrs. Piper, co-operating in her investigation with Richard Hodgson. He became convinced of the reality of the psi faculty and announced that both mental and physical phenomena, surrounded though the true were with the fraudulent, should be studied in the same spirit and with the same thoroughness as other natural phenomena. His enormous prestige greatly strengthened psychical research and encouraged other scholars to consider it a field worthy of research. His writings upon psychical research have been edited and collected in the volume *William James on Psychical Research*, 1960.

Carl G. Jung, 1875-1961. Psychiatrist. Jung became interested in paranormal phenomena as a young man, investigated mediums, co-operated with the great German psychical researcher Schrenk-Notzing, lectured before the SPR in 1919, formulated his concept of "synchronicity" as a possible explanation of the baffling acausal relationships found in psi phenomena, and urged other psychiatrists and psychologists to consider parapsychology as an essential aspect of their discipline. His knowledge of the occult was considerable as well and he insisted, in the face of hostile critics, that whatever the source and validity of occult theories and practices and of paranormal phenomena, the fact that many people held such theories and believed in the reality of such phenomena meant that psychologists must investigate them.

Stanley Krippner, born 1932. Former director of the Dream Laboratory, Maimonides Medical Center, Brooklyn; past-president of the Parapsychological Association; past-president of the Humanistic Psychology Association; and presently director of Saybrook Institute (successor to Humanistic Psychology Institute). Dr. Krippner is a counseling psychologist and speech therapist who was educated at Wisconsin and Northwestern universities. He was the founding editor of *Psycho-Energetic Systems* and has authored several books, including *Realms of Healing* (with A. Villoldo, Celestial Arts, 1976), *Dream Telepathy* (with M. Ullman and A. Vaughan, Macmillan, 1973), *Future Science* (with John White, Doubleday/Anchor, 1977), *Energies of Consciousness* (ed. with D. Rubin, Gordon, 1975), *Song of the Siren* (Harper & Row, 1975), *Human Possibilities* (Doubleday/Anchor, 1980), and the on-going series (as ed.), *Advances in Parapsychological Research*, Plenum Press, 1975 —. In parapsychology, Dr. Krippner has been involved in experimental laboratory work, field investigation, and in education.

G. W. Lambert. Retired civil servant, President of the SPR 1955-1958, former Hon. Secretary of the SPR. Mr. Lambert has proven to be an indefatigable, painstaking and thorough researcher, especially with regard to alternative theories to paranormal causation in reported instances of ostensible psi phenomena. His study of poltergeist cases and the bearing of possible physical factors often overlooked is a major contribution. He has collaborated recently with Mr. MacKenzie in his collection of cases, and has studied the personal references in the cross-correspondence material, especially that of Mrs. Verrall. He has also written important analyses of the famous Versailles "Adventure" and the "Dieppe air raid case."

Gladys Osborne Leonard, 1882-1970. One of the greatest of trance mediums, Mrs. Leonard was exhaustively investigated over a long period by the leading psychical researchers of Great Britain. She participated in the "book tests" and "newspaper tests," especially with Rev. Drayton Thomas, and was one of the principal subjects for Whately Carington's Word Association Tests to determine whether her control, "Feda," was a secondary personality or an ostensible discarnate. Made famous by Sir Oliver Lodge's book, *Raymond*, in which he recounted his conviction that he had communicated with his dead son through her mediumship, Mrs. Leonard for some time accepted sitters exclusively through the SPR, and many were convinced of survival by evidential material received. Unlike Mrs. Garrett, Mrs. Leonard was a spiritualist, and utterly sure of survival; but this personal conviction did not deter her from co-operating in every controlled experiment proposed by researchers. Her personal and professional integrity were above reproach and she remains an extraordinary example of remarkable psi abilities. Her most significant book is *My Life in Two Worlds* (1931).

Sir Oliver J. Lodge, 1851-1940. Physicist; educator; psychical researcher; President of the SPR 1901-1903, 1932. A distinguished physicist, renowned for his research into electricity and radio among other scientific projects, Lodge pursued investigations into psi from the mid 1880's. He studied the mediumship of Mrs. Piper and Mrs. Leonard exhaustively, participated in the cross-correspondences, led in the "book tests" and the development of "proxy sittings" to help eliminate telepathy from the sitter as alternative explanations to discarnate sources for veridical data. At length convinced of survival, he wrote voluminously and created a sensation with his work *Raymond* (1916), in which he detailed why he was convinced of the survival of his son killed in World War I, through the mediumship especially of Mrs. Leonard and Vout Peters. He devised a posthumous test to try and demonstrate his own survival; and while the test itself has been assessed quite differently as to its success, it has led to other more sophisticated ideas in such tests.

William McDougall, 1871-1938. An eminent dualist psychologist and philosopher whose interest in psychical research was aroused by the work of William James at Harvard. When McDougall became Professor of Psychology at Harvard, he urged that psychical research be accepted as a regular discipline of study. His opportunity to put this concept into action came when he was invited to chair the department of psychology at Duke University, and from this came the Parapsychology Laboratory headed by Dr. J. B. Rhine. McDougall's international eminence as a psychologist and philosopher made his support for psychical research especially useful.

William Stainton Moses, 1839-1892. Medium; clergyman. Best known as one of the earliest practitioners of automatic writing, there was some evidence of physical phenomena in the earlier stages of his mediumship, but these had apparently subsided by the time Moses participated in the founding of the SPR in 1882. Convinced of survival and of the discarnate source for evidential material as well as the religious teachings in his automatic writing, Moses resigned from the SPR because he felt its leaders were unfairly critical of spiritualism. His best known work is *Spirit Teachings* (1883).

Gardner Murphy, 1895-1979. Psychologist; psychical researcher; President of the SPR 1949; President of the ASPR 1962-1971. An eminent psychologist, Dr. Murphy studied at Harvard when McDougall was there, and was interested in psi throughout his career. His numerous articles reflected his concerns with both the experimental and theoretical aspects of parapsychology, for he wrote about telepathy, clairvoyance, precognition, survival, the body-mind issue, mediumship, and the bearing psychical research has upon religious views. He was greatly concerned that a repeatable experiment be developed, for this, he felt, would be essential if psi phenomena and their investigation are to become an integral part of psychology in general. His general work on psychical research, *The Challenge of Psychical Research* (1961), is one of the finest overall treatments of the discipline.

Gilbert Murray, 1866-1957. Professor of Greek, Oxford University; President of the SPR 1915-1916, 1952. Murray was one of the foremost classical scholars of his generation and moved in a distinguished academic community, some of whom were more than surprised at his interest in psychical research. His chief contribution to the field centered around reports of his own remarkable telepathic abilities. The demonstration of this gift took the form of Murray leaving the room while a group of family and friends decided upon a scene or idea for him to discover. He then was recalled, held the hand of the person with the concept, and in an unusually high percentage of instances, guessed the precise scene or idea. Some critics have credited Murray with a "telaesthesia" or greatly heightened hearing and sensing ability rather than telepathy, intimating that he physically heard the discussion despite his distance from the room. The participants in the tests, however, have discounted this due to the nature of the building and its heavy walls. The Murray tests, while not easily quantifiable, are probably the most impressive qualitative demonstrations of telepathy on record.

Frederic W. H. Myers, 1843-1901. Poet; classicist; psychical researcher; founder of the SPR; President of the SPR 1900. His interest in psychical research sprang from two roots: first, his close friendship and great admiration for Henry Sidgwick; second, his intense desire to prove for himself and for all the reality of survival. During the twenty years between the founding of the SPR and his death, Myers devoted time, energy, and a considerable sum of money to the investigation, publication, and publicizing of psychical phenomena. Although a classicist by training and a poet by inclination, he steeped himself in the rudimentary psychology of his day, and based upon that and his own deep knowledge of the evidence so far gathered for psi, he postulated bold theories, insisted upon high standards for the new discipline, and laid the foundation for what has ensued. Probably more than any other, Myers could be called the founder of psychical research. His perceptive ideas in the classic *Phantasms of the Living* (which he prepared with Gurney and Podmore in 1886), plus many articles in the *SPR Proceedings*, and the extraordinary insights of the most important single work in the literature of psychical research, the mammoth *Human Personality and Its Survival of Bodily Death*—these contributions are unexcelled.

Eugene Osty, 1874-1938. Physician; psychical researcher; Director of the Institut Métapsychique International in Paris. Osty worked closely in his psychical studies with Charles Richet, Gustave Geley, Henri Bergson, and Emile Boirac. His critical acumen, insistence upon careful experimental controls, lucid writing, and thorough investigation were all outstanding. While especially interested in mental phenomena, he became convinced of the reality of PK through investigation of Rudi Schneider. Like Richet, he rejected the spiritualist hypothesis and argued that psi phenomena and faculties were other aspects of human nature that must be studied in the same dispassionate, scientific manner as the physiological factors. Like many researchers of his generation, he was overly optimistic as to the early establishment of the reality of psi among the orthodox scientists; but he repeatedly challenged them to investigate the evidence, repeat the experiments, and see for themselves. Besides the vast numbers of articles he wrote, probably his most significant work is *Supernormal Faculties in Man* (1925).

Eusapia Palladino, 1854-1918. Possibly the greatest physical medium since Home, or possibly the cleverest of fraudulent mediums, Palladino was certainly the most controversial of her time. No other medium except "Margery" has so divided the psychical researchers in their assessments. Studied by virtually every important investigator in Europe, Great Britain, and America during her career, she undoubtedly cheated when she could or needed to; but many shrewd experts were convinced of the reality of her phenomena under stringent conditions. These phenomena, ostensibly under the direction of her control "John King," included levitation of Eusapia herself, of tables, chairs, tambourines, trumpets, strange flitting lights, the playing of a small guitar, raps, etc. The distinguished investigator, Hereward Carrington, possibly was closest to the truth when he held that Eusapia, a highly erotic, mischievous, impatient woman, enjoyed fooling investigators, was uninterested in proving her gift, and cheated when she could not or would not produce real phenomena. The most thorough investigation of Eusapia Palladino's mediumship is in the volume by Feilding, Carrington, and Baggally dealing with their series of sittings in 1908, *Sittings with Eusapia Palladino and Other Studies*.

Michael Perry, born 1933. Clergyman; writer, editor and publisher's assistant. Author of *The Easter Enigma* (1959), *The Miracles and the Resurrection* (1972), *The Resurrection of Man* (1975), and *Psychic Studies—A Christian View* (1984). The Venerable Mr. Perry is archdeacon of Durham, Church of England, and currently serves as Editor of *The Christian Parapsychologist* for the (English) Churches' Fellowship for Psychical and Spiritual Studies.

Leonore E. S. Piper, 1859-1950. Medium. Mrs. Piper was "discovered" by William James in Boston, where she was a member of a socially prominent family. Sure that she did indeed have a paranormal gift, he arranged for Richard Hodgson to come from England to investigate her; Hodgson was not only certain of her psi faculty, but became convinced of survival through her mediumship. For thirty years, Mrs. Piper was investigated thoroughly by the most prominent and careful of American and British researchers, and all attested to her utter integrity, constant co-operation despite the considerable inconveniences caused by the stringent precautions imposed, and the remarkably consistent quality of her gift. Her trance work was both oral and through automatic writing. She participated in the cross-correspondences, in which the material of a recondite classical nature completely foreign to her own limited knowledge is especially impressive. There are numerous articles dealing with her mediumship in the publications of both the ASPR and the SPR, and her daughter, Alta, wrote a sympathetic and perceptive brief biography, *The Life and Work of Mrs. Piper* (1929).

Frank Podmore, 1856-1910. Psychical researcher; government official. Podmore was converted to spiritualism early in his life, but the widespread fraud among mediums severely disillusioned him and he swung to the highly critical point on the spectrum, a position he retained for many years. His massive study, *Modern Spiritualism* (1902), is sharply critical of the entire movement but it is thoroughly researched and remains a principal volume in the literature. He collaborated with Myers and Gurney in the preparation of *Phantasms of the Living* (1886), investigated many cases of ostensible poltergeist and apparition phenomena, studied Mrs. Piper, postulated a variation of the hallucinatory theory of apparitions, and followed the cross-correspondences closely. The high evidentiality of the latter caused him to indicate that his anti-spiritualistic hypothesis position was changing shortly before his death. He was one of the most thorough and skeptical of the early researchers and his contributions to the discipline are manifold.

J. Gaither Pratt, 1910-1979. A world-renowned experimental parapsychologist, Dr. Pratt worked with Dr. J. B. Rhine at Duke University for thirty years before joining the staff at the Parapsychology Unit of the University of Virginia. His tests with Pearce and Woodruff are considered, together with Dr. Soal's experiments with Shackleton and Mrs. Stewart, the most impressive statistical evidence for ESP yet produced. He conducted extensive tests with the Czech sensitive,

Pavel Stepanek, on the "focussing effect," continued the investigation of the "thoughtography" of Ted Serios begun by Dr. Eisenbud, studied the possibly paranormal faculties of homing pigeons, the Seaforth poltergeist case, and developed, with Birge, a method for quantifying qualitative material for statistical analysis and assessment. He collaborated on several works with J. B. Rhine, and wrote his own account, *Parapsychology: An Insider's View of ESP* (1966).

Harry Price, 1881-1948. Psychical researcher; writer. A rather flamboyant and controversial figure in his lifetime, Price has continued to arouse dispute posthumously over his most famous case, the "haunting" of Borley Rectory. A study of the case by Eric Dingwall, K. M. Goldney, and Trevor Hall (published by the SPR) argued that Price himself had fraudulently produced some of the most striking phenomena through his excellent legerdemain (he was an outstanding amateur magician). Recently Robert J. Hastings has written a refutation of those charges, and the controversy continues. Price established his own investigative organization, the National Laboratory of Psychical Research, in London. He developed an enormous personal library of about 15,000 volumes dealing with magic, the occult, and psychical research, which he left to the University of London. He wrote hundreds of articles and many books of a popular nature, and investigated many mediums including Rudi Schneider, Helen Duncan, Frau Silbert, Eleanore Zugun, Stella C., and Eileen Garrett. His apparent interest in publicity and the popular nature of his writings set him at odds with the scholarly pursuits of the SPR and other scientific bodies, but he did arouse public interest in psi phenomena and did point out the fraudulent practices of some mediums. One's assessment of Price remains a matter of personal predilection.

H. H. Price, born 1899. Professor of Logic, emeritus, Oxford University; President of the SPR 1960-1961. An exceedingly distinguished academic philosopher, Professor Price has concerned himself principally with telepathy, mediumship, and the survival issue. Regarding the latter, he has written several articles postulating possible forms survival could conceivably take, and has argued that a "bodiless" survival is really unthinkable due to our need for personal identity, social acceptance, and love—all of which are premised upon some type of "bodily" recognition. Consequently, he has suggested that the tradition of an "astral" or "etheric" body may be a productive line of thought. He has also dealt with the problem of precognition, the mind-body issue, and other philosophical implications of psi.

Walter Franklin Prince, 1863-1934. Psychical researcher; minister; psychologist; President of the SPR 1930-1931. The ablest and most experienced American researcher of his day, Dr. Prince combined his knowledge of psychology, religion, and psychical research with a highly developed critical ability, natural shrewdness, and thorough scrutiny of every aspect of a case. His study of "Doris Fischer's" multiple personality is a classic of abnormal psychology, while his large volume, *The Case of Patience Worth* (1927), is a major contribution to mediumistic literature. He remained highly skeptical of PK and other physical phenomena, but felt that there was no doubt at all of telepathy, clairvoyance and precognition. He pointed out the inherent difficulties of proving survival, but held that the best evidence (such as the cross-correspondences and the Chaffin will case) made the alternative hypotheses tenuous; consequently, while he believed in survival, he felt that psychical research had not established it empirically, nor was he sure it could. This realistic appraisal of the problems involved was unusual at that period and demonstrates the remarkable qualities Dr. Prince brought to the discipline.

J. B. Rhine, 1895-1980. Possible the most widely known of all parapsychologists, no one has had a greater influence upon research during the last forty years. Following the establishment of the Parapsychology Laboratory under his direction, with the encouragement of William McDougall, at Duke University, Rhine undertook to devise repeatable and statistically measureable experiments. His early successes aroused a storm of controversy, and easy and frequent replication proved less likely than had been supposed. Soal vindicated Rhine's findings impressively after initial failure, and other statistical studies have followed by the dozens. After the mathematics, randomness, laboratory controls, record-keeping, and possible sensory clues had all been investigated, some flaws corrected, and the general conclusions verified, the final and unanswerable criticism has been made by Hansel: collusion, involuntary and voluntary fraud among both subjects and investigators as the most likely hypothesis to cover the extrachance results, since ESP is intrinsically impossible. Dr. Rhine has joined other parapsychologists in replying vigorously to this and other attacks upon the scientific integrity of investigators.

His numerous books, some scholarly, others directed to the general public, have made ESP a household term. The statistical evidence for psychokinesis has also been gathered by Rhine's co-workers, but this has met with less acceptance among other parapsychologists. Investigation of psi in animals, psychological traits and conditions conducive to and inhibitory of psi, their effects upon psi, and other topics have been undertaken, while the collection of spontaneous cases has proceeded under the direction of his wife, Dr. Louisa Rhine. After his retirement from Duke University, Dr. Rhine formed the Foundation for Research on the Nature of Man where he continued his research and supported other approaches to parapsychological investigations.

Louisa E. Rhine, 1891-1983. Dr. Rhine was a full partner in the lifetime work of her husband, J. B. Rhine, in development of the experimental method to establish and evaluate the psi function. However, she will be best remembered for her work in collecting, cataloging, classifying and analyzing her collection of more than 20,000 spontaneous cases of psi in normal life. From that work grew the bulk of her writing, resulting in many articles and six books: *Hidden Channels of the Mind* (1961), *Mind Over Matter* (1970), *ESP in Life and Lab* (1967), *Psi—What Is It?* (1975), *The Invisible Picture* (1981), and (posthumously) *Something Hidden* (1984). Since her husband's death, she served as Executive Director of the Foundation for Research on the Nature of Man, and was elected president of the Society for Psychical Research (London) in 1981.

Charles Richet, 1850-1935. Physiologist; psychical researcher; President of the SPR 1905; winner of the Nobel Prize in 1913. An outstanding physiologist, Richet was a cautious, careful, skeptical investigator who had strongly criticized William Crookes' acceptance of paranormal phenomena in the 1870's. However, he undertook his own studies and became a leading figure in European psychical research. Especially interested in physical phenomena, he studied Eusapia Palladino, Eva C., Kluski, Rudi Schneider, and other important mediums, coined the term "ectoplasm" for the quasi–physical substance supposedly used in materializations; with Geley, he obtained what he considered fraud-proof evidence for the reality of ectoplasmic phenomena under laboratory conditions; he wrote extensively about telepathy and precognition—particularly premonitory cases—and held firmly to an anti-spiritualistic interpretation of paranormal phenomena. Like Osty and other experts, he challenged scientists to experiment and investigate with an open mind and discover the reality of psi for themselves. His most important work is probably *Thirty Years of Psychical Research* (1923).

W. H. Salter, 1880-1970. Barrister; psychical researcher; President of the SPR 1947-1948. Mr. Salter served the SPR in a variety of capacities over forty years and came to know all the key figures in psychical research in Great Britain and most of the non-British investigators as well. He was an excellent reseracher, expert in dissecting testimony, postulating alternative explanations, and elucidating the issues in an unusually clear and judicious manner. Together with Piddington, Alice Johnson, and Gerald Balfour, Salter was a principal expert upon the cross-correspondences. His interest in these important cases was strong because his wife was Helen Verrall, whose mother was one of the "SPR group" of automatists and who also was an automatist, while her father was a member of the "Myers group" of ostensible discarnate communciators. In addition to his involvement with the survival issue, Salter studied apparitions thoroughly and wrote an excellent treatment of the subject, *Ghosts and Apparitions* (1938). His last and largest book, *Zoar* (1961), is one of the most important studies of survival yet produced.

H. F. Saltmarsh, 1881-1943. Psychical researcher; businessman. Saltmarsh was an important contributor to SPR work during the 1930's. He was among the earliest to attempt a quantifying method for qualitative material; he made a thorough study of the cross–correspondences, and his book, *Evidence of Personal Survival from Cross Correspondences* (1938), remains the best brief introduction to that complex mass of data. He also wrote a clear account of the evidence for precognition and the various frustrating attempts to explain it in *Foreknowledge* (1938).

Gertrude R. Schmeidler, born 1912. Psychologist; parapsychologist. Best known for her "sheep and goat" experiments in which she demonstrated that belief or disbelief in psi tends to affect the subject's psi performance so that it is congruent with his predilection, Dr. Schmeidler has also studied how various psychological conditions and patterns affect psi, the inter-relationship of the experimenter-subject rapport and successful results, and other laboratory-oriented projects. The book she wrote with Dr. McConnell, *ESP and Personality Patterns* (1958), brought together many of the results of her research. She has also written many articles for the *ASPR Journal*. She was president of the Parapsychological Association for two terms.

Rudi Schneider, 1908-1957. A prominent physical medium in the 1920's and early 1930's, Rudi and his older brother, Willy, were investigated by leading researchers such as Schrenk-Notzing (who discovered them in Austria), Richet, Osty, various SPR researchers, and Harry Price. Very stringent conditions were generally imposed, including a complete physical examination, sewing into a one-piece suit with luminous markings which showed in the dark, sitting in a cage, infra-red photography, etc. Rudi's phenomena included the apparent psychokinetic movement of small objects such as a trumpet, bell, doll, strumming a zither, and the ectoplasmic materialization of a three-fingered hand. While Price and others said that Rudi had on occasion cheated when the conditions were lax, a large number of investigators were convinced that truly paranormal phenomena were produced under fraud-proof conditions.

Albert von Schrenk-Notzing, 1862-1929. Physician; psychical researcher. His medical training led to his interest in hypnotism and thence to psychical research, an interest which was encouraged through his friendship with Charles Richet. Schrenk-Notzing studied many aspects of psi, but was best known for his forty years of work on physical phenomena, in which he co-operated with Osty, Geley, Lodge, and earlier figures such as Myers. He devised many of the precautionary procedures which were widely adopted, such as the complete physical examinations, one-piece luminous suits, and dyes in fluids to detect if ectoplasmic material had been regurgitated fraudulently. He investigated major physical mediums such as Eva C., Eusapia Palladino, Tomcyzk, and the Schneider brothers; and he became convinced, as did Osty, Richet, Geley, and some others, that materializations did occur under fraud-proof conditions. He translated some non-German works into his own language, established his own laboratory, and wrote numerous articles and books, principally upon physical phenomena. It is interesting to note that, like most European researchers who accepted the reality of the controversial physical phenomena, he rejected the spiritualistic explanation and felt that virtually all cases could be explained upon psychological and physiological grounds.

Emilio Servadio, born 1904. Psychoanalyst; parapsychologist. Dr. Servadio is a prominent Italian psychoanalyst who helped found the Italian Society for Psychical Research in 1937. He has written about various facets of psi phenomena such as precognition, dowsing, dreams, and healing, but is especially concerned with telepathy and its relationship with psychoanalysis. His Myers Memorial Lecture in 1963, entitled "Unconscious and Paranormal Factors in Healing and Recovery," has been published by the SPR and is an important discussion of psychosomatic and psi factors in healing.

Harold Sherman, born 1898. He was probably the first of the American psychic-sensitives who, in the tradition of Ossowiecki of Poland, induced scientists to test and evaluate his psychic gifts. In 1937 Sherman teamed with polar explorer Sir Hubert Wilkins to receive daily messages in New York City from the North Pole area, which he mailed each night to the American Society for Psychical Research. His own ESP Research Associates Foundation in Little Rock has, for thirty-five years, pioneered scientifically oriented conferences on psychic issues. An established writer before developing his psychic gifts, Sherman produced a long series of books to explain the psychic and demonstrate its practical uses. (His work closely paralleled that of psychic Eileen Garrett whose skeptical attitude toward her own gifts charmed many scientists who tested her; they were featured in her books and attended her annual conferences held to explore specific scientific features of the psychic scene.) Sherman has been best known in the past two decades for his national workshops on unconventional healing that have often featured spiritual healers such as the late Olga and Ambrose Worrall.

Eleanor M. B. Sidgwick, 1845-1936. Psychical researcher; educator; editor; President of the SPR 1908-1909. Mrs. Sidgwick, wife of Henry Sidgwick, sister of Arthur and Gerald Balfour, was a brilliant woman with a highly developed critical acumen, literary ability, and determination to investigate ostensible psi phenomena thoroughly. She was prominent in the SPR from the early 1880's until the 1930's and contributed greatly to its growth in prestige and to its accumulation of knowledge about paranormal phenomena. She studied many mediums, including Mrs. Piper, Mrs. Leonard, and Eusapia Palladino, and wrote numerous perceptive articles in the *Proceedings* of the PSR. While she doubted the survival hypothesis during a large part of her career, she was much impressed by the cross-correspondence material and indicated a few years before her death that she tended to accept that survival was a distinct possibility. Her writings are well worth study even today because of their acute analysis of the data, shrewd judgments of people and their motives, original hypothesis, and insistence upon objectivity.

Henry Sidgwick, 1838-1900. Philosopher; educator; founder of the SPR; President of the SPR 1882-1885, 1888-1892. Sidgwick was the key figure in the founding of the SPR since many of the original members who responded to Barrett's call for such an organization agreed to its formation only if Sidgwick would act as President. His prestige, reputation for integrity, and brilliant abilities all attracted members of high repute and standing and helped set the tradition of excellence. He was a careful and skeptical investigator and took a leading part in the important Census of Hallucinations published in 1894, as well as studying the mediumship of Mrs. Piper, Eusapia Palladino, and others. His various Presidential Addresses remain important in shedding light upon the genesis of psychical research and in reminding the student of the remarkable consistency of the criticism and problems faced over ninety years by researchers.

S. G. Soal, born 1889. Mathematician; psychical researcher; President of the SPR 1949-1951. Dr. Soal has long been the most prominent statistical researcher in Great Britain. A distinguished academic mathematician and retired lecturer in mathematics at London University, he has brought to the statistical work an unusually strong knowledge of the mathematics of chance, as well as many years of study in psychical research. Before launching his statistical experiments, Dr. Soal spent some years investigating mediums and reported the very important Gordon Davis case in 1925. Through the mediumship of Mrs. Blanche Cooper, Soal received communications purporting to be from a friend, Gordon Davis, which were highly evidential, only to learn later that Davis was still alive. This pointed out, as did the Réallier case and some others, the highly developed dramatic faculty latent in mediums and the inherent difficulty, if not impossibility, of eliminating telepathy, precognition, and/or clairvoyance (Super ESP hypothesis) as alternative explanations for ostensible discarnate sources of veridical data. Dr. Soal's most important work is doubtless his impressive statistical evidence for psi through a long series of experiments with Mrs. Stewart and Basil Shackleton. He undertook this work only after Whately Carington suggested that the displacement effect might be responsible for Soal's complete failure earlier to replicate Dr. Rhine's results. This proved to be true in the case of these two subjects, and in the new series extraordinary results were gained, especially by Shackleton, in precognitive tests. Besides numerous articles on psi, Dr. Soal's two most significant works are *Modern Experiments in Telepathy* (1954), written with F. Bateman, and *The Mind Readers* (1959), written with H. T. Bowden.

Ian Stevenson, born 1918. Professor of psychiatry; parapsychologist; physician. Dr. Stevenson has been especially concerned with the evidence for survival and reincarnation, as well as the psychological concomitants of psi research and precognition. He has devised both a questionnaire and a padlock test for survival research which may shed light upon the Super ESP hypothesis and upon the nature of veridical survival evidence. Currently, he is probably the leading American parapsychologist working on the survival issue, after quite some years in which little attention was paid to this facet of psychical research. His principal publications have been *Twenty Cases Suggestive of Reincarnation* (1966), and *Telepathic Impressions* (1970).

W. H. C. Tenhaeff, 1894-1981. Director of the Parapsychology Institute of the State University of Utrecht, Dr. Tenhaeff is the leading Dutch parapsychologist. While he has investigated virtually the entire spectrum of psi phenomena, his greatest interest in recent years has been in the study of the psychological characteristics of psychic sensitives. He has worked extensively with the well-known Dutch sensitive or "paragnost," Croiset, and has co-operated with researchers in other lands in the "chair tests" through which Croiset precognitively describes the person to sit in a particular chair at a given future date. These tests have provided some impressive instances of precognition. Dr. Tenhaeff has been exceedingly active in lecturing about parapsychology before a large number of organizations throughout Europe and has written many books upon different facets of psi phenomena.

C. Drayton Thomas, died 1953. Clergymen; psychical researcher. Rev. Thomas studied the mediumship of Mrs. Leonard more thoroughly than anyone, having had about five hundred sittings with her over thirty years. Convinced that he had received veridical communications from his father and sister as well as others, he was a leading survivalist. He helped devise the "book tests" and "newspaper tests," the former of a clairvoyant nature, the latter of a precognitive; and some of the results were impressive. While he disagreed with Whately Carington's conclusion that "Feda," Mrs. Leonard's control, was a secondary personality, he co-operated fully in the Word Association Tests to test this hypothesis. He wrote a considerable number of articles for the SPR about mediumship, proxy sittings, and various evidential cases; he also published several books embodying the results of his survival research. While other researchers did not share Thomas's conviction of survival, he was held in very high repute for his integrity and care in research.

Robert H. Thouless, 1894-1984. Psychologist; parapsychologist; President of the SPR 1943-1944. Dr. Thouless has concerned himself with PK research, statistical studies of ESP in the manner of Rhine and Soal, possibilities of improving guessing performance in such tests, and the issue of survival. In connection with the latter, he devised a complex cryptogram test for survival to obviate the drawbacks of the ealier posthumous tests, such as those of Myers and Lodge, which were useless once the key to the test had been used. Over the following years, he refined this test and through this line of thought engendered other survival tests, such as the padlock test of Dr. Ian Stevenson. He wrote several articles about psi, and his book for laymen is an excellent contribution: *Experimental Psychical Research* (1963).

H. C. Thurston, 1856-1939. Historian; priest; psychical researcher; writer. Probably the leading Roman Catholic expert upon psychical research, Father Thurston studied the field for thirty years. While he supported the Roman Catholic ban upon mediumistic contact with the discarnates and could not, therefore, study mediums firsthand, he was a close student of the literature and was in contact with some of the leading British researchers. Few have had a deeper knowledge of the evidence dealing with poltergeists. His principal work is *The Church and Spiritualism* (1933), in which he disagreed with other

Catholic writers that spiritualism was all fraud. This is a remarkably balanced and fair account of the movement as seen from the Roman Catholic viewpoint and remains an important contribution.

G. N. M. Tyrrell, 1879-1952. Engineer; mathematician; psychical researcher; President of the SPR 1945-1946. Tyrrell, a pioneer in the development of radio, devoted his full time to psychical research for forty years. He became a leader in experimental work and also a prominent theoretician about psi. His devices for mechanical randomness and for testing both telepathy and precognition were significant developments; and through the use of these machines with Gertrude Johnson, he obtained highly significant statistical evidence for telepathy and precognition. Tyrrell wrote exceedingly well and brought his great knowledge and experience to bear upon the theoretical and philosophical meaning of psychical research in a series of very important works: *Grades of Significance* (1930), *Science and Psychical Phenomena* (1938), *The Personality of Man* (1946), and *Human Personality* (1953).

Montague Ullman, born 1916. Psychiatrist; parapsychologist. Dr. Ullman has been the leader in the field of dream research at the Dream Laboratory of Maimonides Hospital in New York. Here he and his staff have studied telepathic exchange of ideas and images through dreaming, and they have greatly deepened the knowledge about the nature of dreams, the dramatic faculty of personality, and the different types of stimuli which seem to enhance telepathic rapport. He was the President of the ASPR, and traveled to Russia where he learned about Russian parapsychological research.

L. L. Vasilyev, 1891-1966. Physiologist; parapsychologist. Vasilyev was the most prominent student of psi in Russia, established the first laboratory for parapsychological studies at Leningrad University, and urged that research into psi was a matter of the greatest importance. Like many physiologists and physicians in the field, he rejected the non-physicalistic properties of psi and insisted that it was an atavistic remainder from earlier forms of evolution which probably operated through some form of so far undiscovered energy in the brain. His most significant work is *Mysterious Manifestations of the Human Psyche* (1959).

Margaret D. G. M. Verrall, 1859-1916. Classicist; automatist. Mrs. Verrall was the wife of a distinguished Cambridge classical scholar, A. W. Verrall, and a member of the Cambridge group of academic figures prominent in the SPR. She investigated both Mrs. Thompson's and Mrs. Piper's mediumship before developing her own automatic writing. She was a leading member of the "SPR group" of automatists involved in the cross-correspondences, in the course of which she received veridical information purporting to originate with Frederic Myers, her husband, Henry Sidgwick, Richard Hodgson, and others. The complex and recondite classical allusions were typical of Myers, Verrall, Butcher and Sidgwick, but since she was herself a fine classicist, some students have argued that the cross-correspondences emanated from Mrs. Verrall's subconscious, telepathically triggering the jigsaw pieces found in the automatic writings of her daughter, Mrs. Piper, Mrs. Willett, Mrs. Forbes, and Mrs. Holland, although the mediums were as far apart as India and America. Mrs. Verrall was herself convinced of the discarnate source of the data.

Leslie D. Weatherhead, 1893-1976. Clergyman. One of the most famous preachers and religious authors in the world, Dr. Weatherhead was interested in psychical research, especially in healing and survival. He argued that knowledge of so-called paranormal phenomena sheds light upon the numerous similar instances in the Bible, upon the resurrection, and upon the nature of miracles. He wrote several books upon facets of psychical research, including *The Resurrection of Christ in the Light of Modern Science and Psychical Research* (1959), but his major work was the massive volume, *Psychology, Religion, and Healing* (1951).

Rhea A. White, born 1931. Ms. White was one of the organizers and founder-council-members of the Parapsychological Association in 1957-1958, and is about to embark upon her second stint as its president. She is presently editor of her own periodical, *Parapsychology Abstracts International* (semi-annual), and additionally edits two quarterlies, *Theta* and *Journal of the American Society for Psychical Research*, plus the annual *Research in Parapsychology* for the Parapsychological Association, as well as operating her Parapsychology Sources of Information Center in Dix Hills, New York, and serving as librarian at her neighborhood library. Somehow, she finds time to write several major papers a year.

APPENDIX

RESEARCHING SURVIVAL OF DEATH BY HUMAN CONSCIOUSNESS*
Frank C. Tribbe

Why do most parapsychologists ignore the Survival question? Because it is claimed that the so-called "Super-ESP Hypothesis" removes the issue (survival of death by human consciousness) from the arena of serious scientific studies. But, is that reason itself scientifically sound? Robert Ashby thought not.

Robert H. Ashby got his training in psychical research during postgraduate study at Edinburgh University, through the Society of Psychical Research, and as Research Officer for the College of Psychic Studies, London, during his years as High School principal for the American School, also in London. From September 1971 until his death on August 22, 1975 he was Director of Research and Education for the Spiritual Frontiers Fellowship. From his study and research Ashby ultimately came to the firm conclusion that the so-called super-ESP theory was untenable insofar as it was asserted in opposition to data supporting the claim of spirit survival of bodily death, especially since the super-ESP claim has never been supported by data.

Unfortunately, Ashby died before his arguments could be formulized publicly and I wish to set forth Ashby's views on the survival problem. The information is either pure Ashby or Ashby-inspired. It

*Reprinted with permission from *Theta* (Journal of the Psychical Research Foundation), Volume 12, Number 3, Autumn 1984. Original title: *Robert Ashby and the Super-ESP Hypothesis*. An earlier version of this paper was read at the 1982 meeting of the Southeastern Regional Parapsychological Association.

is based on my extensive correspondences with him, on his files which I obtained from his widow, and on information from the Spiritual Frontiers Fellowship headquarters and the SFF research chairperson who succeeded Ashby. I also worked from his handwritten notes, and from information I obtained from conversations with him or with others who knew him. Although the ideas set forth here are his, almost all the supporting data are mine.

The data from mediumistic communications provide the most common, and perhaps the most relevant, evidence for spirit survival. However, many scientists do not accept such evidence because of the alternative super-ESP theory. This theory presumes that if a fact physically exists anywhere on earth, or any living person has knowledge of same, it is more reasonable to assume that the medium obtained that knowledge by his or her own ESP rather than by communication with the claimed spirit of a deceased person. The assertion of such skepticism is usually coupled with a claim of parsimony—that super ESP is simpler than the claim of spirit survival and is therefore preferable scientifically.

In a well-known psychiatric journal, Ian Stevenson (1977) called for a renewal of research on the survival problem (discussed below). In a subsequent issue three readers (Lief, 1977; Roll, 1977; Ullman, 1977) wrote letters endorsing Stevenson's call. In response to that call, I will survey the pros and cons in the literature in respect to the super-ESP theory, and I will reason that the theory should no longer be considered a bar to meaningful research.

The standard approach to the problem of survival by the super-ESP proponents is to state that clairvoyance and telepathy do occur, whereas we have no independent evidence for spirit survival of bodily death; ergo, although super-ESP has never been demonstrated, it *must* be the answer. This can also be termed the "eyes closed" approach, for one must refuse to look at the numberless cases of evidential mediumistic material and related data throughout history in order to be able to say that "we have no independent evidence for spirit survival of bodily death." Further, the survival skeptics must ignore the impressive apparitional data, which Professor Hornell Hart (1959) found to be very significant, as well as reincarnation and possession cases, communications, and physical phenomena such as phone calls, dictaphone communications, electronic voice phenomena, materializations, and spirit photography.

As will be obvious, the survival skeptics espousing super-ESP are mostly parapsychologists and psychical researchers already committed (at least tentatively) to the probable existence of telepathy and clairvoyance. Initially, such persons challenged the early survival research on the basis of possible "telepathic leakage," but when later sittings and experiments were tightly structured and controlled to preclude such leaks, super-ESP was hypothesized as a fall-back proposition. Most present-day scholars credit the late Hornell Hart, a sociology professor and parapsychologist, with popularizing (if not actually coining) the term "super-ESP" in his book, *The Enigma of Survival* (1959). Hart cities the writings of Charles Richet which, as early as 1923, contained the thought but without the catch phrase, and the later writings of skeptics E. R. Dodds (1934), Antony Flew (1953), Gardner Murphy (1945a, 1945b, 1945c, 1948, 1957), and H. H. Price (1953), but acknowledges that while such views "are no more than guesses," they perhaps apply at least some of the time, at least in part. Hart concludes with a very involved philosophy that he calls the "persona theory" and describes it as a personality structure. This view, he suggests, accommodates super-ESP and yet validates survival—however, I know of no writer on the subject that he convinced. Hart ultimately voted for the reality of survival; nevertheless, his excellent summary of the super-ESP theory has had the effect of generating continuing support for it among the skeptics.

It may be worth noting that Gardner Murphy devoted an ASPR lecture to a discussion of Hart's book, and it was later published (Murphy, 1961). Murphy refers repeatedly to what Hart calls the "I-Persona," without himself taking a position for or against it. Murphy's paper was followed by a rather sharp reply from Hart, who wrote: "*The 'I-Persona' expression is actually Murphy's, not Hart's.* The expression . . . which Dr. Murphy uses repeatedly . . . is actually a composite of two different concepts which must be clearly distinguished from each other if the analyses presented in *The Enigma of Survival* are to be understood in the sense which the author intended" (Hart, 1961, p. 19). Thus, there clearly was no "meeting of the minds" on the question of Hart's persona theory.

Prominent philosopher C. J. Ducasse, in his book, *A Critical Examination of the Belief in a Life after Death* (1961), concluded that he had to agree with earlier giants in the field, such as Mrs. Sidgwick, Lord Balfour, Sir Oliver Lodge, Professor Hyslop, and Dr. Hodgson, who had individually decided that the balance of the evidence was on the side of the reality of survival. However, Professor Alan Gauld (with A. D. Cornell), in the excellent volume, *Poltergeists* (1979), barely leaves opens the possibility that such phenomena might be the work of excarnate entities. Both in Gauld's lecture to the Society for Psychical Research, "The Super-ESP Hypothesis" (Gauld, 1961), and in his chapter, "Discarnate Survival," in Wolman's definitive *Handbook of Parapsychology* (Gauld, 1977), his conclusion is that a "virtual stalemate" exists between the survival and the super-ESP theories (he takes no personal position). This seems to be a fair summation, since neither side has changed the attitudes of those on the other side. Gauld's chapter on survival does demonstrate the strength of the SPR's cross-correspondences as survival evidence, data which were much favored by Ashby.

Perhaps the latest professional handling of the subject appears in the article, "Research into the Evidence of Man's Survival after Death," by Ian Stevenson (1977), referred to above. He mentions the super-ESP hypothesis, but concludes that survival evidence is strong enough to *permit* belief in survival, but does not *compel* such a belief. In reporting his investigation of hypnotized subjects through whom an alleged deceased entity spoke in a foreign language not known to the subject (e.g., Stevenson, 1974), he makes the point (as had C. J. Ducasse) that speaking a foreign language responsively is a "skill" that must be learned by practice and cannot be transmitted by ESP, thus necessitating survival, plus either possession or reincarnation (in most valid cases). This is a point which no survival skeptic has attempted to answer, perhaps because of the several well-documented cases of extensive mediumistic communications in languages of which the medium had no earthly knowledge, conscious or unconscious (Bozzano, 1932; Kelsey, 1968; Stevens, 1945; Stevenson, 1974; Van Eeden, 1902; Wood, 1955).

Similarly, those who cite the super-ESP hypothesis as the explanation for survivalist data are the very ones who, with the shoe on the other foot, insist that theory must follow data—yet data never have been put forward as preliminary to the super-ESP theory.

In the few modern instances where super-ESP might plausibly be claimed, e.g., Uri Geller's ESP experiments at Stanford Research Institute—now SRI International—(Targ & Puthoff, 1977, Chap. 7); long-distance remote viewing at SRI International (Puthoff & Targ, 1976); Ingo Swann's (Swann, 1975) and Harold Sherman's (Sherman, 1981) reports of OBE or clairvoyance data of Jupiter, Mars, and Mercury months before the NASA Pioneer probes reached the planets; and Douglas Dean's plethysmograph experiments between New Jersey and southern France (Dean, 1966), very little notice has been taken of them in the parapsychological journals. (In fact, researchers Targ and Puthoff were only able to publish their results through their affiliation with the Institute of Electrical and Electronic Engineers [Puthoff & Targ, 1976]).

In my judgment, the super-ESP theory is flawed, in that any statement of it must of necessity incorporate explicitly or implicitly the requirement that the medium provide an unconscious dramatization ability of the subconscious mind. H. H. Price (1959), particularly, considered he had proven the feasibility of super-ESP by citing the apparent ability of our subconscious minds to fabricate, during dream-time, such plausible fiction with no real meaning. Most of the proponents of super-ESP, as cited above, were writing before the era of modern dream research which began only eighteen years ago. With the body of knowledge now available from that source, it begins to become highly probable that such unconscious dramatization in dream production is *not* a fabrication, but rather may be a combination of higher-self guidance, innate therapy and catharsis, ESP, and communications *and visits* from entities who are incarnate, excarnate, and discarnate.

In the same vein, Paul Beard (1966) points out three serious weaknesses of the super-ESP hypothesis: (1) It offers no explanation of how the medium selects, from his omniscient resources, the particular items needed. (2) If the subliminal mind really does possess these very extensive powers, why have they not long since been discovered and harnessed to useful ends? (3) Why would not the subliminal mind *frequently* have some knowledge, however imperfect, of the *sources* of its information? Also, Beard reminds us, in the three best sets of evidence developed by SPR investigators (the cross-correspondences, the book tests, and the newspaper tests), not one research project was initiated by researchers, but all were suggested, designed, and carried out by the alleged communicators.

Similarly, C. J. Ducasse (1961) argued that it is one thing for a medium to obtain by super-ESP certain relevant items of *information*, but it is quite another matter for him or her to acquire paranormally the *mental abilities* or *skills* known to be characteristic of a deceased personality. The latter, he insists, has never been demonstrated in any experimental context, whereas it is a striking feature of some of the more impressive survivalist evidence, especially of the celebrated SPR cross-correspondences where only one of the many independent automatists involved (Mrs. Verrall) possessed the classical scholarship that typified the alleged communicators.

It is worth mentioning at this point the views of some of the other present-day premier researchers (in addition to Beard and Stevenson) who find the survivalist view worthy of belief and/or active research. Gertrude Schmeidler (1979) succinctly says: "Must super-ESP always seem a reasonable alternative? I think not" (p. 14). "The super-ESP hypothesis," says Karlis Osis (1979), is "that strange invention which shies like a mouse from being tested in the laboratory but, in rampant speculations, acts like a ferocious lion devouring survival evidence" (p. 31). "The super-ESP hypothesis," says the Venerable Michael Perry, "argues for such fantastic powers in the living mind that human survival is thereby made more rather than less credible" (1981, p. 65). And John Beloff (1970), parapsychologist at Edinburgh University, without opting for the survival theory, nevertheless points out:

> In appealing to the super-ESP hypothesis we must be careful not to abuse Occam's razor [the rule of parsimony, or simplicity]. Undoubtedly we should always aim to avoid if possible a multiplication of entities in science. . . . And, if the alternative is to stretch the *ad hoc* basis of our explanation beyond endurance, it may well be preferable to settle for the additional entities. Perhaps a parallel may be found in the field of nuclear physics. Nothing could be more offensive to the spirit of Occam than the proliferation of "fundamental" particles that has been such a notorious feature of modern physics. Yet presumably the physicists know what they are doing, and if extra particles are required in order to make intelligible their observations—in this case the visible tracks made by colliding particles—then they have no hesitation in postulating such entities. Parsimony is important in scientific theorizing, but it is not all-important; intelligibility is at least as important and, in certain circumstances, may have to take precedence. Hence, if by acknowledging the intervention of discarnate intelligences we succeed in simplifying or clarifying the existing parapsychological picture, then, as scientists, we would be fully justified in doing so. (p. 330).

In one of his last publications, J. Gaither Pratt (Hintze & Pratt, 1975) wrote:

Some parapsychologists go so far as to say that we should abandon all scientific effort on the survival problem unless we can rule out the super-psi hypothesis.

It seems to me that there is another choice open to us, one that is to be preferred because it offers a better prospect of achieving a significant advance in scientific knowledge. *Research effort should be increased when we are confronted with an "either/or" situation, and we should actually favor the more novel explanation, in this case the possibility of survival, during the evidence-gathering stage of research.* If as a consequence, the novel explanation should eventually prove to be the correct one, science would have benefited through our venturesomeness (p. 236).

My personal conclusions and beliefs on the question are doubtless clear by now, so I think it appropriate to give my good friend, Robert Ashby, the last word (based on the unpublished records in my possession). In response to Hart's (1959) explication of the super-ESP theory, Ashby countered:

In order to "explain" the cross-correspondences, one must suppose that the subconscious selves of the mediums concerned were engaged in a gigantic conspiracy to provide evidence for survival, and that some of the mediums had gained by paranormal means at least a slight knowledge of the languages with which they believed themselves to be unacquainted.

As to the Gauld writings, Ashby commented:

Gauld argues that Myers' "subliminal self" is an illogical construct which does not explain anything. Unconscious or subliminal motivation is invoked to *explain* an observable behavior, and later that same behavior is thought of as being *caused* by the unconscious. A peculiar type of circular reasoning is involved. Therefore, the "subliminal self" cannot be thought of as a scientific theory. Also, because the super-ESP theory is forced to invoke the "subliminal self" theory, it, too, must be thought unscientific, since it assumes communication between subliminal selves.

Ashby was well aware of the survival views of Dr. J. B. Rhine—of Rhine's early interest in survival, and his later determination that meaningful survival evidence could not be scientifically obtained (Rhine, 1956, 1971). In the summer of 1974 Ashby spent a very exciting (for him) day of wide-ranging discussions with Rhine at his Durham laboratory. Shortly thereafter Ashby wrote:

It is Rhine's point that while the thesis of super-ESP is damaging to the spiritualist position, parapsychology, in demonstrating that there is a psi faculty (or faculties) that is non-physical, contrary to the rules of a physical universe, supports the postulate of a kind of consciousness which spiritist evidence indicates does survive. In short, parapsychology tends to view that man is more than merely physical; and, if man is more, then physical dissolution of the body and brain would not necessarily mean the dissolution of the "I" that is the individiual.

REFERENCES

Beard, P. (1966). *Survival of Death: For and Against*. London: Hodder & Stoughton.

Beloff, J. (1970). C. J. Ducasse on survival. *Journal of the American Society for Psychical Research*, 64, 327-332 .

Bozzano, E. (1932) *Polyglot Mediumship (Xenoglossy)* (I. Emerson, Trans.). London: Rider.

Dean, E. D. (1966). Plethysmograph recordings as ESP responses. *International Journal of Neuropsychiatry*, 2, 439-446.

Dodds, E. R. (1934). Why I do not believe in survival. *Proceedings of the Society for Psychical Research*, 42, 147-172.

Ducasse, C. J. (1961). *A Critical Examination of the Belief in a Life after Death*. Springfield, IL: Charles C Thomas.

Flew, A. (1953). *A New Approach to Psychical Research*. London: G. A. Watts.

Gauld, A. (1961). The "super-ESP" hypothesis. *Proceedings of the Society for Psychical Research*, 53, 226-246.

Gauld, A. (1977). Discarnate survival. In B. B. Wolman (Ed.), *Handbook of Parapsychology* (pp. 577-630). New York: Van Nostrand Reinhold.

Gauld, A., & Cornell, A. D. (1979). *Poltergeists*. London: Routledge & Kegan Paul.

Hart, H. (1959). *The Enigma of Survival*. Springfield, IL: Charles C. Thomas.

Hart, H. (1961). Some basic reactions to Gardner Murphy's lecture. *Journal of the American Society for Psychical Research*, 55, 19-23.

Hintze, N., & Pratt, J. G. (1975). *The Psychic Realm: What Can You Believe?* New York: Random House

Kelsey, M. (1968). *Tongue Speaking: The History and Meaning of the Charismatic Experience*. Garden City, NY: Doubleday.

Lief, H. I. (1977). Commentary on Dr. Ian Stevenson's "The evidence of man's survival after death." *Journal of Nervous and Mental Disease*, 165, 171-173.

Murphy, G. (1945a). An outline of the survival evidence. *Journal of the American Society for Psychical Research*, 39, 2-34.

Murphy, G. (1945b). Difficulties confronting the survival hypothesis. *Journal of the American Society for Psychical Research*, 39, 67-94.

Murphy, G. (1945c). Field theory and survival. *Journal of the American Society for Psychical Research*, 39, 181-209.

Murphy, G. (1948). An approach to precognition. *Journal of the American Society for Psychical Research*, 42, 3-14.

Murphy, G. (1957). Triumphs and defeats in the study of mediumship. *Journal of the American Society for Psychical Research*, 51, 125-135.

Murphy, G. (1961). Hornell Hart's analysis of the evidence for survival. *Journal of the American Society for Psychical Research*, 55, 3-18.

Osis, K. (1979). Research on near death experiences—A new look. In W. G. Roll (Ed.), *Research in Parapsychology 1978* (pp. 30-31). Metuchen, NJ: Scarecrow Press.

Perry, M. (1981). Near death—and surviving it. *Christian Parapsychologist*, 4, 65-66.

Price, H. H. (1953). Survival and the idea of "another world." *Proceedings of the Society of Psychical Research*, 50, 1-25.

Price, H. H. (1959). Personal communications to Hornell Hart, Feb. 28 and May 2, 1958. Quoted in H. Hart, *The Enigma of Survival* (p. 144). Springfield, IL: Charles C Thomas.

Puthoff, H., & Targ, R. (1976). A perceptual channel for information transfer over kilometer distances: Historical perspective and recent research. *Proceedings of the Institute of Electrical and Electronic Engineers*, 64, 329-354.

Rhine, J. B. (1956). Research on spirit survival re-examined. *Journal of Parapsychology*, 20, 124.

Rhine, J. B. (1971). News and comments. *Journal of Parapsychology*, 35, 302-310.

Roll, W. G. (1970). Comments on Ian Stevenson's paper: Some assumptions guiding research on survival. *Journal of Nervous and Mental Disease*, 165, 176-180.

Schmeidler, G. R. (1979). Survival research. *ASPR Newsletter*, 5, 13-14.

Sherman, H. (1981). The Sherman-Swann psychic probes (out-of-body?) of Jupiter, Mercury, and Mars. *Spiritual Frontiers*, 13, 87-93.

Stevens, W. O. (1945). *Beyond the Sunset*. New York: Dodd, Mead.

Stevenson, I. (1974). *Xenoglossy: A Review and Report of a Case*. Charlottesville, VA: University Press of Virginia.

Stevenson, I. (1977). Research into the evidence of man's survival after death. *Journal of Nervous and Mental Disease*, 165, 152-170.

Swann, I. (1975). *To Kiss Earth Goodbye*. New York: Hawthorn Books.

Targ, R., & Puthoff, H. (1977). *Mind-reach: Scientists Look at Psychic Ability*. New York: Delacorte Press/Eleanor Friede.

Ullman, M. (1977). Discussion of Dr. Stevenson's paper: "The evidence of man's survival after death," *Journal of Nervous and Mental Disease*, 165, 174-175.

Van Eeden, F. (1920). Account of sittings with Mrs. Thompson. *Proceedings of the Society for Psychical Research*, 17, 75-115.

Wood, F. H. (1955). *This Egyptian Miracle* (2nd ed.). London: Watkins.

GLOSSARY OF TERMS

The definitions of those terms marked with * are used with the permission of and through the kindness of the Editor of *The Journal of Parapsychology.*

Agent: * The "sender" in tests for telepathy, the person whose mental states are to be apprehended by the percipient. In GESP tests, the person who looks at the target object.

Apparition: An hallucination with some paranormal cause. Some students hold that some apparitions have a spatial reality, but most researchers feel that an apparition is an exteriorized hallucination corresponding to some veridical person or occurrence and caused by some psi linkage. The process or psychologically triggered mechanism involved is not known, although various theories have been advanced, principally by Myers and Tyrrell.

Apport: An object which appears at seances, ostensibly by means of penetration of matter, i.e., an object is "dematerialized," transported through intervening material obstacles such as walls, and "rematerialized" in its original form. The evidence for apports under anything like satisfactory controls is very scanty, and known fraudulent instances have been numerous. Most apports are small objects like stones, but live animals, plants, and flowers have also appeared. This phenomenon is much more rare today than in the heyday of physical mediumship.

Astral Body: Also frequently termed "etheric body." Said to be an exact, non-physical replica of the individual physical body which separates at death and occasionally before death. Accordingly to spiritualists and theosophists it is the vehicle for the spirit in the first state after death and is sometimes faintly perceived as apparitions, phantasms, ghosts, or haunts.

Astral Projection: See *Out-of-the-Body Experience.*

Automatic Writing: Writing done in a dissociated state of varying degree. The writing is done without conscious muscular effort or mental direction.

Basic Technique (BT):* The clairvoyance techinque in which each card is laid aside by the experimenter as it is called by the subject. The check-up is made at the end of the run.

Cabinet: An enclosed space, generally surrounded by curtains, often no more than a curtain drawn across a corner of a room, which physical mediums claim they need in order that they can concentrate or condense the "psychic force" or energy by means of which they perform ostensible materializations, raps, etc. Some mediums sit within the cabinet, others at the entrance, while a few, notably D. D. Home, have dispensed with one.

Call:* The subject's guess (or cognitive response) in trying to identify the target in an ESP test.

Chance:* The complex of undefined causal factors irrelevent to the purpose at hand. *Mean Chance Expectation* (also *Chance Expectation* and *Chance Average*): The most likely score if only chance is involved.

Chi-Square:* A sum of quantities, each of which is a deviation squared divided by an expected value. Also a sum of the squares of CR's (q.v.).

Circle: A group sitting with a medium, generally in a circle, possibly holding hands or with knees touching, or both, the reason given being that this establishes an ostensible "psychic current" which can be utilized by the medium and/or discarnates for paranormal manifestations.

Circle for Development or *Development Circle*: Is one which meets for the purpose of leading to the improvement and growth of mediumistic powers among the members, under the guidance of an acknowledged medium.

Clairaudience: Extrasensory data perceived as sound. Generally considered a facet of clairvoyance.

Clairsentience: Extrasensory data perceived as heightened feeling or awareness. Generally considered a facet of clairvoyance. Sometimes also termed *telaesthesia*.

Clairvoyance:* Extrasensory perception of objects or objective events.

Communicator: A purported discarnate personality, or surviving personality of a deceased individual, which manifests through a medium.

Control: A personality or purported discarnate entity which frequently or regularly seems to take control of the medium during trance. An example is Mrs. Leonard's control "Feda." Also used for any personality controlling or directing the speech and/or actions of the medium.

Critical Ratio (CR):* A measure to determine whether or not the observed deviation is significantly greater than the expected random fluctuation about the average. The CR is obtained by dividing the observed deviation by the standard deviation. (The probability of a given CR may be obtained by consulting tables of the probability integral, such as Pearson's.)

Cross-Correspondences: A highly complex series of mediumistic records, in the form of automatic writings and speech, which have been shown to fit into exceedingly recondite patterns of veridical information, principally dealing with classical allusions. The plan for such puzzles purportedly originated with the early leader of the Society for Psychical Research, F. W. H. Myers, after his death, to demonstrate survival by eliminating "telepathic leakage," i.e., the medium's tapping of the sitter's mind by telepathy, as a possible explanation for veridical information which seemed to come from a discarnate. Bits of information, clues, and hints, meaningless in themselves, were received by several automatists as far apart as India, America, and Great Britain, within brief periods of time, often containing references to the other automatists concerned, and purporting to originate with the discarnate Myers and/or several other deceased former leaders of the Society for Psychical Research. The numerous pieces of the puzzles had to be fit together into a meaningful whole by investigators, one of whom, Alice Johnson, was the first to notice the corresponding references among the scripts. The painstaking and most scholarly study of the *cross-correspondences* was carried on for many years and covers many hundreds of pages in the *Proceedings* of the Society for Psychical Research. The most recent case of this type, "The Palm Sunday Case," a most impressive instance, was first published in 1960. Many students consider the *cross-correspondences* the most impressive evidence yet obtained in support of the *dualist hypothesis* (q.v.)

Cryptothesia: Older term for *General Extrasensory Perception* (*GESP*) (q.v.).

Crystal Gazing: See *Scrying*.

Deviation:* The amount an observed number of hits or an average score varies (either above or below) from mean chance expectation of a run or series or other unit of trials.

Differential Effect:* Significant difference between scoring rates when subjects are participating in an experiment in which two procedural conditions (such as two types of targets or two modes of response) are compared.

Direct Voice: An ostensibly paranormal isolated voice without any apparent source. Most frequently manifested through a small "trumpet" or megaphone by a physical medium, it is rare today. It was often shown to be fraudulent, and the evidence for the phenomenon under controlled conditions is sparse.

Discarnate: Disembodied. Used in mediumistic communications to refer to the surviving personality of a deceased person. The term implies that the surviving personality no longer has a "body" in any physical sense of the word.

Displacement:* ESP responses to targets other than those for which the calls were intended. *Backward Displacement*: ESP responses to targets preceding the intended targets. Displacement to the targets one, two, three, etc. places preceding the intended target are designated as (-1), (-2), (-3), etc. *Forward Displacement*: ESP responses to targets coming later than the intended targets. Displacement to the targets one, two, three, etc. places after the intended target are designated as $(+1)$, $(+2)$, $(+3)$, etc.

Dissociation: Division of the mind or personality with one or more parts behaving as if independent of the rest.

Down Through (DT):* The clairvoyance technique in which the cards are called down through the pack before any are removed or checked.

Dowsing: The apparent ability of some people to locate water, minerals, or objects through the use of a Y-shaped "dowsing rod," most often of wood, but frequently of metal or other materials. When the two ends of the rod are held with the apex pointing outwards from the dowser, it is claimed that the apex will dip and point to the ground over the water or other object sought. Some dowsers have used pendulums, and some claim success through using the rod or pendulum merely over a map of the area concerned. The evidence that some dowsers are successful in locating water, minerals, pipes, electrical conduits, etc. far more often than could reasonably be attributed to chance is quite strong; many commercial firms have paid considerable fees for their services and have vouched for the success of the dowser. Whether dowsing is paranormal, however, is a matter of considerable controversy among psychical researchers. Some have held that the dowser clairvoyantly perceives the object of the search, and involuntary muscular action then dips the rod; others that success is due to shrewd knowledge of topography, and that failures are forgotten or ignored.

Dualist Hypothesis: The tentative view that the psi faculty is non-physical in nature, demonstrating that the human mind, at least in part, is non-physical, and could, therefore, theoretically, survive the physical dissolution of the body and brain at death; also that a surviving discarnate mind or personality or fragment of such might be able to communciate through and, on occasion, control a medium, and is therefore responsible for some paranormal veridical information or other phenomena produced. It should be noted that many who have held this view have not been *spiritualists* (q.v.). The principal distinctions are that the dualist holds this standpoint as a working hypothesis with which to examine the data, not as a religious belief, and would generally consider the hypothesis as applicable only in cases where other paranormal sources, such as ESP, precognition, or PK, could be eliminated. The spiritualist, on the other hand, has tended to accept discarnate origin and control for a much larger proportion of paranormal phenomena.

Ectoplasm: Term introduced by Charles Richet to describe the "exteriorized substance" ostensibly emitted by some physical mediums through various bodily orifices. From ectoplasm, it was claimed, faces, limbs, and even full figures of discarnate personalities were formed and recognized by relatives as life-like in appearance. Darkness has been said to be essential as the substance is sensitive to light. This has made fraud easy, and many exposures of "ectoplasm" as muslin and other substances have been made. Conversely, some highly trained and critical experts like Richet and Geley were utterly convinced that they had obtained irrefutable evidence for ectoplasms under the most rigidly controlled laboratory conditions. Manifestations are extremely rare today.

*ESP Cards:** Cards, each bearing one of the following five symbols: star, circle, square, cross, and waves (three parallel wavy lines). A standard pack has 25 cards. *Closed Pack*: An ESP pack composed of five each of the five symbols. *Open Pack*: An ESP pack made up of the ESP symbols selected in random order.

Extended Telepathy: See *Super ESP*.

*Extrasensory Perception (ESP):** Experience of, or response to, a target object, state, event, or influence without sensory contact.

*Expectation:** See *Chance*.

*Extrachance:** Not due to chance alone.

Foreknowledge: See *Precognition*.

General Extrasensory Perception (GESP):* ESP which could be either telepathy or clairvoyance or both.

Ghost: See *Apparition.* As popularly utilized, this term denotes only the apparition of a deceased person, and is not sufficiently precise for use in psychical research.

Hallucination: Experiencing or perceiving sensory data which have no physical or objective case; e.g., "seeing" a table that is not there spatially. *Veridical Hallucination:* A hallucination corresponding with some degree of accuracy to an external object, person, or event, but *not* caused by that object, person, or event directly.

Haunt: Ostensibly paranormal phenomena seemingly connected with a certain location, especially a building. The reported phenomena have included apparitions, poltergeist manifestations, cold drafts, sounds of steps and voices, and various odors.

Hit: A correct response in a test for some facet of psi.

Illusion: An erroneous interpretation of sensory data actually obtained normally; e.g., mistaking a tall bush waving in the wind for the figure of a person.

Levitation: The purported rising into the air of persons or objects without any apparent agency as required by known physical laws of motion and gravity. There are numerous well-attested instances of this phenomenon, some under excellent conditions. As the statistical evidence for PK has grown, the evidence for the possibility of levitation theoretically has also been strengthened, but reports of levitation today are extremely rare.

Mean Chance Expectation (MCE):* See *Chance.*

Medium: A person who perceives, communicates, and/or demonstrates ostensibly paranormal phenomena regularly and/or with some degree of ability to do so at will. A term less favored by psychical researchers than "sensitive" or "psychic," since "medium" implies a "go-between" and is used by spiritualists to indicate the person acting as a means of communicating with purported surviving discarnate personalities.

Miss: An erroneous response in a test for some facet of psi.

Ostensible: Seeming; indicating that there is a possibility of paranormal causation or of a paranormal factor being present, but that such causation or factor has not been conclusively demonstrated.

Ouija Board: From "oui" and "ja," meaning "yes" in French and German. A wooden board with letters and numerals arranged in crescent shapes, it is used with a tripod at whose apex is a pointer. When one or more persons place their fingers lightly upon the pointer it spells out "messages" by stopping at letters. Some important cases in psychical research have begun with paranormal information coming through the ouija board, e.g., Mrs. Curran and "Patience Worth." Unquestionably, much, if not all, of the material is derived from the subconscious of the operator(s) who unconsciously directs the pointer. Some students have held, however, that there is evidence of discarnate influence or direction. Many researchers have pointed out the inherent dangers of using the ouija board or of taking its "messages" seriously, because of the possibility of dredging up some very unpleasant and potentially disturbing attitudes and facts from one's subconscious. There may have been numerous instances of persons who have become very upset emotionally from the use of the ouija board.

Out-of-the-Body Experience: Also frequently termed "astral travel" or "astral projection." The purported detachment, voluntary or involuntary, of the *astral body* (q.v.) from the physical body, the two generally remaining connected by a distended "cord." In this state of "projection," percipients have claimed to perceive their physical body lying inert, to see and hear people while remaining imperceptible themselves, to perceive and remember people, places, objects, and occurrences which were beyond the reach of their physical senses. While there are excellent cases of ostensible astral projection which demonstrate paranormal perception or veridical information, many researchers would hold that ESP can account for the data, while the experience itself of astral projection would be hallucinatory in nature.

Probability (P):* A mathematical estimate of the expected frequency of a given result or set of results from chance alone.

Paranormal: Generally synonymous with *parapsychical* (q.v.). Refers to those faculties and phenomena which are beyond "normality" in terms of cause and effect as currently understood.

Parapsychical (Parapsychological):* Attributable to psi.

Parapsychology:* The branch of science that deals with psi communication, i.e., behavioral or personal exchanges with the environment which are extrasensorimotor—not dependent on the senses and muscles.

Percipient:* The person experiencing ESP; also one who is tested for ESP ability.

Phantasm: See *Apparition*.

Placement Test:* A PK technique in which the aim of the subject is to try to influence falling objects to come to rest in a designated area of the throwing surface.

Planchette: A *ouija board* pointer with a pen or pencil thrust through the apex. The operator then allows the planchette to write "messages" by placing the fingers lightly upon it as it glides over the paper. See *ouija board*.

Poltergeist: Literally "noisy spirit." Termed *Recurrent Spontaneous Psychokinesis* (*RSPK*) by some modern researchers, the ostensibly paranormal manifestations including the throwing, lifting, and breaking of objects, the setting of fires, and, occasionally, personal injuries to people involved. There is very frequently a child near puberty at the center of the activity. While many cases have been shown by researchers to be fraudulent or attributable to natural causes, there are some very well attested instances of clearly paranormal phenomena of the poltergeist type.

Precognition: Prediction of random future events, the occurrence of which cannot be inferred from present knowledge.

Preferential Matching:* A method of scoring responses to free material. A judge ranks the stimulus objects (usually pictures in sets of four) with respect to their similarity to, or association with, each response; and/or he ranks the responses with respect to their similarity to, or association with, each stimulus object.

Preternatural: An older term for *paranormal* (q.v.).

Proxy Sitting: A sitting at which the sitter acts as a substitute for someone in attempting to obtain paranormal information through the medium. There have been instances where the proxy sitter did not even know the name of the person for whom he was sitting. This helps eliminate "telepathic leakage" from the sitter as a possible source of any veridical information furnished by the medium.

Psi: The general term for extrasensory perception and extrasensorimotor activity. *Psi* includes telepathy, clairvoyance, precognition, retrocognition, and psychokinesis.

Psi Missing:* Exercise of psi ability in a way that avoids the target the subject is attempting to hit.

Psi Phenomena: Occurrences resulting from the operation of *Psi*.

Psychic: A general adjectival term for paranormal events, abilities, studies, etc. Also a synonym for *sensitive* or *medium* (q.v.).

Psychic Photography: See *Spirit Photography*.

Psychical Research: Generally synonymous with *parapsychology* (q.v.), this is the name for the study of paranormal phenomena and the psi faculty originally used and still widely utilized, especially outside of the United States.

Psychokinesis (PK):* The extramotor aspect of psi; a direct (i.e., mental but non-muscular) influence exerted by the subject on an external physical process, condition, or object.

Psychometry: The technique of obtaining ostensibly paranormal information through touching or handling an object. Generally considered a facet of clairvoyance, many students would consider that the object touched acts as a focal point or catalyst psychologically for the exercise of the psi faculty, much as a crystal ball does in *Scrying* (q.v.) Many mediums, however, consider that there is a "psychic residue" upon the object, collected during its use and available through psychic touch and clairvoyance to give veridical information about the person who owned or used the object.

Purported, Purporting: See *Ostensible*.

Recurrent Spontaneous Psychokinesis (RSPK):* See *Poltergeist*.

Retrocognition: Paranormal knowledge of past events beyond the range of influence or memory on the part of the subject.

Run:* A group of trials, usually the successive calling of a deck of 25 ESP cards or symbols. In PK tests, 24 single die-throws regardless of the number of dice thrown at the same time.

Score:* The number of hits made in any given unit of trials, usually a run.

Screened Touch Matching (STM):* An ESP card-testing technique in which the subject indicates in each trial (by pointing to one of the five key positions) what he thinks the top card is in the inverted pack held by the experimenter behind a screen. The card is then laid opposite that position.

Script: An example of *automatic writing* (q.v.) or of a record of automatic speech.

Scrying: Also termed *crystal gazing*. A technique of focussing the psi faculty, especially *clairvoyance* (q.v.) by staring into a crystal ball, pool of water, coffee grounds, tea leaves, or like focal point; this seemingly may act upon the psi faculty and cause pictures, sometimes of veridical data, to form a type of exteriorized hallucination. In all probability, the staring induces a type of dissociation which aids in the exercise of the psi faculty.

Seance: A sitting (q.v.), generally of a group of six to ten persons.

Second Sight: A term used in Celtic folklore, especially, for ostensibly paranormal ability, possibly of the psi faculty.

Sensitive: *Medium* (q.v.). Preferred by many psychical researchers because it does not have the implications of acceptance of the spiritist hypothesis which the term *Medium* has.

Series:* Several runs of experimental sessions that are grouped in accordance with the stated purpose and design of the experiment.

Set:* A subdivision of the record page serving as a scoring unit for a consecutive group of trials, usually for the same target.

Significance:* A numerical result is significant when it equals or surpasses some criterion of degree of chance improbability. The criterion commonly used in parapsychology today is a probability value of .02 (odds of 50 to 1 against chance) or less, or a deviation in either direction such that the CR is 2.33 or greater. Odds of 20 to 1 (probability of .05) are regarded as strongly suggestive.

Singles Test:* A PK technique in which the aim of the subject is to try to influence dice to fall with a specified face up.

Sitting: A session with a medium, generally by an individual, or a small number of persons.

Spirit Photography: The purported photographing of the faces or forms of discarnate spirits, called "extras," upon photographs otherwise taken normally and ostensibly upon a plate or film which has not been tampered with in any way to produce such "extras." Also termed *psychic photography*, it flourished in the late nineteenth century and the first third of this century. A great many spirit photographers were exposed as fraudulent, and the evidence for the genuineness of this phenomenon as paranormal under controlled conditions is very slight.

Spiritualism: The religious movement which holds that: (1) man's personality (spirit) survives death as a *discarnate* (q.v.); (2) discarnates can and do demonstrate this individual survival by communications of veridical information and by physical manifestations such as raps, apparitions, poltergeist activity, and materializations, generally through psychically gifted individuals termed *mediums* (q.v.) who act as vehicles or communication between the two spheres of existence; (3) man's individual survival as a self-conscious, idiosyncratic, remembering personality can thus be an empirically proven fact, and not merely a hopeful article of faith.

Spiritualist: A follower of *spiritualism* (q.v.).

Spontaneous Phenomena: See *Spontaneous Psi Experience*.

Spontaneous Psi Experience: * Natural, unplanned occurrence of an event or experience that seems to involve parapsychology ability.

Standard Deviation (SD):* Usually the theoretical root mean square of the deviations. It is obtained from the formula $\sqrt{npq}$ in which n is the number of single trials, p the probability of success per trial, and q the probability of failure.

Subject:* The person who is tested in an experiment.

Subliminal: Beneath the "threshold" of consciousness.

Super ESP Hypothesis: The hypothesis that any veridical information is theoretically available to the percipient via telepathy, clairvoyance, precognition, or retrocognition, and, therefore, to postulate a discarnate source, as the spiritist hypothesis does, is unnecessary and, therefore, unjustifiable as an additional assumption to explain the paranormally obtained information. Since there are no known limits to the psi faculties, any human knowledge, even if only in someone's subconscious, any extant document or object may be accessible to the percipient; thus, if the information is verifiable as veridical, it is theoretically possible that the percipient could obtain the information by means of the exercise of *super ESP*. Until such a possibility can be eliminated, the *dualist hypothesis* is not the most parsimonious explanation, and should be rejected in favor of the *super ESP hypothesis*. Some students, however, hold that in the cases of the most impressive mediumistic data, such as the *cross-correspondences* (q.v.), the instantaneous selection of pertinent data from the billions of potentially available items, and the construction of a realistic, idiosyncratic personality with the proper characteristics to impress the highly critical investigators concerned presupposes a range, power, and sophistication of exercise of the psi faculty far beyond that for which there is any other evidence. They hold, therefore, that the *super ESP hypothesis* is not so direct or parsimonious as the *dualist hypothesis*.

Supernormal: See *Paranormal*. *Paranormal* is preferred by psychical researchers since it does not imply that the faculties or phenomena in this category are in any sense superior to other faculties or phenomena, merely different and not currently congruent with known norms of causation or behavior.

Supraliminal: Above the threshold of consciousness.

Survival Hypothesis: See *Dualist Hypothesis*.

Table Tipping: Also termed "table turning." A method of receiving "messages" purportedly from discarnates. Sitters place their hands lightly on the table and by levitation and tapping the table spells out the messages by giving a rap with a leg when the sitters come to the relevant letter of the alphabet as they repeat the alphabet aloud.

*Target:** In ESP tests, the objective or mental events to which the subject is attempting to respond; in PK tests, the objective process or object which the subject tries to influence (such as the face or location of a die).

Target Card: The card which the percipient is attempting to identify or otherwise indicate a knowledge of.

Target Face: The face of the falling die which the subject tries to make turn by the PK.

Target Pack: The pack of cards the order of which the subject is attempting to identify.

Telaesthesia: An older term for *clairvoyance* or *clairsentience* (q.v.).

Telekinesis: An older term for PK (*psychokinesis*) (q.v.).

Telepathy:* Extrasensory perception of the mental state or activity of another person.

Trance: A state of psychological dissociation varying in degree of depth among mediums. Generally self-induced.

Travelling Clairvoyance: The paranormal perception of persons, events, objects, or places by ostensibly "travelling" to another location psychically while remaining in the present location physically. Often practiced under hypnosis *or* self-induced trance, it is not to be confused with *astral travel* (q.v.). The percipients have sometimes given strikingly veridical data. The percipient's sense of being "there" while his body remained "here" would generally be regarded as a veridical hallucination, as he paranormally perceived the veridical items via some aspect of the psi faculty.

Trial:* In ESP tests, a single attempt to identify a target object; in PK tests, a single unit of effect to be measured in the evaluation of results.

Veridical: Corresponding to or conveying fact. Utilized with reference to items obtained paranormally which have been verified. See especially its use in connection with *hallucination* (q.v.).